INTERPRETATION AND BELIEF

Austin Farrer

INTERPRETATION AND BELIEF

Edited by Charles C. Conti
Foreword by E. L. Mascall

WIPF & STOCK · Eugene, Oregon

Wipf and Stock Publishers
199 W 8th Ave, Suite 3
Eugene, OR 97401

Interpretation and Belief
By Farrer, Austin and Conti, Charles, Ph. D.
Copyright©1976 SPCK
ISBN 13: 978-1-62032-322-9
Publication date 6/1/2012
Previously published by SPCK, 1976

Contents

Acknowledgements	vi
Editor's Introduction	vii
Foreword by E. L. Mascall	xiii
Prologue: On Credulity	1

CANON
The Inspiration of the Bible	9
The Mind of St Mark	14
Messianic Prophecy	23
The Gospel as 'Good News'	32
Inspiration: Poetical and Divine	39
On Looking Below the Surface	54

CREED
The Christian Doctrine of Man	69
Justification	95
Mary, Scripture and Tradition	101
Very God and Very Man	126
Gnosticism	138

CRITERIA
Infallibility and Historical Revelation	151
Can Myth be Fact?	165
The Theology of Morals	176
Free Will in Theology	186
Analogy in Common Talk	202

Acknowledgements

Thanks are due to the following for consenting to the reproduction of material which has been published elsewhere:

George Allen & Unwin Ltd: 'The Christian Doctrine of Man' in *The Christian Understanding of Man* (Church Community and State, Vol. 2), ed. T. E. Jessop.

The British Broadcasting Corporation: 'The Inspiration of the Bible', a broadcast talk delivered on 29 June 1952, and 'The Gospel as "Good News"', delivered in 1963.

Darton, Longman & Todd Ltd: 'Mary, Scripture and Tradition' in *The Blessed Virgin Mary: Essays by Anglican Writers*, ed. E. L. Mascall and H. S. Box, and 'Infallibility and Historical Revelation' in *Infallibility in the Church: An Anglican-Catholic Dialogue*, ed. A. Farrer et al.

Illuminatio: 'On Credulity' in Vol. I, No. 3, 1947.

The Oxford Society of Historical Theology: 'On Looking Below the Surface' in *Proceedings of The Oxford Society of Historical Theology*, 1959–60.

The Society for Old Testament Study, and Professor F. F. Bruce: 'Inspiration: Poetical and Divine' in *Promise and Fulfilment*, ed. F. F. Bruce, first published by T. & T. Clark Ltd.

The Society for Promoting Christian Knowledge: 'The Theology of Morals' in *Theology*, Vol. 38, 1939, and 'Messianic Prophecy' in Vol. 54, 1951.

Stella Aldwinckle, ed. *Socratic Digest:* 'Can Myth be Fact?' in No. 3, 1945.

'Free Will in Theology' by Dr Austin Farrer is reprinted by permission of Charles Scribner's Sons from *A Dictionary of the History of Ideas*, Copyright © 1973 Charles Scribner's Sons.

Editor's Introduction

In *Reflective Faith* Farrer undertook a philosophical analysis of the language or logic of theistic belief; here he considers the origins of Christian faith, evaluating and, if necessary, reformulating its historical expression. As companion-volumes these books illustrate 'faith . . . balanced by a luminous philosophical wisdom':[1] an evident continuity with the classical tradition of faith and reason. Comparison of Farrer's later pieces with his earlier ones reveals another continuity: namely, a mind that constantly built on itself and, where necessary, emended itself in the light of criticism; and both forms of continuity point to the durability of rational theology.

In an era inclined to substitute theological method for theology itself, it is appropriate to ask 'How has Farrer achieved this timeless quality in his writings?' Partly—though it is no consolation to us—it is, as Mascall observes, through the sheer originality of his thought and partly by the careful way he examines biblical and historical sources, reaching philosophical conclusions after painstaking exegesis. Thus, to take an issue discussed in one essay and implicit in others (if not indeed underlying the book), Farrer rejects the doctrine of papal infallibility[2] in favour of a 'corrigibilist' view of dogma, leaving his treatment of the content of an historic faith capable of critical self-assessment. It is because the Church has but the unsure factual conclusions of the historian upon which to dogmatize that he insists credal formulations be in principle emendable, even though they provide the historic delineation (or, in the case of Chalcedonian Christology, the delimitation[3]) of faith.

It is my special concern, as a reformed Christian, to emphasize the necessity of a constant overhaul of dogmatic development by the standard of Christian origins; and 'Christian origins' can only mean in practice the *evidences we have* for Christian origins. . . . To admit primitivity as a judge or as a control is to submit to scholarship or historianship; and the scholar or historian is fallible; his work is endlessly corrigible, or subject to revision.[4]

Thus, Farrer avoids the rigidity of an infallibilist tradition without going to the other extreme of making faith its own arbiter. Given exclusive control of their subject-matter, those forms of theology which base their pronouncements either on irrefutable authority or what has come to be known as 'the existential situation' cancel each other out. Dogmatic theology has little or no contact with the culture it addresses; while cultural (or secular) Christianity offers no continuity with the faith it presupposes.

Accordingly, if there is a unifying motif in *Interpretation and Belief*, it is that only a well-reasoned approach to theological problems can evaluate a faith which grows out of facts not easily ascertained:

> We do not either simply appreciate the divine in the facts, or else simply fail to appreciate it: *we interpret it*, and we may do so inadequately or erroneously; and no mere historical expertise or scholarly soundness in settling the human facts will assure a correct reading of the divine meaning.'[5]

How then—admitting the provisional and corrigible nature of our 'reading the divine meaning'—is the believer to conduct his inquiry? Primarily, Farrer tells us, he must ask himself whether the belief adhered to is 'reasonably educible from the known historical evidence'.[6] His choice of the word 'educible'—drawing out implications—rather than the one we expect, 'deducible', is deliberate; because where the evidence is *not* straightforward (given that unusual events are alleged to have occurred), the theologian may be forced to admit that certain credal statements represent 'the presumption of inferring from one unique divine act another unique divine act'.[7]

Presumption is unavoidable, Farrer would have us believe, because what constitutes divine action is often shrouded in mystery or the miraculous: 'No one can think of the continuous action of God through a whole train of events without filling in a few gaps in the evidence.'[8] It is not so much that the thread of divine action is imperilled by lack of causal explanation,[9] as that the divine initiative is often hidden in natural events. Hence inference from effects to underlying divine cause, or from clear examples of divine intervention to ones less clear, not only explains how the concept 'divine action' came about but is our only method of checking its content:

> And the extreme case of a fact made credible in this way is the fact of Christ's virginal conception; for not only is the fact physically improbable, the evidence for it lies in testimonies both late and (though capable of harmonization) not *prima facie* harmonious.[10]

What this means to the historical theologian, besides his having to 'piece together' the divine story from subsequent accounts, is the denial of strict deductive inference. That is, Farrer denies any direct inference *from* the facts of faith *to* the beliefs or formulations which grew up round those facts. There are two reasons for this: (1) we can never dig below the level of interpretative response to artifacts of faith uninfluenced by the Church's own attempt to promote her title-deeds; and (2) if God is, as faith proclaims, a supernatural being, it follows that not every link in the causal chain between divine mysterious act and perceptible human effect can be forged on visible evidence.[11] If then faith shapes 'the half-chaos of historical fact',[12] the theologian has no alternative but to start with those beliefs handed down as central to faith, and reason backwards to those antecedent events thought capable of producing such beliefs: not deductive, but a sort of *retro*-ductive inference.[13] Likewise, because the events of Christ's life were, by the time of compilation, reminiscences overlaid by a rich oral tradition, the Gospel writers went through a similar mental process in composing their accounts. Therefore, although the Church believes that what was transmitted was under the guidance of the Spirit and so preserved from error in matters essential for salvation, variations in the Gospels convince us that the inspiration of their authors ought not to be conceived on the model of automatic writing.[14]

Failure to admit that God's invisible acts, being discerned only by their perceptible effect, are inference-ridden lands us, as discussed in 'Mary, Scripture and Tradition', with unsatisfying alternatives. (1) By adhering to a verbal, plenary doctrine of inspiration, we may take Gabriel's announcement to Mary as literal—an interpretation which the Lucan Greek fails to support, entailing as it does a word-play,[15] and which further supposes, in a way that strains the imagination, *either* that St Luke was privy to the event and so recorded 'the very words Gabriel spoke, as it were, out of the mouth of God'[16], *or* that the details of the annunciation were inerrantly transmitted by oral or written tradition, a thesis which synoptic study renders implausible. (2) Alternatively, we may believe the doctrine of the Virgin Birth on papal authority which, in that it claims 'a *charisma* for miraculously knowing historical fact over the evidences, or, indeed in default of any'[17] gives the impression of 'an infallible fact-factory going full-blast'[18]—in effect, vouchsafing the details of the divine drama long after the event has passed. (3) Finally, we may insist that the post-Apostolic Church was 'inspired' to use such language, but:

> If we say that the Church or her hierarchy was *inspired* to acknowledge the virginity of Mary, by using that word we do not excuse ourselves from logical considerations.... The inspired process of mind, being itself human, should be either visible or inferable, and its divine rightness should be appreciable, anyhow after the event.[19]

Thus, what makes the doctrine acceptable—if it is deemed such —is its consistency with the miraculous nature of Christ's life, death, and resurrection: an example of reasoning backwards from the supernaturality evident in certain historical facts to ones less easily documented.

If then we accept, as it seems we must, Farrer's thesis of inferring previous events from resultant beliefs, the problem of assessing the content of faith is more difficult than simply weighing up, or marshalling, the evidence. Not only is the evidence (in some cases) slight, as with the birth-narratives, but 'it was some while before the set-form of Gospel story was stretched to include them'.[20] Justification for the claim of historicity must therefore proceed along the following lines: First the theologian must decide whether the logical steps between the experience of faith and its subsequent formulation were immediate or betray certain historical accretions: i.e., whether the Church's proclamation was passed on as 'simple fact' or 'inspired tradition'. (The resurrection with its appeal to 500-plus witnesses might be an example of the former; Mary's conception, appealing to Old Testament Davidic or Messianic[21] passages for intelligibility, possibly the latter.) Secondly, if we conclude—as Farrer maintains—that revelation represents an amalgam of 'fact' *and* inspired tradition, the theologian must ask: 'What is being testified to, or proclaimed, here?'

From this we must conclude that knowledge of the circumstances and thrust of the Church's original formulation of faith—its creeds and/or doctrinal statements—can't help but influence our current attempts to assess doctrine; and this assessment requires a special sensitivity to the interplay between faith and fact.

It is our author's characteristic *un*willingness to dodge troublesome issues either by retreating into dogma or falling prostrate before the shrine of contemporaneity that commends this collection as a prime example of faith seeking to understand itself, reason thinking with integrity out of the past.

A posthumous publication of this sort invariably raises the question of an author's right of self-determination. The fact that this collection contains a number of reprints means that much of what is presented has met Farrer's own publishing standards; and I think the reader will agree that failure to put the final polish on hitherto unpublished essays—seven to be precise, nearly half the contents of this volume—does not mar Farrer's full scripted, meticulous style.

I am indebted to Professor Basil Mitchell and the Reverend Dr E. L. Mascall for advice over the years in connection with the Farrer manuscripts. I also take this opportunity to thank The Southern Fellowships Fund for the generous grant which enabled me to start the project, the Trustees of the Farrer estate for permission to continue it, and my parents for the support that allowed me to complete it.

The University of Sussex   CHARLES C. CONTI

[1] *Faith and Speculation*, p. 14.
[2] Farrer rejects 'infallibilism' (in 'Infallibility and Historical Revelation' because, as he put it elsewhere, our understanding of revelation-history is 'flecked with creaturely imperfection'. (*Faith and Speculation*, p. 173). Therefore, the theologian (a) may deny 'a pure datum of revelation prior to those necessary evils, reflection and communication'; (b) must 'rethink ancient thoughts,

removing irrelevance and correcting bias'; (c) hold firm to the belief that 'God reveals himself effectively through fallible minds and takes care that their imperfections shall not frustrate his purpose' (*FS*, 101–2).

'Corrigibilism' is also evident in Farrer's essay 'Revelation' (*Faith and Logic*, ed. B. Mitchell): 'The history of revelation is largely the history of false prophecy and a sifting of much sand to find a grain of gold' (p. 106).

3 Thus, he recommends that the Chalcedonian formula, 'Very God, Very Man', be understood in a dynamic, rather than formal, sense; and sees the Pauline doctrine of 'Justification' as primarily 'corrective'.

4 p. 158 below.

5 pp. 156–7 below (my italics). Consequently, 'a fallible historian and an infallible dogmatist make strange bedfellows' in that 'the infallible dogmatist accepts from the fallible historian data upon which he infallibly dogmatizes' (p. 158 below).

6 p. 121 below.   7 p. 122 below.   8 p. 123 below.

9 The concept 'divine action' is preserved, according to *Faith and Speculation*, because 'the grid of causal uniformity does not (to any evidence) fit so tight upon natural processes as to bar the influence of an over-riding divine persuasion.' (p. 62; see also pp. 78–85 where he contends that because the basic component of matter is energy—and not, as Newton's predecessors thought, impenetrable *corpuscula*—there is sufficient room for God to pierce the web of natural event or influence the direction of natural evolution.) Farrer also uses this argument to define a libertarian position in '*Free Will in Theology*', p. 186 below.

10 p. 116 below.

11 Appeal to 'the miraculous' (as proof of 'divine action') does not avoid the problem of inference; for in the absence of strong induction—i.e., sufficient examples—the question becomes 'Is this (highly unusual, singular or unique) event inference-worthy? That is, does it confirm the interpretation "act of God"?'—for which the criteria evoked, of identification and ascription, are subject to rational assessment.

The problem of identifying divine action is further complicated when the miraculous lies embedded in myth—e.g., 'Can Myth be Fact?' and 'On Credulity'.

As regards the divine activity in nature, detection is made doubly difficult, Farrer maintains, by the fact that, being neither overthrown nor violated in yielding to the divine persuasion, nature is 'perfectly mute' (see esp. *Love Almighty and Ills Unlimited*, pp. 93–9, and *FS*, 72). Nevertheless from the fact that the believer experiences divine causal efficacy (in his reception of grace), Farrer infers a theology of nature; for how else could spiritual creatures emerge from natural process without an overriding divine effect? (See *A Science of God?*, pp. 88–91).

12 p. 169 below.

13 See p. 122 below for the comparison between 'the eduction of implications' and 'inference to antecedents'.

14 See 'The Inspiration of the Bible' for how words mediate the Living Word without relying on a notion of literal inerrancy. In 'Inspiration: Poetical and Divine', Farrer argues that the biblical writers played an active part in shaping their material, analogous to the creative imagination; and this supposition, examined in his two essays on Mark's Gospel in this volume, forms the basis for his rejection of Form Criticism and a pre-Marcan Q-source (cf. 'On Dispensing with Q', *Studies in the Gospels*, ed. D. Nineham).

15 p. 121 below.   16 Ibid.   17 p. 154 below.   18 p. 164 below.

19 pp. 116–7 below.   20 p. 118 below.

21 See 'Messianic Prophecy'; and 'Gnosticism', in which Farrer discredits by implication the Gnostic idea that, matter being corrupt, Christ's human nature (or physical lineage) ought to be denied.

Foreword

Dr Conti, to whose enthusiasm and skill we owe the collection and editing of the volumes of papers and sermons by Austin Farrer which have appeared under the titles *Reflective Faith* and *The End of Man,* has increased our obligation by delving into highways and byways to rescue the writings which comprise the present volume. Some of them have been published before in one form or another, but almost all were in danger of falling into oblivion; and both those of us who are old enough to have dim memories of their first production and those of us who were in their theological cradles at the time will profit by their gathering together and re-presentation.

It is easy for the writer of a Foreword to slip into writing a review, but the temptation to do this must be resisted. For the reviewer must assume that his readers have not read the work in question and will properly inform them of its contents and, in the light of his own judgement, urge them to buy it or else to refrain from buying it. In contrast, the writer of the Foreword must assume that his readers already have the book in their hands and are capable of forming their own judgement about it. The most he can hope to do, perhaps, is to reassure them that, even in these days of high prices, they have not wasted their money in buying it.

To me at least, one of the chief reasons why it is still worthwhile to read Austin Farrer's writings seven years after his death and anything up to forty years after they were first published is provided by the amazing originality and independence of his thought. His views on New Testament criticism in particular were often looked upon as highly speculative and even in some cases fantastic, but they were no more so than many of those which he controverted; and he was convinced—and had the courage to say so—that many of the theories which it has become almost blasphemous to criticize were in fact ill-founded, implausible, and ham-fisted. Being himself a man of delicate sensibility, whose mind had the rare combination of the qualities of the philosopher and the poet, he was painfully aware of the philistinism of much biblical scholarship, especially that of Germanic origin. And if his own views were often alarmingly speculative, he was only too anxious that they should be searchingly criticized; he was the very opposite of the pundit. He once remarked in my hearing that, while he seemed to have the gift of producing new theories, he was the last person in the world who was competent to assess their value. In defending himself, in the presidential address which is printed in this book, against some obviously unexpected criticisms by a distinguished literary and historical scholar, he wrote: 'Has not Miss Gardner noticed that, in matters of literary or scholarly fashion, theology is always a quarter of a century behind the times? We are not just due to recover from the typological measles; we are only beginning to come out in spots.' What he would have said about some of the quite recent developments of redaction-criticism we can ourselves only speculate, for, as E. C. Bentley lamented at the tomb of Wordsworth, man is always born too late or else he dies too soon. But it was of course not only in the biblical realm that Farrer showed this daring originality combined with readiness to engage in dialogue. To the end of his life he was developing a Christian apologetic that was both thoroughly orthodox and thoroughly contemporary. And, although he was agonizingly conscious of the problem posited for faith by moral and physical evil, he was deeply convinced that the answer was orthodox Christian theism or nothing. As many of the papers in this book show, he had no use for any reduced form of Christianity. The development of his thought from the formidable work *Finite and Infinite* to the more finished and manageable form of *Faith and Speculation* has been the subject of a brilliant doctoral thesis by Dr Conti which itself well merits publication. And, although Farrer himself clearly felt Scripture rather than philosophy to be his true theological love, it may well be on his philosophical theology and not on his biblical studies that his lasting reputation will rest.

E. L. MASCALL

Prologue: On Credulity

There are various ways of offending against truth, and different environments stress different types of falsity. In the nursery they punished us for evasive lying: in the world of practical affairs evasive lying is considered in many circumstances to be a duty, but you must not enter into engagements that you do not propose to fulfil, or go back on those you have made. In universities, the crime is credulity: you must not believe, still less assert, what evidence does not warrant. What is the use of studying anything—history, science, what you will—if in the end you are going to make up the answers, and believe what you choose? Every society will punish by penalty or contempt the vice which frustrates its peculiar aims, and credulity will get short shrift in universities.

And Christianity appears to be credulity. The Christian believes, as faith, general truths which he must suppose to be the concern of philosophy, and particular facts which cannot be exempted from the scrutiny of history. He does not live long in a university without discovering that what passes there for philosophy does not oblige its practitioners to believe in God, and that history indeed obliges us to reckon with the Christian movement, but not necessarily to accept the Christian's account of the facts in which it originated. The Christian comforts himself for some while with the reflection that nothing, anyhow, has been proved *against* him; and then goes on to ask whether to believe without compelling evidence is not, after all, credulity.

At this point, perhaps, he picks up the New Testament, to see whether the apostolic writers have anything to say in their own defence. Not a word. Defence, indeed! They are putting their opponents through it, asking how men can look truth itself in the eye, and turn away to believe and practise lies. And this is plainly not the pose of propagandists. It is the only way in which these Christians can see things. And our perplexity is not simply that apostolic men once felt like this, but that a part of our own minds has often shared their view. We have often just seen (so we have thought) the inexorable truth that we are rebellious creatures under the eye of our Creator, and that our Creator has come upon us in Christ. Credulity, here, is the crime of pretending to believe that there is any way out of this situation but one—to reconcile ourselves to the truth of our nature, which demands our submission to the God who made us.

Unless our minds in fact function in these two ways: unless we sometimes see God as truth, and evasion of him as credulity, at other times the proved facts of the special sciences as truth, and the outrunning of them as credulity—unless this is so, we are not confronted with the specifically religious problem of truth. If we do feel the problem, the most reasonable attitude to start with is that two ways of thinking which exercise an undoubted sway on the truth-seeking mind both have their rights: it is a matter of finding the proper relation between them, not of allowing one to oust the other.

So it seems natural to ask whether there are not more sorts of truth than one. At the first brush we must answer that there is only one sort of truth, if by truth you mean 'being true', in the sense in which our acts of mind can be true. To be true is to conform to fact, and we know what we mean when we say that an act of mind so conforms to facts as to be true about them. Professional philosophers can write volumes about the sense in which the statement 'There is a lamp-post in the High Street' is true, because it is their business to sharpen the wits of boys by the dissection of trivial questions. But unless the result is to make them and their students better fitted to attack questions which are not trivial, they will not have used their time well. Truth is the conformity of thought to act, and that is all there is to it. When we suggest to ourselves that there may be various sorts of truth, we must mean something else, for instance, that there may be facts of different sorts. Well, but that's a platitude: facts can be classified in all sorts of ways. Yes, but what we mean is something more special, there may be several classes of fact which are differently related to our faculties, so that what our minds can 'do' about them is different. If our minds do it right, the result will be truth; and truth will be conformity to fact, and fact will be the way things are in themselves: nothing will differ except the way in which our minds deal with these different classes of fact.

To put the same point differently: the word 'truth' is used in three senses, and only one of these is meant when we talk about 'different sorts of truth'. 'Truth' is used to mean:

(*a*) the facts to which true thinking corresponds;
(*b*) an act of thought which is, as it happens, true;
(*c*) the truthfulness of an act of thought.

We are talking about (*b*). There are various sorts of 'truths' (truths of science, history, etc.) because the subject-matters of several disciplines oblige them to use different sorts of thinking. It is not the *truth* of these thinkings that differs, it is their nature as thinkings: the difference between erroneous scientific thinking and erroneous historical thinking is just the same as the difference between true scientific thinking and true historical thinking. Naturally, it is only because scientific and historical thinkings are *capable* of truth that we are interested in their differences, but the difference between them lies not in their truth but in the way they are thought.

So much for generalities; and now, unless our indiscreet scorn of certain professional philosophers is to topple back upon our own heads, we shall have to put our definitions to some use, and make a division of sorts of 'truth' which may help to clarify the religious problem of truth from which we started. Four sorts will, for our purposes, be plenty. So we will list the truths of (1) science; (2) personal understanding; (3) formal ethics; (4) religion. We will try to show that as (1) is related to (2), so (3) is related to (4).

(1) Science of all sorts obtains precision by artificially limiting its subject-matter. Modern physics began to get under way when it began resolutely to refuse to consider anything but the *measurability* of physical process. Not that physical process can possibly be nothing but its own measurability, but that the question of its measurability is a tidy question which leads to exact answers. The same artificial limitation has been brought into the study of human affairs. The economist may concentrate on man in so far as he is an economic agent, but if the economist concludes that *because* it is possible to get sound results this way,

man is nothing but an economic agent and all the rest of his apparent action is economic activity under a disguise, then the economist is a fool. So, again, with the psychologist's study of man's subrational impulses, or any other limited inquiry.

(2) As soon as a man stops asking tidy questions about a single aspect of things and asks the very untidy question 'What *whole* reality is confronting me here?', science stops. Science may lay down the lines within which the answer can be found; but it cannot supply the answer. If we ask our question about *physical* realities, we shall not get an answer, anyhow. No one is going to know, or guess, what the whole being of physical substance is. But if we ask it in the human field, we do get some sort of an answer. I may consider very scientifically a man's economic relationships and the probable psychology of his instinctive urges, but the answers I shall get will do no more than point to what it is I am up against in dealing with this man. I have just got to know him through interacting with him. That is personal understanding.

(3) Science is true when it conforms to certain abstract patterns which real things or processes exhibit, and personal understanding is true when persons are (or, in history, were) as we understand them to be (or to have been). It does not matter whether the facts are such as to be approved or deplored, whether the persons are acting a lie or living sincerely. As long as we get the deplorable facts right and understand how insincere the insincere agents are, our science and our personal understanding are true. But we open up a completely new dimension of questions when we ask what is that true essence of man which the insincere betrays and the fool misses and the callous ignores and the perverse distorts. This time we are up against an object which is quite differently related to us from the objects of science or personal understanding. It isn't *out there*, it is, so to speak, *within*; not 'within' as our states of mind are within, for our states of mind, worse luck, are not the standard of the just and the worth while. The standard of the truly human is something even more deeply 'within', which our states of mind ought to be expressing, but very likely they are not.

Now there are two ways in which the mind may relate itself to this essence of the truly human which it is our life's work to express. We may think about it abstractly, and that is ethical philosophy: we may think about it whole and in the round, and that is religion. The ethical philosopher is like other scientists of human nature—like the economist or the psychologist. He limits the issue and picks out a tidy question. He says: 'I do not propose to allow myself to be bemused by anything so overpowering or confusing as the attempt to see my whole human nature in its place in the world of real beings, and how I, as a mind and will, am related to it. I shall limit my scope. Anyhow, I shall say, men do feel themselves to be under obligations; and they habitually codify them in moral rules. And they, less clearly perhaps, but nevertheless effectively, build up ideals which outrun the letter of the rules. So let us talk about the limited fact of moral thinking—the recognition of obligation, the attempt to make moral rules consistent, the problems of particular duty.' All right, then, let's.

(4) But, say we, that cannot be the end of the matter. The ethical philosopher remains the master of his subject-matter by limiting his question. But in the end there is something more important than remaining the master of your subject-matter, and that is that you should undergo the impact of the whole fact. Just as you cannot become aware of the personal reality of your friend by trying on him preconceived questions of psychological or economic science, but only by undergoing the impact of his existence, so it is with awareness of your own being and destiny, and of its demands on you. You cannot say: I propose to open just a crack of my mental door and admit only those facts to which I have already issued blue tickets. You have to throw the door open, however mysterious, or terrifying, or overwhelming the body of fact may be that tumbles in.

Now when the New Testament writers said that in Christ they had met the truth, they meant that in him they recognized what was demanding admittance through this door. It is of no use, of course, for Christians to pretend that on this ground everybody is bound to agree with them straight away, but anyhow on this ground their position is immensely strong and need fear no antagonist. There is no constraint, no embarrassment here; here we can take on all comers. We do not need to worry whether all philosophers agree with us, for the philosophers are for the most part discussing carefully limited questions and their opinion on the total question may be of little interest even if they are prepared to plead guilty to having one. Certainly it is up to us to think as clearly and philosophically as we can about our own beliefs; but what sort of logical structure belongs to theological propositions is a very complicated and special question, and I do not propose to start upon it here.

As to the historians, we shall have to treat them with great respect, because it is vital to us that Christ was, in the field of history, what we say he was. We must have no bogus history. But at the same time many historians are limiting their scope to the search for 'truths' of the (1) and (2) type; such men are not going to see truths of the (4) type breaking out at them through the façade of history, for they have discounted them from the start. There is no question of proving the Christian view of what happened in the year A.D.30 out of 'mere' history. Indeed historians who take the precepts of their own art for the laws of being, and decide that what 'mere' history does not prove cannot reach the human mind, are the men of all others least likely to admit the Christian fact. But the historian whose mind is open to the fourth type of truth, and who has some awareness of the abyss of divine being which underlies his own existence, may meet a voice and a visitant out of that abyss, when he weighs the strange history of the year 30 as it is mirrored in the witness of those who most intimately responded to it.

CANON

The Inspiration of the Bible

They say the Bible makes good reading, but unless you are concerned for the everlasting salvation of mankind, you will prefer to look for your reading elsewhere. It is a sort of sacrilege to recommend the Bible as culture or amusement. The story of David and Absalom is a better piece of literature than Matthew Arnold's *Sohrab and Rustum*; but that has nothing to do with the reasons for which we read the Books of Samuel. Christ promised many additional blessings to those who put the kingdom of God first, and readers who listen for the commands of a divine King in Scripture will enjoy all sorts of incidental satisfactions. But that is on the side, and if you read the Bible otherwise than as the word of God, you will yawn over most of it.

Christians read the Bible because they want to listen to God. Sentimentalists and moralizers find God a handsome subject to make speeches about, but true believers would rather hold their tongues and let God speak. Here am I speaking about God at this moment; if, by a miracle, you could change the wavelength and hear God himself, I take it that you would turn me off. And so Christians in all ages have turned from the theologians and philosophers who write about God, to the Bible in which they hope to meet God's Spirit.

You will say to me: Yes, that's what Christians have done; that's what my great-aunt did; I know that without being told. Christians used to be able to do that because they were as simple-minded as children, but now we have grown up, and we can't do it any more. My great-aunt read Isaiah or St Paul, and said, 'These are the words of God.' But I (you will say) read the same texts, and I say 'These are the words of a couple of ancient Jews, giving their ideas about what God wants, warns against, or promises.' Now which of us is right, my great-aunt or I? Did God put St Paul, or Isaiah for that matter, into a trance, and make them do automatic writing under his control; or did these men stay awake and write their books by the use of their own wits, like any one else?

Well, if I am to try and answer the question, I will begin by saying that Christians do not believe, and never have believed, that the Bible writers were out of their ordinary senses when they composed, except where they tell us themselves that they are undergoing visions or ecstasies, and that is not often. But in the second place I shall say that it is a disastrous mistake to suppose that God can only make men his instruments by suspending their normal consciousness and wagging their tongues and hands for them as a showman does for his puppets. If that were so, God would be no better than a puppet-master, and the obedience of faith would be no better than a dance of dolls. By that doctrine you don't make nonsense of Bible inspiration only, you make nonsense of religion altogether. For what does religion amount to, if we cannot even do what the children do, and ask God to make us kind or brave? How do you expect him to make you kind and brave, except by inspiring and heightening and guiding your mind and conduct? When God inspires us, he does not make us any less ourselves, he makes us twice the men we were before. And St Paul does not cease to be St Paul, he is twice the Paul he was, when the Spirit of Jesus possesses his pen.

There is, of course, a great difference between the inspiration God gives us and the inspiration he gave St Paul. I do not merely mean that St Paul's inspiration was stronger than ours, or that he obeyed it more completely, though no doubt both those things are true. I mean that what he was inspired to do was something different. We are inspired to care for good things and to do good actions; we are not inspired to speak to our fellow men the words of God, as St Paul was. We may be inspired to embrace what St Paul revealed: he was inspired to reveal it. We may be inspired to expound what he taught: but he was inspired to teach it. Inspired, not manipulated: he spoke for God and he remained himself.

But if so, surely the practical result for the Bible-reader remains perplexing. For, when God inspires us to do a good action, and, as I was saying, makes us twice the men we were in the doing of it, is there anyone alive clever enough to put our good action through a filter, strain out all the part of it which is merely ours, and isolate the part of it that is purely divine? And, similarly, if God inspires St Paul to speak, how are we to strain out St Paul, so as to be left with the pure word of God? We do not want St Paul's national prejudices or personal limitations, which, good man as he was, he could not wholly escape; no one can, it is like trying to jump off one's own shadow. How then are we to draw the line between the Apostle's oddities and the word of God?

It would save us a lot of trouble if we could find a cut-and-dried answer to that question; but cut-and-dried answers to spiritual questions are always false, and in the special matter of understanding God's word Christ rules such answers out. 'He that hath an ear to hear, let him hear', said he. We cannot hear the voice of God in Christ's words, let alone in St Paul's or Isaiah's, unless we have an ear attuned. After we have done our best to understand the words by the aid of mere honest scholarship, there is still something to be done, and that is the most important thing of all: to use our spiritual ears. If we do not believe that the same God who moved St Paul can move us to understand what he moved St Paul to say, then (once again) it isn't much use our bothering about St Paul's writings. 'God is his own interpreter, and he will make it plain.'

'God is his own interpreter.' Does that mean that each of us is to take any given text to signify just what we happen to feel about it at the moment of reading? Certainly not. God is his own interpreter, but he does not interpret himself only by speaking in the single reader's mind, he interprets himself by speaking in the Church, the whole organized body of Christian minds; we are not alone, we have the mind of Christendom, the Catholic Faith, to guide us. God is his own interpreter in another way, too: he gives us one text by which to interpret another. The God who spoke in St Paul spoke also in St John, he who inspired one page of St John also inspired the next page, and the one will cast light upon the other. And above all lights, most clear and most brilliant, is the light of Christ.

People used to talk about the *verbal* inspiration of Scripture, that is, the inspiration of the actual words. In one sense that is absolutely right, but in another sense it is misleading. Verbal inspiration is a misleading expression, if it means that every word is guaranteed to be free from human error or bias, so that (for example) St Luke's dates, St John's history, and St Paul's astronomy are absolutely beyond criticism. That is not so: St

Paul's astronomy is (as astronomy) no good to us at all. St Luke appears to have made one or two slips in dating, and St John was often content with a very broad or general historical effect, and concentrated more on what things meant than just the way they happened. It does not matter. God can and does teach us the things necessary to our salvation in spite of these human imperfections in the texts.

But in another sense *verbal inspiration* is a proper expression; indeed it stands for the very thing we need to think about most. It is not true that every word is guaranteed, but it is true that the inspiration is to be found in the very words and nowhere else. What God inspired St Paul to do was to use the very words he used; just as, when God inspires you to do a good action, the action itself is what God inspires. He doesn't put some sort of vague blue-print for action into the back of your head, and leave you to carry it out according to your own ability. He inspires the action, and if we want to see God's spirit expressed in the lives of his true servants, we don't look for it in any general ideas, policies, or attitudes they may have, but in the particular things they do. Every detail counts; the tone of the voice, the gesture of the hand can make the difference between social hypocrisy and Christian kindness. So too it is in the detail of expression, in the living words of divine Scripture that we hear the voice of the divine Spirit, not in any general (and therefore dead) ideas. We are listening to the voice of God, not reading a text book of theology; we must attend, therefore, to the homely phrases, the soaring poetry, the figures of speech, the changes of mood; for these are the alphabet of the divine utterance.

I take up the Bible and I read. Here are a million or so printed words, in which divine gold and human clay are mixed, and I have to take the gold and leave the clay. Is there clay everywhere mixed with the gold, does no part of the text speak with a simple and absolute authority? Indeed it does in some part, for some part of it is the voice and recorded action of Christ, and in Christ the divine does not need to be sorted from the human, the two are run into one, for here is God in human nature by personal presence. Christ is the golden heart of Scripture. Indeed, if he were not there, the rest would not concern me. Why do I read St Paul? Because he sets Christ forth. Why do I read the old Testament? Because it is the spiritual inheritance Christ received, it is what he filled his mind with, it is the soil in which his thought grew, it is the alphabet in which he spelled, it is the body of doctrine which he took over and transformed. So whenever I am reading the Old Testament I am asking, 'What does this mean when it is transformed in Christ?' and whenever I am reading the New Testament I am asking, 'How does this set Christ forth to us?'

There is no part of the Bible which is not inspired, because there is no part that does not either illuminate, or receive light from, the figure of Christ. But obviously not all parts are equally important, and some of them are more the concern of theologians than of laymen. Begin from the most important parts; read the Gospels and Epistles, read Genesis, Exodus, Deuteronomy, Psalms, and Isaiah, and when you are full of those, spread your net wider.

People will always ask why God gives us his truth in such a mixed form; just as they will always ask why God made the world such a mixed affair. And those who are looking for excuses to live without God will say that, until God speaks more clear, they cannot be bothered to listen; but people who care about God will listen to him here, because this is where he can be heard and because it's a matter of life and death. What is the Bible like? Like a letter which a soldier wrote to his wife about the disposition of his affairs and the care of his children in case he should chance to be killed. And the next day he was shot, and died, and the letter was torn and stained with his blood. Her friends said to the woman: The letter is of no binding force; it is not a legal will, and it is so injured by the accidents of the writer's death that you cannot even prove what it means. But she said: I know the man, and I am satisfied I can see what he means. And I shall do it because it is what he wanted me to do, and because he died next day.

The Mind of St Mark

When we undertake to interpret Scripture, what question do we undertake to answer? I would say, 'Any of three'. Taking the text to convey divine revelation, a believer may ask, 'What does it teach us? What on the basis of it are we either to hold for truth or to fulfil as destiny?' But this, you may think, is the last question to be asked. We must first settle the question, what an author as a matter of historical fact intended to say. For a written book is simply the expression of a writer's mind; to understand the text is to understand the author: not the author outside the book, but the author as author of the book. It is peculiar to legal documents that they should be allowed to bear whatever sense can fairly and logically be placed upon the words composing them. We do not read a book—you do not, I trust, read mine—to discover what it can be fairly made to mean; we read it to perceive what its author does or did mean.

That is, if you like, the basic question; on our answer to it must depend our answer to all further questions, whether theological or moral, speculative or practical. Nevertheless there is another question which partly precedes and partly overlaps it; and it is this: What did the author set himself to do? No doubt St Mark set himself to write a story of Christ; and so everything he does write has its meaning as contributory to that story. But a story can be written with quite different aims, all perhaps equally serious—historical, theological, hortatory; and the general purpose of a writer will not leave unaffected the meaning of what he writes in detail. It would be a simple misunderstanding of the author to take as historical information what was intended (let us say) as dramatized theology, or *vice versa*.

It may be presumed that no scholar or critic worthy of the name would make a simple downright choice between the alternative aims we have just suggested for St Mark's writing. It was not either historical or theological parenetic: it was historico-

Introduction to an incomplete Ms. on St Mark found among Farrer's literary remains.

theologico-parenetic. But such a conjoint description gives us no positive guidance; it is rather in the nature of a warning. (Beware of assuming a plain historical, or doctrinal, or moral meaning in any passage; for perhaps the intention was otherwise. If the interpreter plunges in one direction, he has a two-thirds chance of being wrong!) To determine the intention of any passage, or any detail in it, we need something more than general maxims; we need to see what the author was at.

That, certainly, is a difficult enterprise—not in every case, of course, but in the case of our Evangelist. There is no difficulty in appreciating what the writer of a technical treatise is at in each section of his work—always supposing that we can understand what he states; that indeed may be difficult. Whereas there is no difficulty in understanding the mere statement, that at the great cry with which Christ died, the veil of the Temple split from top to bottom. But it is by no means so clear what St Mark is at—why he regards the event as a significant part of the Passion Narrative; whether indeed he means it as a literal fact or as symbolical comment. The rending of the veil is an extreme example. The withering of the fig tree is perhaps equally extreme, but in a less acute form the question arises at every point in the book.

If we are puzzled about the intention of an author, we are greatly assisted by a knowledge of the existing material in view of which he wrote, that is, if we have any such knowledge. St Matthew, for example, is often rewriting St Mark (so at least most of us believe). Thus St Mark's text is one part of the stuff he has in view. Equally it is evident that he writes with his eye on Old Testament models, or prophecies; sometimes he quotes them, more often he alludes to them. But then in the third place, at every paragraph after his first St Matthew is writing in view of what he has written already. Authors who write without regard to the previous part of their own text can scarcely be called authors, or anyhow not authors of books: a man might put together an anthology of anecdotes as does Aelian, but that is not what is meant by writing a book. If then we can appreciate the three relations in which St Matthew stands at any point—if we can see how he reacts to a Marcan text (or complex of texts), to an Old Testament text (or complex of such), and to the run of his own narrative up to the point taken, then we shall be well on the way to grasping what St Matthew is at.

If now we turn from St Matthew to St Mark and apply the same model of procedure, we find ourselves less happily placed. There are the Old Testament texts, right enough, sometimes quoted, sometimes alluded to, sometimes silently mirrored in St Mark's story. And there is the run of his own previous narrative, suggestive of developments which his next paragraphs will carry forward. But where are his Christian authorities? That St Mark was rewriting a Gospel tradition we few of us doubt. St Paul alludes to, or quotes, part of it—Christ's teaching on marriage, his company of Twelve, his charge to missionary apostles, his last supper with his disciples, his death by Roman execution on Jewish initiative, his burial and resurrection, his prophecy of a second Advent to follow upon severe trials for his Church. None of the Pauline allusions fails to find an echo in St Mark's pages; but (*a*) we have reason to suppose a far more extensive deposit than St Paul has occasion to mention and (*b*) the Pauline tradition, where it is at all fully written out, offers the manifest text for St Mark's corresponding paragraphs. I say the manifest text. It might be possible to make hypotheses explaining why St Mark, having before him much of what St Paul records, should have wished to rewrite it as he did—should have refashioned the apocalyptic prophecies in the Thessalonian Epistles to form the thirteenth chapter of his Gospel, or the Institution of the Supper as it is in Corinthians 11 to take the place it holds in his fourteenth. But such hypotheses are unverifiable conjectures. We cannot claim to possess St Mark's Christian sources otherwise than as St Mark has reproduced (or transformed) them.

If our concern is to understand what St Mark is at, the moral of this state of affairs is clear. We can observe his responses to Old Testament prophecies, texts, or models, and we can observe the way in which his later paragraphs take direction from their predecessors in his own narrative. We cannot observe his handling of his Christian sources, for we do not possess them.

Suppose, however, that our concern is not with St Mark or with what he is at. Our overwhelming desire may be to reconstruct his Christian sources. For we want above all to collect evidence from which to establish historical fact about the human life of Jesus and about his teaching; and if we can work back from St Mark to his sources we come nearer to the fountain head. A most natural, indeed a laudable, line of inquiry, if a hazardous one. How are we to pursue it? St Mark at every point is writing in view of three factors: ancient Scripture, his own developing narrative, his Christian sources. Of these the first two are observable, the third is not. It is the x in our equation. How are we to determine its value? How else than by working with the factors we can observe? It is only by seeing what St Mark does with the known factors that we can begin to conjecture how the unknown factor needs to be conceived or postulated. For (let us suppose) what St Mark writes is not easily intelligible as a reaction to the two known factors alone; another factor makes its influence felt and, from the influence exerted, we conjecture the cause.

Such a line of argument sounds speculative, and it is so. But how can we make it less speculative, or pursue a less conjectural path? If we work in this way, we do at least argue to a conclusion about St Mark's use of sources; we do not simply postulate a hypothesis about it. What would be an example of such a mere postulation? We might choose to suppose that everything in St Mark that allows of being viewed as (unmodified) tradition material really is such, our task being simply of a removing what *must* be editorial; for then we have the source material neat. How shaky this hypothesis is we can see by inverting it. Why not throw the burden of proof on the other side? Let everything be freely recast by St Mark except what *cannot* be attributed to his free writing. If our purpose is to establish source material with any sort of firmness, the second hypothesis is unquestionably the safer.

But to revert to the first hypothesis. How do we show what must be 'editorial'? Here is St Mark at work—you can read his book and see what belongs to the continuous progress of his thoughts—if that is what you mean by detecting the editorial element. But somewhat to our amazement we find another method commonly preferred. You start from the other end, with the invisible and unknown. You *conjecture* the form which the tradition must have taken in those pre-Marcan decades. It must, you think, have consisted of short, mutually independent, anecdotes or dicta; it must have dealt with a certain range of topics; and so on. Whatever, then, is in contradiction or in excess of your postulated rules will be 'editorial'.

The rules, as the learned determine them, are indeed no

baseless suppositions. They are constructed on a good deal of sound analogy. We know, for example, in what sort of units oral tradition about famous rabbis and their sayings was preserved. Suppose, then, we allow that scholarly doctrine about the pre-Marcan state of Gospel tradition is roughly correct. What we still cannot allow is any justification for ruling out St Mark's having freely composed paragraphs conforming to the criteria for pre-Marcan oral tradition. Why should he not? He was (it is reasonable to suppose) a preacher and oral narrator before he was a writer. What other style would he know, when he took to the pen, than that which had directed his tongue? If he adopted literary models, they were presumably scriptural. And what tract of Scripture was best adapted to his purpose? Which, in fact, most visibly influences his narrative writing? What but the histories of Elijah and Elisha? And in what do those histories consist but in a pile of anecdotes, suitable for oral narration? Some of them are quite short and disconnected; others are longer and more complex. St Mark contains no very long narrative complex except the Passion; but he has some considerable pieces, for example, the Stilling of the Storm and the Exorcism of Legion. If for St Mark to become literary was for him to write like the author or authors of the Elijah or Elisha cycles it gave him little reason to depart from the style of oral narrative or of traditional anecdote, whether he was closely reproducing current anecdotes or not.

The conclusion to be drawn is that St Mark's Gospel contains many paragraphs which are persuasive examples of the pre-Marcan oral genre; few if any which can be accounted certain and actual pre-Marcan entities as they stand. If you examine the continuous development of St Mark's story, and his systematic use of Old Testament types, you can form a probable opinion as to the extent to which he rephrases his Christian material. That he has Christian material to rephrase is a conclusion in which you can also hope to find yourself established; and you may even reach a reasonable supposition about its general content.

But are there not critical arguments of a more detailed kind which enable us to do better than this? Can we not see St Mark fall into editorial clumsiness in what can only be the stitching together of traditional units? Or again, cannot we see that certain verses or paragraphs reflect an earlier situation and are not St Mark's?

To take these types of argument in reverse order—the second is extremely difficult to apply. If a traditional unit ceased to be relevant to St Mark or to his readers, why would he record it? And in fact, are there any such elements in his record? If it was relevant, still you may say, it is cast in the form of primitive circumstances. Well, but are you sure that St Mark had no historical imagination, no conception of the old Palestinian scene? How do you know that he had not a first-hand acquaintance with it? If he modified tradition, was he bound to introduce detectable anachronisms *at every stroke*? No doubt he occasionally does, or so it is commonly thought—but always? Ah, but there are cases in which St Mark has manifestly misunderstood—or, to put it more politely, revalued—the sense of a primitive tradition. Are there, though? I have yet to see an instance which convinces me. Theologians find it convenient to think so, in their defence of reconstructions of the Gospel story at variance with St Mark's. It is certainly possible or even plausible to view 4.11–12 as a revaluation of expository parable as theological riddle, and as thereby changing the natural sense of 4.13. It is equally possible to understand the passage as the continuous development of St Mark's thought, carried by two scriptural allusions (Num. 12.8; Isa. 6.9) and by a play on the double sense of *parabole*. Asked by his following, including the Twelve, for the sense of his parables, Jesus replies:—To you (as to Isaiah in the Temple) is revealed the hidden Royalty of God; it was to those outside that (as JHVH said elsewhere in contrasting Moses's vision with other men's) everything was to come riddlingly (in parables), that . . . 'hearing they might hear, and not understand. . . .' And so it now is. And Jesus proceeds: 'If *you* do not understand this parable [which is about understanding], how are you to understand any parables? The Sower sows *the word*. . . .' What is the matter with this? The thought is pregnant and allusive; but so it is elsewhere in St Mark. His critics want the evangelist to make Jesus reproach his disciples for not understanding what is offered to general comprehension. St Mark makes him reproach them for not understanding what they are specially qualified to understand. Compare 7.17–18 (here once more the disciples 'ask of him the parable' and he replies: 'Are *even you* so uncomprehending?'—surely to be taken as a summary restatement of 4.10–13; 7.18 goes on from 7 but brings back from 4 the eyes and no eyes, ears and no ears theme), 8.17–21, and the whole drift of 9—10, in which those who have been shown the Secret of the Kingdom on the mountain keep failing to grasp the doctrine. To complain that Jesus is made to *exclude* the crowds from understanding, and that this cannot have been how the first witnesses took his parabolic teaching, is to neglect the well-established principle that a Jewish teacher was inclined to say one thing at a time, and to say it with unqualified emphasis. The text of Isaiah shows that incomprehension may be expected among 'those without'; but to find so entire a lack of understanding among those privileged to look Glory in the face! What degree of incomprehension is to be expected 'outside' is a subject for another moment, but not, in this case, a moment very far removed. For what is the Parable of the Sower itself about? The seed is broadcast; much is wasted, but some takes root. Either the learned critic will say that we have here a fine example of the Semitic juxtaposition of complementary truths; or he will say that St Mark's text is in flagrant contradiction with itself and betrays unskilful editing of old material. Which the critic will say may seem to depend on whether he is in a good temper or a bad.

In developing this example we have run over on to the ground of the first among the two arguments listed above—the argument from 'editorial clumsiness betraying itself'. Well, clumsiness always betrays itself if it is seen to be clumsy. But what else does it betray? When St Mark is not in the midst of a lively anecdote, he is frequently careless, awkward, or ambiguous. But awkward bridge sentences or phrases joining the episodes on which a writer's interest centres need not show that those episodes existed already in set verbal form before he joined them. Or is the patchwork sometimes unmistakable? So often, different views are possible. For example: let us assume (though the evidence conflicts) that St Mark really did write as follows:

> And he made twelve to be with him and for him to send preaching and with power to cast out demons. And he made the twelve and gave Simon the surname of Peter; and James the Son of Zebedee and John the brother of James, them he surnamed Boanerges. . . .

Now on the one hand we may judge that the second sentence which so pointlessly repeats the exordium of the first was evidently the set beginning of a narrative about the renaming of the twelve and that St Mark in overtaking it fails to digest it into the flow of his story. But on the other hand we may compare 15.24–5:

> And they crucify him and part his garments among them, casting lots for them, who should take what. And it was the third hour and they crucified him.

Then we may judge that what we have in both cases is naive semitic parataxis and that the meaning of 15.25 is 'And it was nine o'clock *when they crucified him*', while that of 3.16 is 'And *in making the twelve* he gave Simon the surname of Peter', etc. If that is the way to take it, the absence of the definite article from 'twelve' in 3.14 and its presence in 3.16 are equally proper. 'He made twelve to be with him. . . . And in making the twelve, surnamed. . . .' There may be passages which manifestly betray the botcher of set pieces; but I have yet to find them.

The stripping of St Mark down into pre-Marcan entities is surely a desperate question-begging business if it is done on the basis of paragraph form and the self-betraying editorial hand. The best way to judge what St Mark has done to his material is to see what he does with it, and to consider how probable it is that it lent itself just as it was to the shape he puts upon it. Our conclusion need be by no means sceptical; for we may judge that St Mark was working upon material of which the content can be roughly inferred. It may seem that the principles of interpretation which we have sketched are more negative in tendency than 'orthodox' form-critical procedures. For the form-critic hopes by stripping down to obtain nuggets of solid ore, the true metal of primitive tradition; whereas we have advanced considerations which, if sound, undermine that hope. What have we to say to this? The first answer must, of course, be *Magis amica veritas.* If the contentions we have offered are convincing, they must be accepted for that reason alone, whether they are palatable to us or disagreeable, positive or negative. Second, the effect of recommending an inappropriate method is always ultimately sceptical, however positive or dogmatic in form the method may be. The old scholastic recipes for conforming physical method to the method of pure mathematics appeared to make the highest possible claims for the rigour of physical science but led to physical scepticism because the physical subject matter afforded no hold to the proposed method. Form-criticism ends in historical scepticism by failing to work. Third, it is tautological to say that the abandonment of a certain line of investigation is a negative move. But he who abandons one lead may take up another. Form-criticism is atomistic; its aim is to isolate units of traditional material and to reconstruct the history from them. It is possible to reject that approach, to study St Mark's whole story as he presents it, and to see what it adds up to as historical evidence, when we have appreciated his conventions, his standards, his methods, and his aims.

Messianic Prophecy

My subject is messianic prophecy, that is to say, the predictions of Christ in the Old Testament. No one speaks from the pulpit for any other purpose but to publish the truth of God; and it is with the aim of knowing God himself that we must speak of messianic prophecy. We have sufficient warrant. We are Christians, and for us to know God is to know Christ. And Christ made himself, his work, and his glory known to men by an appeal to messianic prophecy. The beginning of wisdom is to acknowledge Christ as what he claimed to be, that is, as Christ, the Messiah, the Lord's Anointed. And if the Old Testament had not taught to Israel the expectation of Messiah, the foundation on which Christ built would not have been there.

It is unquestionable, therefore, that the Spirit of God effectively proclaimed the Messiah through the Old Testament. The whole sense of Scripture, working by the power of the Spirit on believing minds, revealed the messianic promise. That is a simple matter of history. And it is important to distinguish this plain historical fact from a whole range of secondary questions which admit of doubt. It is clear that, through the whole sense of Scripture, God taught the Messiah to the Jews. It is not necessarily so clear that this and that scriptural text was messianic to the prophet who originally conceived it or wrote it down. The fact of messianic prediction is proved by Messiah's having been effectively predicted, and not by any dogmatizing about the original sense of 'A virgin shall conceive' or 'Behold my servant whom I uphold'. The original senses of Old Testament texts are the objects of a praiseworthy historical curiosity, but the inspired word of God for us Christians is the instrument through which God taught that Israel among whom Christ came.

I said that our purpose here is to understand God himself, his action and his ways, how he has bestowed himself and spread abroad his grace through messianic prophecy. Now God is his

Preached before the University of Oxford in the Hilary Term, 1951, and reprinted from *Theology*, Vol. 54, 1951.

own interpreter: we understand one field of his action best by comparing it with another field of the action of the same God; the two will cast light upon one another, and so upon the God who is displayed in both. And what I shall do here is to draw out the parallel between God's self-revelation in prophecy and his self-revelation in nature. Scripture itself makes the comparison: *Caeli enarrant*—'The heavens declare the Glory of God'; but also in the same psalm, a little below, 'The testimony of the Lord is sure, giving wisdom unto the simple.' And the prophet makes the comparison more directly: 'I am the Lord thy God, that stirreth up the sea, that the waves thereof roar; the Lord of Hosts is his name. Moreover, I have put my words into thy mouth, and covered thee with the shadow of my hand; that I may be he who planteth the heavens and layeth the foundations of the earth, and saith to Zion, Thou art my people.'

The first point I will make about revelation by prophecy and revelation in nature is the inadequacy of anything like argument or proof to set forth the form of either. There was a time when theologians argued confidently from the works of nature to prove that their author was divine, and supposed the proof to be logically cogent. And in the same way, and with the same mind, the same men argued from the miraculously exact predictions of Jesus Christ in the Old Testament, and drew the supposedly inescapable conclusion that he was the Incarnate Word. Both arguments can be broken and refuted by consistent unbelief, and for the same reason. If the whole thought and conception of a divine author and first cause is eradicated from a man's mind, then the very questions to which the creator is given as the answer can be rejected as superfluous or illegitimate. All reasoning from nature towards God is the recognition of God displayed in his handiwork; it is a reasoning from God to God, from God seen in nature to God considered in himself. If God is not seen, or half seen, in the beginning of the argument, he will not be seen at the end of it either. As with the light of the sun. From the manifold reflections and radiations of his light, from the world of colour spread over the whole face of things, a child may learn to appreciate the power of the sun; and apart from these tokens, the sun might seem nothing but a hurtful and stabbing point isolated in the blue expanse. But all this reasoning from the reflections to the original presupposes the sun actually there and diffusing his light. Blot out the sun himself, and there are no reflections by which the knowledge of him can be recovered. And so it is with our mental picture of the world. If the divine idea is utterly blotted from the mind, it is no longer reflected in anything, and all evidence perishes. But, happily, it is not so easy as some persons suppose to exclude every vestige of the divine idea from every level of the human soul.

As the reflections of God in nature point back to and enliven and confirm our idea of the first cause and primal bounty, so the shadows of Christ in prophecy point the Christian back to Christ. But here again the same condition holds: the shadows of Christ in prophecy can only be seen as such if we have the body and substance of Christ in the gospel. Blot Jesus Christ out of the Scripture and the messianic anticipations bear no longer any clear or single sense. There remains nothing but a conflicting pile of hopes and images, some beautiful, some barbarous and strange; pictures of Israelite world empire, of a new David, of a jewelled city floating from the sky; motives of sacrificial piety and of bitter self-vindication. True, we may speak, as we did speak, of God's Spirit drawing this matter together and preaching Messiah to the Jews before Messiah came. But that spiritual preaching needed to be fixed and clarified by the actual coming of Christ. Without the Christ of flesh and blood, the Jewish foresight of him is a flickering and transitory gleam. It is in the light of Christ himself that all messianic prophecy is understood.

I will continue the comparison between Christ foreshown in prophecy and God displayed in nature by taking a further point, namely this: that in both fields revelation moves from multiplicity towards unity. The image of the sun and of its radiations will serve us here once more. The whole power and glory of the sun is in the sun, but gathered and concentrated in such a simplicity of incandescent splendour as to baffle our eyes. We turn from the sun, and range over the variety of his innumerable effects, the universe of warmth and growth and light. We gather and collect our impressions, we carry them back and up into their source, and so we enrich our perception of the power of the sun. And thus it is with our knowledge of God through the works of nature. The dazzling simplicity of his being is extended and shaded and pluralized through the variety of his works, and we gain some conception of his glory by gathering the effects of

God's act and drawing them back into his act; into the simplicity of absolute power in which they are all prefigured.

So it is again with the many figures of messianic anticipation and the one Christ. Christ has the intense and blinding simplicity of God. Every circumstance of his life, every word and action, is clear, simple, and meaningful without end. In his death and resurrection all divine truth is summed within a few events. Here is too much light, too much truth, too much reality drawn into a point. But it was never the intention of God that this blinding simplicity should confront the unprepared mind. He had extended and shaded and scattered the truth of Christ in the manifoldness of the messianic images; and those who saw and believed Christ were inspired to draw together into him all this universe of anticipated meaning. What had the promise of a new temple signified? What but the flesh of Jesus Christ, wherein God truly inhabited? Who else but he was the marvellous child, the token of deliverance and bearer of the name *God-with-us*? All the atoning blood that ever ran down under the altar of Solomon, what had it been but a shadow of the death of Christ? And so one could continue endlessly. It is no mere speculation or construction on our part to say that the disciples of Christ understood Christ by seeing his glory scattered in the Old Testament, and by gathering all those scattered lights into his divine splendour. This is no speculation of ours; it is what the men of the New Testament, and Christ himself, manifestly did. The legal and controversial type of mind has misinterpreted the New Testament, just as it has misinterpreted the vision of God in his works. We look upon the works of God to see God, not to prove him; and the primary purpose of the apostles, say of St Paul, when they looked into the Old Testament, was not to demonstrate Christ thence, but to see Christ there. Certainly when they saw Christ in the Scripture it had the force of evidence, for seeing, after all, is believing; and they laboured to show him to others there, that they too might believe. They gathered, or collected, Christ from the Old Testament by the light of the Holy Ghost, and they called upon others to submit to the same illumination. It was not, of course, the manhood of Christ that they collected from the Old Testament. The man stood before them; they took him in with their eyes and ears. It was the supernatural act and being of God in Christ that they sought in the ancient text, where all the images of divine action and divine indwelling were displayed. It is the Godhead that dazzles and blinds, that drives our eyes from the centre towards the circumference, to judge of the centre from there; to judge of him that sits upon the throne from the rainbow that surrounds his majesty.

I shall advance a third point of comparison between knowing God from his works and knowing Christ from the prophetic shadows of him. I will show that what is called the coincidence of opposites occurs in the second no less than in the first. How is it that a certain coincidence of opposites arises in a conception of God collected from his works? It arises through our inability to see how the diversity of the creatures is prefigured in the simplicity of the Godhead. We find several similitudes of God in the world, and we run them all back to their source in God, and we say that God is that very point in which these several lines of glory meet and are united in a single being. Certain things in the world, and certain aspects of the world, suggest to us the ideal of changeless permanence, of exemption from the tyranny of process, sequence, time. Other things, and very different things, present us with the ideas of consciousness and life. Nothing here below, nothing that we can remotely conceive, can combine life and changelessness in a single being. The changeless does not live; the living changes by the very act of living. Nevertheless we define God by the coincidence of these opposites; he is that changelessness which lives, or he is that life which does not change; *Deus est sua vita*, but also *Deus est sua eternitas*. And this coincidence of opposites in God is not a difficulty about the idea of God; it is the idea of God. It is not something to be cleared up in a philosphical footnote; it is something to be set in the middle of the theological page, and proclaimed as the hallmark of Deity. God is God, God transcends our world and our conceiving; therefore his being holds together in unity what neither our world nor our mind can truly unite.

Ascending, then, from the creatures to God, we fall into a coincidence of opposites. But so we do in advancing from messianic anticipations to Jesus Christ. Christ is seen to be God incarnate and no bare creaturely fulfilment of the prophetic types, by everywhere forcing opposites into an undreamt-of union. To take a famous example. The story of Abraham's sacrifice is wholly based on the distinctness and oppositeness of the two sacrificial victims, Isaac and the ram caught in the thicket. Isaac was a moral sacrifice, not actually offered. The ram was a slaughtered sacrifice, but morally no more than a token. Isaac is human obedience and self-oblation; the ram is divine mercy and providential redemption. Isaac is the $υἱὸς\ ἀγαπητός$, the only or Beloved Son: the beast is the $ἀμνὸς\ τοῦ\ θεοῦ$, the Lamb of God which takes and bears the sin, the indebtedness, of man, that man may live. The whole meaning of the story, in its Old Testament dress, turns on the distinction between these two figures. The New Testament, again and again, points to the ancient story, but only to show that in Christ the opposites have coincided; the beloved son and the Lamb of God are one. The merciful redemption and the willing self-oblation, human devotion and divine deliverance, death and the exclusion of death—all these are one, when the Son of God is also the Son of Mary, and voluntary death achieves resurrection.

Another example, and one more obviously prophetic, more obviously messianic. Daniel predicted and Enoch elaborated the deliverance of the suffering saints by the advent of the Son of Man. The sufferings were referred to Israel in this age, the glory of the Son of Man to the advent of King Messiah. This was the pathos of the picture: the sufferers looked for a deliverer; and the deliverer came in power divine and irresistible. But Christ, gathering up all things in himself, *omnia in semet ipso recapitulans*, taught this lesson to St Peter: 'The Son of Man must suffer', the sufferings are his as well as the glory, he is both the martyrdom which calls forth the intervening mercy, and also the mercy which intervenes.

The coincidence of opposites in Christ differs for us in a marked way from the coincidence of opposites in the being of God above all worlds. Both are marvellous, but the one marvel is enacted, as it were, before our eyes; the other is invisible. We have not seen the beatific vision, we have not appeared before the face of God nor traced all the rays of glory back to their coexistence in the substance of glory. But the work of Christ is revealed, it is what we have heard, what we have seen with our eyes, says St John, what we have surveyed, and what our hands have handled of the Word of Life. We have made the pilgrimage through the prophecies and arrived at Bethlehem and Calvary; but the pilgrimage through the creatures and through all worlds to the Throne of Glory we have not made; we have not finished it, that is; we are still upon the road. Even so, our thoughts outrun our feet, and aspire after the apprehension of our goal, that living unity who draws all the riches of diversity into himself.

I will take another point of comparison between nature pointing to God, and prophecy pointing to Christ, and I will call it 'signs' or 'indications' of deity. When we survey our natural environment, we encounter two sorts of things which speak to us of God, which I will call respectively signs and evidences. The evidences suggest God by way of reason, the signs by way of mere similarity. The orderliness of nature is *evidence* of the divine government, the existence of spiritual creatures is *evidence* of God's spiritual nature. There is a reasonableness about the appeal of such evidence, however wrong it may be to reduce such reason to the form of a hard demonstration. But the signs of deity do not appeal to reason in the same way at all. For example, the sun appears to us a most striking *sign* of deity, and I have already made several applications of it in this discourse. It is a sign of deity because there is (in our minds anyhow) a vivid similarity between the lordship of the sun in the kingdom of light and the lordship of God in the kingdom of being; and the devout mind is moved to adoration and wonder by a contemplation of the sun. But no theistic *evidence* can be found in the sun particularly; nothing is reasonably concluded about the creator from the fact that among his creatures there exists one large conglomerate of incandescent stuff.

Similarly in the realm of messianic prophecy there are both signs and evidences. The evidences are those texts which represent a serious anticipation of what Christ, when he came, proved to be. Thus the predictions of a Son of David or a Son of Man, or the Isaianic pictures of redemptive suffering conjoined with sanctity—such things as these are evidences of Christ. But there are also to the believing mind most striking signs, which are not evidences, and could scarcely form a part of any argument. How arresting, for example, are those phrases in the psalms which seem exactly to describe the psalmist crucified. *Confoderunt manus meas et pedes*: 'They pierced my hands and my feet, they look, and stare upon me, they part my garments among them, and upon my vesture do they cast lots.' Such words move and astonish us, but they are plainly no part of a messianic prediction, except in so far as all innocent suffering faithfully borne is predictive of Calvary, and all righteous blood shed on earth, from the blood of Abel to the blood of Zacharias, speaks in the blood of Christ. No special messianic evidence can be collected from them, but they are nevertheless to us Christians a sign. And to regard them as such is not superstition. For all things are under the providence of God; the sacred text did not fall into the form it retains without the hand of God. It is the same with the signs exhibited by nature. If the sun is a sign of the divine bounty, it is not so without God's appointment. He made the sun, and he made our minds; he is the master of our thoughts. It is no accident, from the point of view of his contriving wisdom, that the sun signifies the deity to us; for, to the divine wisdom, nothing is mere coincidence.

But if we are speaking of the scriptural signs, the providential configurations of the sacred text, most striking of all, perhaps, is that which (if we are to believe St Justin) most moved the Jew with whom he disputed: I mean the position of the name of Jesus in the Old Testament. The matter is disguised from us by the use of Joshua in the Old Testament and Jesus in the New. But the names are one. Assimilate them, and what do you find? How is it that these words came to stand in the prophecy of Zechariah? 'The angel said, Be silent, all flesh, before the Lord, for he is waked up out of his holy habitation. And he shewed me Jesus the great Priest standing before the Angel of the Lord, and Satan standing at his right hand to be his adversary.' Then, in the sequel, Jesus is justified and Satan condemned, and this is the salvation of all Israel. Or again, lower down in the same prophecy, 'Make crowns and set them on the head of Jesus . . . and speak unto him, saying, Behold the Man, the Branch his name, and he shall branch up out of his place and build the temple of the Lord . . . and he shall bear the glory, and shall sit and rule upon his throne . . . and the counsel of peace shall be between them both.' No less wonderful are the significations that hang about the earlier Jesus, the son of Nun, whom we call Joshua, and after whom, presumably, our Saviour was principally named. For how surprising it is that Moses, the patron and the glory of the ancient law, was unable to fulfil his own work, or to bring the people to inherit the promises of God, but was obliged to leave all fulfilment and all victory to a successor, and that successor no other than Jesus. Moreover, this Jesus alone of Old Testament heroes is associated with the cross. For of him alone it is recorded that he crucified the potentates he overthrew. And this prompts St Paul, applying the principle of the *coincidentia oppositorum*, to reflect that the greater Jesus, by himself willingly accepting crucifixion, crucified the hostile powers in his own flesh. The bond that was against us, he says, he abolished, nailing it to the cross; he put off as a garment the principalities and powers, and publicly gibbeted them, triumphing over them on the tree. These surprising significations which follow the name of Jesus are not evidences, but signs only; but they are wonderful none the less, and they are the providences of God.

The founder of this sermon particularly desired that his preacher should address himself to refuting the cavillings of Jewish commentators. And I hope that my argument has done this, in the only sense in which any person of good will would wish to see it done. There is no place for any dispute on points of detail between Jewish scholarship and our own. Whenever Christians and Jews fight for the possession of a single text, we saying 'This points to Jesus Christ' and they denying it, the two parties are always arguing at cross-purposes. For by the phrase 'points to' the contestants do not mean the same thing. For us Messiah is God, for them he will be but a man. For us, therefore, that which 'points to' Messiah points to him as a created thing points to its creator: it points to a fulfilment which is transcendent, superexcellent, and joins opposites in unity. For the Jews there is none of this. What points to Messiah points to him as one creature points to another; it points to a fulfilment which is literal, and lies in the same plane as itself. There is therefore no dispute between the Jews and ourselves on the exegetical level. They are showing what the prophecies mean in the mere sense in which they were uttered. We are showing how the prophets uttered more than they knew, and how that 'more' was wonderfully revealed and actualized by Jesus Christ. For in him it pleased the Father that all the fullness should dwell, and through him to reconcile all things unto himself, that they might ever so remain, tied in the cords of the Holy Ghost.

The Gospel as 'Good News'

Some notoriously square character—I can't remember who—was told about a new sect of Christians. They were dancing and shouting in their assemblies and conducting themselves (said his informant) with a truly primitive fervour. 'Very primitive indeed' was the comment; meaning that Christianity must be allowed to be its age. There was an element of innocent excitement in New Testament times which it is impossible to keep going and silly to revive.

The beginning of our religion was the shouting of good news from village to village. One might compare the publication of an armistice settling a long and miserable war; especially if one is allowed to suppose that all means of communication have been destroyed and the news has to be spread by messengers running on their own two feet. That might give some approach to the feeling of the situation. The contrast offered by our present position is obvious. Christianity is not published as an item of happy news; it is commended as a way of life. There are various patterns of life, we say, which people have tried; but ours is the right one.

If what I have said is anywhere near true, the change in Christian approach is surely startling. A way of life is a timeless recipe; you can put it into operation whenever the necessary conditions exist. An item of good news is an event, tied to the moment. It either does or doesn't happen within a limited period. If peace has neither been signed today, nor promised in a matter of weeks, then there is no news on the peace front.

I said that it is silly to keep reviving the original Christian attitudes, now that our origins lie so far behind us. That may be all it is necessary to say about attitudes. Why bother with them, anyway? Attitudes can be trusted to take care of themselves if we are healthily engrossed in the thing that claims our attention. But what about the thing? If the thing for New Testament believers

A BBC broadcast, 19 February 1963.

was an event announced in the news, and the thing for us is a way of life, is our thing their thing at all? And if not, then where are we? Christianity claims to be a faith once for all revealed, and the thing, the object of faith, cannot change if the religion is to remain true to itself.

Can we use propaganda as the acid test? What do we put in the window of the shop? The apostles said something like 'Believe the good news and come in on what's happening while you have the chance.' What do we say? Perhaps something like 'There are several ways of life, but here's the only one we know which gives solid satisfaction. Why not try it?' I dare say you will think that such an account of contemporary Christian propaganda is a parody. I would agree that it's a parody of what Christian propagandists *say*. But I suggest to you that it very fairly represents the level at which they make contact with those they address. Are they not taken to be way-of-life merchants? Surely not prophets of a new age, or anything like that.

Their gospel was good news. What was the news? And why was it so good? The news was, or sounded, political. Not quite political, as we understand politics; for government is not to us, as it was to the ancient mind, a divine or magical power. The Greek and Italian republics had, of course, gone a long way in the direction of political rationalism; but the newly established Roman Empire had put itself back into the old series of monarchies by divine right. Because the prince was hand-in-glove with heaven, he could command the essential blessings heaven gave; victory over the barbarians, justice and order, material plenty, happiness and health.

Exaggerated claims are dangerous; they invite disillusion. The early Roman Empire was a tolerable regime, as regimes go; but it wasn't the kingdom of heaven. It supported wealth against poverty and establishment against discontent. It suppressed nationalism. It made its provinces the occasional battleground between rival generals or emperors. It covered the earth with avaricious and corrupt officials. As for the emperors themselves, they were a very average lot. You might fairly hope for enlightened self-interest on the throne; you could not complain if you got incompetence, perversion, or downright lunacy. Nothing but a sport of nature would throw you up a ruler of heroic virtue, like Marcus Aurelius. But that was later, anyhow.

The divine claims of the Empire could be criticized either from the top or from the bottom. Starting from the bottom, you could complain that it didn't deliver the goods. Starting from the top, you could protest that if heaven set a kingdom on earth, it would be worthy of heaven; the prince would be a true messiah, his legates would be saints, grotesque idolatries would be put down, public and private morals would be cleaned up, the rich would share their money with the poor. . . . More than this, the kingdom of heaven would show the magic marks of heavenly favour—equable seasons, sleeping volcanoes, bumper harvests; not a taint of pestilence, not a tremor of earthquake anywhere.

The Christian gospel was very much a criticism from the top: the heathen regime was unworthy of God and in many of its aspects positively Satanic. It had its providential part to play, but then so had Satan. It was commissioned to keep the peace, and was, perhaps, as good a government as the nations deserved. That they deserved no better, was the punishment of their sins and the reward of their idolatrous folly. Still, it was unthinkable such a state of affairs should indefinitely continue. God, the heavenly landlord, would not for ever administer his earthly estate through callous and defaulting agents. He had given them a contract, but he had set a limit to its effects.

So this was the good news, that God was coming through. He would remove the ungodly empire and enthrone his saints over a regenerated world. But how would he do this? In his own divine way. There were traditional symbols, or pictures, of the coming great event. A prince would arrive on clouds, an angel would blow a great trumpet. Jesus and his apostles were content to repeat such figurative prophecies. But they were no more than paintings on the curtains which hid the future from men's eyes. One day the hand of God, and of history, would pull aside the painted curtain of prediction and show the substance of fact. Only then should we know what relation the figures on the veil bore to the realities they typified. 'For eye had not seen, nor ear heard, nor heart of man conceived, the blessings God had prepared for such as loved him.'

But if all Jesus and his apostles could do was repeat time-honoured prophecies, if no one knew when or how God would bring his promises about, then where was the good news? Where was there any news at all? 'Galilean Rabbi offers new interpretation of Daniel chapter 7' is scarcely a front-page item. It would hardly make the back page of the London dailies, the religious press, of course—but then we all know that the news in the religious press isn't news.

No; but the news wasn't the prophecies. The news was that, in his own surprising way, God had begun to act already; and what he had begun to do, he would not leave unfinished. The divine prince, who was to rule the world, was already in it. He had asserted the divine sovereignty with naked spiritual power. The full weight of material force had been thrown against him. The very fact that his enemies had visibly triumphed, and done all they wished to him without hindrance, made the omnipotent presence of God the more unmistakable. For, physically annihilated, he was still there as much as ever and, indeed, more than ever. He had risen from the dead, and, though now hidden from sight, continued to direct the affairs of his kingdom through the inspiration of his followers; he would presently return and establish the rule of heaven.

What, then, was the good news? Not only that the beginning of the divine campaign made the ultimate victory certain, but that there was no need to stand by and wait for the result. Men could be brought to find their places in the divine kingdom now. The new imperial people were already being recruited. They lived in the King's favour, and ruled their actions by his laws. Their faith in the glory to come freed them from the bondage of a doomed order. Above all, they were at one with the victorious will of God.

There was a hidden tension in such a gospel, and it did not take long in coming to light. On the one hand the object of promise was a divine empire replacing the empire of Caesar; and that sounded like a fact of coming history, a new age of this world. On the other hand, the object of promise was the sovereignty of a throne which Christ had mounted through death and resurrection; and this sounded like a reality on quite a different plane, somewhere clean beyond the world, or somewhere clean above it. Christians who died in faith, and especially Christians who died under persecution, were seen as partakers in the victorious quality of Christ's death; death was to them also the gate of everlasting glory. But on the other side there were the Christians surviving in the world, and hoping to survive in it until Christ returned to reform it. We may see St Paul exerting himself to resolve the tension between the two pictures of hope. Those who lived to see the day of Christ (said he) would not die, indeed; but they would undergo the transformation of being which Christ attained through death and resurrection. Flesh and blood could not inherit the kingdom of God; all the animal that death kills in us would drop away from them. They would keep their bodily identity, but transmuted into the stuff and substance of glory. They would be no different from those who had died and who returned with Christ.

No one, surely, can attend to what St Paul says without seeing that Christ's death and resurrection have become the touchstone of doctrine. The old political hope can only survive by being brought into line; and when it is brought into line, it scarcely looks political any longer. For what, essentially, does the apostle bid his friends to hope? Not for a godly empire, but for a transformed existence, assimilated to the heavenly being of Christ.

A similar enlargement, or transformation, of the political idea was reached along a different line of thought, and a line which strikes us as very curious. I was saying just now that Caesar was a false messiah, claiming to rule by the grace of heavenly powers. How should we expect a Christian opposition to meet the claim? Surely, by a downright negative—by denying to Caesar any supernatural backing. And yet they did not take this (as we think it) obvious line; or anyhow, not consistently. They felt the weight of spiritual forces behind the established order; only these forces were not gods, not worthy to be worshipped. They were created spirits of an inferior sort, which operated the energies of nature. In the common view of those times, the circuits of the stars round the earth were the supreme levers working the machinery of nature; and the stars would certainly not perform their gyrations without powerful living agents to drive them. So nature was worked by spirits; but these spirits (said the Christians) were only the spirits of nature. And man, if he were content to be ruled by the spirits of nature, was less than human.

Now the pagans were, by their own admission, nature-worshippers; and the pagan establishment was an empire of mere nature, an obedient servant of the natural powers. The emperor, then, was a messiah of a kind; but he was *their* messiah. It did not matter whether you said that Caesar and his representative, Pilate, had put Christ on the cross, or whether you said what St Paul does say to the Colossians—that the spirits of nature, the so-called Principalities and Powers, had put him there. Indeed the second form of statement might seem the more revealing. The politicians had merely done to Christ what politicians *would* do; there was nothing personal to them about it. But why will politicians behave so? Because it is the way of nature; political man, like economic man, being a natural phenomenon.

So the tyranny which Christ broke by his life, death, and resurrection was the tyranny of the stars rather than the tyranny of Caesar. Christ had taken that piece of nature, which is man, and re-attached it to the ground and cause of its being, the will and the life of God. Meanwhile, the great wheel of the natural order continued to turn on its own centre, in virtual oblivion of its creator's will, and to carry round the mass of mankind with it. But not for ever—the Son of God would complete his work, by subjecting not men only, but all the spirits of nature to the Kingdom of God. As independent powers they are doomed. When the saints take over the domain of Caesar, they will reign in a totally redeemed universe.

Now it must be obvious that modern Christians cannot use the cosmic mythology of the first century just as it stands. What's the use of telling us to regard the energies of nature as a bunch of angels? But we can see that the apostle's cosmic speculations gave expression to a solid conviction. The breaking of the divine life into the world with Jesus could not be confined within categories of political thought. It had overthrown the establishment, yes; but not the establishment of Caesar alone. Caesar's gods must fall with Caesar: the whole condition of existence, not only its political form, had been altered. Even while the world continued to stand, Christians were delivered from the dead weight of natural necessities, and attached to the springing-point of creative life, the will and heart of God. Nothing, they were convinced, could undo their communion with the divine. Must all worlds be remodelled, to give it certainty and scope? Then all worlds would be remodelled from the top to the bottom.

Students of the New Testament will not need to be told that I have drawn a one-sided picture. The sacred writers are far more concerned with the quality of life, and the devotion to God, made possible by the divine breakthrough, than they are concerned with the political or cosmological framework. All the same, the spirituality cannot be simply extracted from the framework, like honey from a comb, without being run into equivalent containers. In fact, the replacement of first-century framework with more suitable categories began immediately and was carried quietly on by the fathers and doctors of the Church. There have been periods of relative stability alternating with periods of more lively reformulation ever since. It may well be that the present time calls for a more drastic reformulation than any and that we are somewhat behind with the job.

Inspiration: Poetical and Divine

Is it infirmity of mind to think of salvaging some elements of truth from one's indiscretions? Anyhow the temptation is strong. In a book called *The Glass of Vision* I pressed the comparison between divine revelation and poetic 'inspiration'. Miss Helen Gardner demolished the literary side of my comparison in her Riddell Lectures, and Professor H.D. Lewis the theological in *Our Experience of God.*

Much of Professor Lewis's criticism is based on the very reasonable contention that revelation is fundamentally a personal encounter. Suppose, then, that we adopt this view and take it as far as we can. By seeing where it begins to fail us, we may find an acceptable place for a supplementary interpretation of revelation in terms of a comparison with the poetic process.

The point I wish to fix attention upon throughout is the role of the imagination. It is a commonplace of philosophy that we see very little of what we claim to see. It would be an ordinary claim to make if I said that I saw a matchbox. Now a matchbox is not a matchbox unless it is a six-sided hollow rectangle put together in a certain way out of certain materials. But, when I say I see the matchbox, I see only three sides at the most out of the six; I do not see whether it is hollow or not, nor how it is put together, nor what it is made of. Imagination, acting on the advice of memory, supplies the missing features immediately; I no sooner see what I see than I imagine the rest.

We come to a more interesting case of this immediate action of imagination when human speech or conduct is the subject. I hear you speak—well, what do I hear? Only a trail of sounds in the air; yet I immediately supply not only the logical meaning—that could be done by code rules—I supply the attitude and the intention expressed and the indefinable quality of you, the person who express them. In this case the imaginative build-up is untraceably complex; the whole of my past history, especially in relation to you, becomes the sounding-board, as it were, for my present hearing of your words. It is the same when you act, and I feel the nerve of your action.

Here we may well suppose that we come nearer to the case of divine revelation. God in the burning bush speaks to Moses; and Moses speaks to Aaron. We suppose that the second speaking is somehow in line with the first. And if Aaron understands Moses by all he has previously known of Moses, and indeed, of other Israelites, does not Moses understand God by all he has previously experienced of him, or heard about others' experiences of him, say Jethro his father-in-law's, or more remotely those vouchsafed to Abraham, Isaac, Jacob, and Joseph? Yes, certainly; apart from such a background of past memory acting through present imagination it is scarcely conceivable that any event or voice or thought could put itself upon any man as the act or utterance of God.

So far the parallel holds: Moses hears God and Aaron hears Moses. But, of course, there is an enormous difference. We said that throughout the experiencing of one human person by another there works the activity of an immediate imagination untraceably complex in its ramifications. Nevertheless, through all this maze there runs one simple unchanging homespun thread of connection. All men are men; their instinctive passions are broadly identical; the relation of their will or purpose to their tongues and hands is essentially the same everywhere; and we hold the clue in ourselves, for we too are human, we have the human recipe for action and discourse. Thus it is only in marginal cases that there is any real difficulty in knowing whether we are up against the expressions of purpose or not. The most perverse of philosophers will be unable to make our flesh creep with the suggestion that our fellow-beings may all be talking waxworks, or super-subtle robots. We cannot consider the supposition seriously. And there is more than this. Though there are fine shades of intention we may easily miss, and some we can never fix, there are many broad and general directions of attitude and purpose in others, about which it is silly to entertain a doubt.

In the perception of God's interventions, there is nothing like this reassuring certainty. It is not evident by any simple criteria when we are ever up against signs of his personal communication or self-manifestation, and when we are not. If revelation takes place, we are, no doubt, subjectively convinced; for if the act or word of God does not put itself upon us as God's there is not even the appearance of revelation. Yet not all apparent revelation is really such; and how can we ever be sure that we are not the dupes of a counterfeit? We have not the clue in ourselves, for we are not divine, nor do we possess the recipe for acting divinely.

When Moses, or when Jesus himself, sees the hand or hears the word of God, whether in the world without or in his own mind, he appears to us to be actuated by a human parable about God: and not just *the* human parable in general—that God's ways are thought of as somehow manlike—but human parable of a particular kind. The God of Moses is the divine archetype of a tribal patriarch, the warrior-champion of his people, a stern disciplinarian, a benevolent provider, a wise leader of their march through desert places. The God of Jesus is a compassionate parent, a universal king, a patient redeemer, a righteous judge—it seems trite, or almost blasphemous, for a Christian so glibly to run through the human figures under which the Father's person appears in the thought and speech of Jesus himself; and indeed, merely to mention these parabolic types is not to do justice to the divine teaching, nor even to touch the substance of it. It is not the mere presentation of the Father under these guises, it is the special twist given to the story in each case, that states for us what Christ has to say.

What is the source, then, of the parabolic form, if we may call it such, in which God's action is seen and his word understood, whether it be by Jesus or by Moses? The source of all parable, in the sense of the quarry from which the materials are digged, is indeed no mystery—all parable draws on the matter of human experience; if it did not, it would signify nothing. So much for the materials—but what of the form, the story into which they are worked up? It is something which comes in the mind of the recipients of revelation, and it never is the construction of any single mind alone. Jesus gave a new twist to the parables, but they were already alive in the faith of Israel.

What, then, is the source of the parabolic form? There can be little doubt of the *locus* in which it takes shape—it is in the imagination of believers; where else? And if we were not believers ourselves, there might be little more that needed to be said. But because we are believers and are convinced by the *content* of revelation, because we find God to have spoken to us through these things, we ask after the source of the parabolic form, or, let us say, after the control under which it took shape; for we cannot suppose it to have taken shape idly or casually.

It is at this point that the analogy of great poetry, or even some prose fiction which reaches an epical level, appears attractive. For poetry arises in the imagination; and not under the direct control of fact, so that it should be the literal transcript of it. Yet it is not a silly or vain day-dreaming, either; it is controlled by realities, but the control is looser or more elastic than in the case of literal description. The poet's inventions respond somehow to the deep nature of human existence, and give it an expression all the more powerful because inventive and free. Moreover, the expression is often cast in parabolic or symbolic form, as when Shelley sees the poetical vocation embodied in the skylark. What is perhaps most significant for our purpose is that in poetical composition there is, or anyhow need be, no conscious attempt to envisage realities in their naked lineaments, and then to translate them by conscious art. Art is conscious enough, but not commonly in this way; the poet works at his poetry, developing his images; but the manner in which his sense of human existence (or whatever is the control) comes to expression through his inventions may be largely hidden from him while he writes, and perhaps most where the poetry is best.

The last thing I want to do is to lay down the law about the function, or principal aim, of poetry, or even (say) of epic poetry. I should be horrified if you carried away the impression that I had made it the business of poets to express the quality of human existence or anything of that sort. Poetry seems to me to be almost stifled nowadays with a sense of its own importance. I would prefer to say, if I had to say anything, that the business of poets is to make pleasing inventions, though I should have to go on to define the sort of pleasure they rightly give and the sort of means they properly employ. And if the poet is to give the sort of pleasure we look for in epic or in tragedy, his inventions must not be fantasies; they must be inventions so made from the stuff of existence that they cannot fail to illuminate its character and to move under its control.

The moral we should wish to draw is that the parabolic form through which revelation is received, though it takes shape in the human imagination, may do so under a similar objective control. Many unbelievers would agree with us and say that the religious picture is precisely this—a racial or cultural poetry, bringing out the deep qualities of human existence. So religion may be healthful; and yet God need not exist, let alone intervene, or reveal himself by special action in the world.

It is plain by way of contrast that the believer cannot regard the religious parable as just poetry like any other; the control must be for him another control; not the general quality of the life we live but the special action of a self-revealing God. Now in a sense we can see that the figures of the religious parable are under the control of fact. For those who receive revelation are called upon to live in the parable that is revealed; and the parable is then tested against the hard reality of facts. Jesus lives in the parable of messianic Kingdom, and Sonship to omnipotent Mercy; the parable takes on a strange form, when the facts of history, under the hand of Providence, put down the kingdom and crucify the Son.

We may say, then, that the parabolic form is under the check of fact. Yet to say that facts shape or alter the parable is literally nonsensical. Facts can do no such thing. In face of the facts, the parable needs to be recast; but to recast it calls for fresh inspiration, it is not done by dead-reckoning. We may compare the absurdity (an absurdity not committed by Marxists) of an exclusively material interpretation of history. It may be, as Marxists hold, that nothing but material necessities will ever set the problems to which culture finds the answers. The material problems may be inexorable—we must find the answers or perish; but it is still human inventiveness which works out the solutions. Not any solution will do; but whatever solution there is, invention has found it, facts have not dictated it.

To apply the analogy to the matter before us—the death and resurrection of Jesus did not *dictate* the fresh way in which the kingdom of God was seen; it had to be imagined.

Thus, whatever imaginative overplus there is in divine revelation cannot be referred simply to the control of facts outside us; it is in some manner the invention of the human mind.

What shall we say to this conclusion? Is it scandalous? Is it an admission of defeat? Only if we allow ourselves to be lured on to untenable ground and to conceive our question falsely. When we are seeing the human mind reactive to external facts, we naturally wish to see the reaction as controlled by those facts if it is to sustain any claim to objective truth; and so every admission of a subjective element not capable of external verification awakens our doubt and our disquiet. And when I think of God as addressing man in revelation, I naturally fall into the same posture and become the victim of my own parable. If you address me you are outside me; so, then, I suppose, is God. But then, on serious reflection, none of us can really maintain this. God is no more outside me than within; I am his creation just as much as you are, or as the physical world is. He has the secret key of entry into all his creatures; he can conjoin the action of any of them with his will in such fashion as to reveal himself specially through them. God speaks without and within; he reveals himself both through the situation with which he presents the recipients of revelation, and through the imagination, in terms of which he leads them to see and hear the voices and the sights surrounding them. How should it—how could it—be otherwise? The process is gradual; God has employed, he has not forced, the action of his creatures; he teaches us also to discern revelation from revelation and see where the flower and fruit borne by the branching plant of sacred truth are to be found. The occurrence of revelation cannot be guaranteed by the nature of the process, but only by the convincingness of the communication. All we can do about the process is to show what it is, and the relation in which it stands to other processes of the human mind, and especially of the human imagination.

Before we go any further, let us pause and try to add up the score. We have spoken of the analogy of revelation to poetry on the one hand, and personal encounter on the other. These two analogies, however, are not rivals to one another, nor do they lie in the same plane. It is not as though we should say that jerusalem artichoke tasted something like sweet potato and something like celery-root. The recipients of revelation see themselves to be addressed by God, whether through events or other persons or visions or their own thoughts. And this is nothing like poetical experience, anyhow on the face of it; it is like personal encounter. When, however, *we* reflect on such an experience, we see that the God who speaks to them speaks out of a parable, as though a person in a story came alive and addressed us. The parable, indeed, only speaks because it has clothed itself with the living world; it is God's action in some feature of our world which speaks to us in terms of the parable. Nevertheless, we must say that the revelation as we receive it is a function of two things equally—partly a function of the divinely controlled event, and partly a function of the parable in terms of which we personalize, or theologize, the event. Now if we are *believing* enough to accord validity to the revelation, we must be *tough* enough to claim validity for the parable as well as for the event. We look about for analogies with which to support our belief; for though religious faith deals with mysteries which are *sui generis* because God himself is absolutely unique, at the same time we expect religious mysteries to bear some analogy with natural realities because they are revealed in the stuff of our human experience. So it seems that God's encounter with us must be a sort of encounter, analogous to our encounters with men; and that the parables or symbols through which God teaches us to imagine his action must be some sort of symbols parallel, perhaps, to the symbols of valid poetry.

We have been thinking so far of primary revelation, as when Moses at the burning bush is assured that God has come down to deliver, or as when Peter sees Jesus to be the Anointed of God. In such cases attention is fixed on the moment of action. What is seen is seen in the parable; but the parable is taken for granted. If the symbolism undergoes development then and there, the Moses or the Peter is hardly aware of it; nothing appears to happen in his mind, like the free growth of poetry in the invention of a poet.

But we can think of a more reflective occasion, when the seer is inspired to explore the mysteries, so that he may know all that God has to show him about them. In such a case the facts may be taken as fixed; it is the symbolism investing them that will move and grow. The Messiah *was* crucified; he *did* rise again and manifest himself alive; he sent the apostolic mission. So much for the facts. But, in the supernatural dimension, what does all this mean? What was the heavenly counterpart of these earthly events? To ask these questions is to invite symbols to grow in the mind.

Now if the seer sat down and worked it out, if he simply constructed and elaborated, his experience would not have to himself a revelatory character. If it is to seem to him that God is opening the mysteries to him, the images must impose themselves. There is, of course, no psychological mystery about images getting out of hand and seeming to dictate to us; and it would be puerile to suggest that wherever this happens there is special revelation. We are reasoning the other way round. Supposing that our Creator wishes to speak to us in the mode of revelation, will it not be our imaginative faculty that he employs because of its capacity of presenting to us a seemingly independent object?

Because, in this sort of experience, the revealing image imposes itself, it presents itself as a symbol, not as an allegory. The seer sees the imaged object; it comes as something charged with divine significance. What significance, and how much, he does not at first know. He may read several allegories off it, and still not exhaust it.

Although the Scripture abounds with passages in which imagery or symbol is seen to grow, impose itself, and suggest applications or decipherings, the most continuous and concentrated example of such writing or thinking (for these men thought with their pens in their hands) is the Revelation of St John the Divine.

St John's task is, in broad outline, comparable to that undertaken by many poets. Virgil sets out to see and fill out and bring alive the bare bones of a tradition about the origins of Rome. So St John has the naked shape of things to come in the prophecy Christ uttered on the Mount of Olives, with its background in the Old Testament prophecies. He is called upon to experience these future mysteries through living symbols; and the starting-point is a returning to him of the Christ who formerly prophesied to open the secrets he had then adumbrated. Let us follow the growth of images in St John's mind from the beginning of his vision. He is himself an apostolic minister, carrying the Seven Churches of Asia in his heart, and he is, for the present, a suffering witness, or martyr, for the word of God and the witness of Jesus. Jesus is the supreme witness, or martyr, but now in heaven—'the Faithful Witness in heaven', says the psalmist speaking evidently of the Sun (Ps. 89). But Jesus is the Sun—anyhow, the Sun's day is the Lord's Day; and it is on this day that St John has his rapture and sees the Lord of Sunday, the Christ of the Resurrection; and he sees him with a countenance that shines like the sun at midday. St John falls before him as though dead and himself receives a resurrection from his touch: 'Fear not,' he says, 'I am the First and the Last, the Living that was dead, and lo, am alive for evermore, and have the keys of Death and Hell.' He is the First and the Last in the great week of the world's ages; his is the Sunday of creation and, when the week of history has run through, his, in his Advent, is the Sunday of universal regeneration. So too, in the little week of days which gives shape to Christian life, running from Sunday to Sunday, he is the first and the last, embracing in his grasp the days of the seven planets (for it is after these seven that the weekdays are named). And so St John sees him whose face shines as the sun, holding the seven planets in his right hand.

St John sees Jesus in vision, and St John is a prophet: what more natural, than that he should see through the eyes of a former prophet, Zechariah, who had seen in vision a former Jesus, God's High-Priest, under the solar name of Dayspring, and manifested as a type of the Resurrection, 'as a brand plucked from the burning'. The vision in which Zechariah saw him was paired with a vision of worshipping Israel which he saw under the form of a sevenfold candlestick; and what can the seven flames mean to St John but the seven worshipping congregations of Christ's new Israel in the Province of Asia, the subjects of his own pastoral care? Seven flaming wicks in the seven Churches, seven shining stars in the grasp of Christ, seven earthly and seven heavenly fires, how are they related? Stars are gods to the heathen, to Israel they are angels: the Churches' candles shine on earth, their angels in the heavenly grasp of Jesus. In Zechariah's vision, the seven lamps were in one lampstand, which are Israel; the lampstand held the centre of the scene, while like heraldic supporters on either side stood the two oiltrees, the two anointed stocks of principality and priesthood, feeding the lamps from the oil of their anointing. In St John's vision the pattern cannot be the same. The two anointed stocks are united in one and fuse at the centre of the scene; Christ is Zorobabel as well as Jesus, he is as much prince as high-priest. Moreover, the seven lamps are not combined in one lampstand; the congregations of God, that is, are no longer contained in one city or one temple as formerly: they are planted out upon the earth in several cities. Their union lies in this, that their life is hid with Christ in God—their angels are stars clustering in the hand of Glory.

The lineaments of Glory are seen by St John in the feature scriptural vision, such as showed to Daniel, Isaiah, or Ezekiel either the figure of God or the angel-figure representative of him. It would take us into too much detail to trace the web of allusion, or the pattern of meaning it makes for the seer. Let us continue to follow the development of the symbols we have already brought into play.

There are the candles, or to speak more exactly, the lamps of the Churches, planted round Christ's feet; and there are the stars, their Churches' angels, in the keeping of his hand. In the world of the image someone is responsible for the burning of the lamp, as in Christ's parable of the wise and foolish virgins—it burns brightly only if the wick is trimmed and if it is supplied with oil. A lamp does not perform these services for itself. So the lamps of the vision can only stand for the objective fact or phenomenon of the Churches' worship or witness; the admonitions which Christ metes out according to merit must go to the address of the angels; just as it is the virgins of the parable, not their lamps, that are foolish or wise. And so St John feels the divine dictation—'To the angel of the Church in Ephesus, write: . . . I will remove thy lampstand out of its place, except thou repent. . . .' The several messages are addressed, indeed, to the Churches; but in their invisible, spiritual, and (as it were) angelic aspect, in respect of that life which they have in Christ, and indeed, in heaven. For, either motived by that very development of images we have just been following, or by a prior conviction with which the imagery wonderfully chimes, St John is henceforth consistent in maintaining that Christians, *qua* Christians have their existence in heaven: the description 'dwellers upon earth' is pejorative, and refers to those alone whose spirits know no better habitation.

We may notice in retrospect that whereas the seven planets owe their place in the hand of Christ to the symbolism of the sacred week, in which Jesus, the Lord of Sunday, being the first and the last, is master of time, the developed application of the image is in another direction. It is controlled by the significance of the sevenfold lamplight as expressing a sevenfold Israel, and by the parallel between seven lamps and seven stars, as between earthly and heavenly fires. Yet, if the weekday significance of the seven is pushed aside, it is only for the present; it comes back with full force in the sequel.

St John has seen the countenance of Glory on earth, presented in the person of Jesus Christ. His next vision translates him to heaven, to see Glory enthroned in the person of the Father. As in the previous vision, seven lamps of fire burn before the divine figure, and a sevenfold cluster is in the grasp of his right hand. But not a cluster of stars this time, a cluster of seals, securing the scroll of a book. What is the sealed book in the right hand of the Almighty? It is the book of his purpose, the book of prophecy, or of destiny. As the seven seals are broken one by one, the destiny of the world will begin to unroll in seven successive acts: like the seven days of action by which God in the beginning both created the world, and appointed the Sabbath, and with it the sacred week imposed on Israelite observance, and transformed in Christian experience.

In the former vision the series of seven messages to seven Churches arose out of a relation between the sevenfold cluster in the divine hand and the seven lamps before the divine feet; and in the second vision a similarly dynamic relation obtains. The seven lamps are the seven powers of the Holy Ghost; and how is it conceivable that the sevenfold seal upon the mystery of God should be broken by any interpreter but one on whom the sevenfold power of Spirit has descended? An angelic herald issues the challenge; who is worthy to open the book and to break the seven seals thereof? None is found able to open the book, or to scan it, until there appears the figure of a Lamb, his head crowned with seven horns and ringed with seven eyes, declared to be the seven powers of the Holy Ghost which range the world—manifested here as horns of strength, to take and open the book, and eyes of vision, to scan its pages. So the Lamb endowed with the sevenfold plenitude of spirit breaks one by one the seven seals of the book, and as he breaks them a series of seven events, a 'week' of divine judgements unrolls, the first of three such weeks, which taken together give shape to the Apocalypse and carry it forward to its destined consummation.

For convenience of exposition one takes a single strand of imagery and follows it through. But to do this, as we have perfunctorily done, is to give no idea of the complexity of the total imaginative process. There are so many such strands, and none of them is dominant; the miracle is that concrete images of vision, briefly and simply presented, conform at once to so many principles of symbolical sequence. In the more interesting visions the interweaving of sequential themes is subtle and self-concealing. In the more perfunctory passages it is mechanical and obvious. For example in the trumpet-visions. The blowing of the seven trumpets expresses a piece of directly preceding liturgy, the scattering of coals from an angelic censer after the incense has been offered. This means that the acceptance of the prayers of the saints (the incense) draws, as its consequence, coals of fire on the heads of their persecutors. So now the trumpets of advent blow; and every blast brings a different sort of fiery thing—a falling star, a comet, lightning—down from the sky to the earth. But now each of these fiery agents falls upon a distinct element of nature, taken in order—on land, on sea, on freshwaters. By so doing it produces one of the plagues of Egypt, as recorded in Exodus; and it must be a plague appropriate to the smiting of that particular element by that particular fiery agent.

Here, then, St John in the most deliberate manner has felt moved to impose *a priori* a threefold bondage on his inspiration: each little vision, each trumpet-plague must be so conceived as to meet three distinct requirements. Not that any of these is arbitrary; all arise from the general movement of the Apocalypse. We have seen why the judgements are 'coals of fire'; their smiting of the elements in order shows that nature turns all her constituent forces against God's enemies; the echoing of Egyptian plagues shows the continuity of judgement through recorded history into a prophesied future. The threefold chain is meaningful; yet when St John lets himself be tied by it, he is not only conforming to requirements of meaning, he is adopting a technique of inspiration. For to be so bound is, in fact, no bondage but a liberation to the creative faculty. The setting of the conditions challenges, directs, and supports the act of the imagination.

The comparison here with the procedure of poets is obvious. Since we mentioned Shelley and his skylark, we may as well return to that example. Before he has written the poem, he does not know, at least in any detail, what he is going to say. By the time he has projected the first stanza, he has laid down the following rules for every succeeding sentence until the end. (*a*) It must fill its place in the metrical stanza; (*b*) it must supply the rhyme-words demanded by the scheme; (*c*) it must continue the address to the skylark; (*d*) it must so speak to and about the skylark as to make what is said appropriate in a treatment of her as no bird, but a 'blithe spirit'—in fact, as a poetical soul.

Now all poets have groaned, from time to time, under the bondage of the formal conditions they accept; the metre, for example, and the rhyme. It may often happen that the poet discovers what he wants to say and projects it in a formulation which he is sorry to sacrifice, and then hacks it into the required stanza or couplet. Such is, almost chronically, the condition of verse-translators, because what they have to express already exists in a complete verbal formulation, though in another language; and the translator will show almost superhuman restraint if he keeps himself from rendering his French or his Latin into a literal English prose equivalent before he tries to knock it into English verse. And so the requirements of rhyme and metre seem to be there for the express purpose of stopping his saying just what he wants to say. But the poet composing freely in his own language need not be in so painful a fix. He may allow the rhyme and metre to help him discover what he wants to say; as Hudibras has it:

> For rhymes the rudders are of verses
> Whereby like ships, they steer their courses.

For the poet is not trying to make a prose communication under wantonly unfavourable conditions; he is trying to create a piece of verbal music in which sound and sense have each their part to play. No doubt one of the elements in the compound will often take the lead and require to be checked by the others; but taking it all in all the total set of formal requirements challenge a writer's invention to the harmonious satisfaction of them all together.

Now it is evident, by contrast, that the inspired writer such as St John is not set to create a pleasing or even a noble piece of verbal music; he is the mouthpiece of the Spirit in revealing mysteries and it would be incongruous that rhymes should be the rudders of his verses. It is true indeed that the prophets of the Old Testament spoke in verse, but a form of verse so adapted to the rhythm of their language and with so elastic a pattern that it was as easy to extemporize as the measure of Longfellow's *Hiawatha*. It added something no doubt, but very little, to the requirements which supported their inspiration. One can hardly think of a prophet prophesying in sonnet-form. Anyhow, we are talking of St John, who writes no kind of verse, but at the most (like the author of the *Imitatio Christi*) a rhythmical prose:

> Καὶ ἀνέβη ὁ καπνὸς τῶν θυμιαμάτων
> ταῖς προσευχαῖς τῶν ἁγίων
> ἐκ χειρὸς τοῦ ἀγγέλου
> ἐνώπιον τοῦ θεοῦ.

So, then, if he is to set himself a complex of formal requirements, comparable in the stringency of their demands with those accepted by a poet, he must multiply sense-requirements to compensate for the diminution of sound-requirements. And this, anyhow, we see him to do; he is always at any point under the combined control of so many trains of significance, always plaiting so many strands of allusion into his rope.

The Apocalypse of St John is an extreme example of its kind; but an extreme example will suffice to overthrow a universal negative. If St John could seek and gain inspiration by such means, it cannot be universally true that spiritual and Christian writers of the first age could never have received inspiration through such means. Yet it is this universal negative with which we are met when we timidly suggest (say) that St Matthew has written the beginning of his Gospel in antitype to a train of events running through Genesis into Exodus. 'Nonsense,' it is said: 'how could he? He gives us a narrative which develops by its own logic, and a narrative which does justice (we presume) to the traditions about Christ which the writer had received. How could he have made it a continuous antitype to Old Testament narratives without the whole structure's creaking at the joints? People just do not write in this way, keeping (like jugglers) half a dozen balls in the air at once.' To which we can only reply: 'Don't they, though? Don't they just!' and show them a few of the obvious examples. Nor do we need to be content simply with exhibiting the examples. We can call attention to the psychology of poetical composition and the way in which a multiple control may liberate, not fetter the pen.

We have fallen from the universal to the particular. From the most general considerations about poetry and divinity, we have slipped into the consideration of one particular proceeding which inspired writers and poets have in common. And even here it is most necessary to emphasize the limitations attaching to the parallel. Religious seers and secular poets may be led to seek inspiration in these similar ways; but the fact casts no light whatever on the fundamental mystery of divine inspiration. Shelley uses certain methods to set his imagination acting; and this gives his imagination scope to act. St John uses similar methods; and this gives the Holy Ghost scope to move his imagination. Looking into a crystal or into the embers of a glowing fire gives the imagination of the clairvoyant the opportunity to project its images; what comes, comes from within the crystal-gazer, it does not come out of the crystal. It comes from within; and Shelley is within himself; St John is also within himself, but so (in his belief, which we share) is the Spirit of God. Belief in inspiration is a metaphysical belief; it is the belief that the Creator everywhere underlies the creature, with the added faith that at certain points he acts in, as, and through the creature's mind. We have argued that if this really happens a part will be played by imagination. Imagination, in such an employment, will be suppled and made responsive or creative; there will surely be an analogy here to the workings of the poetic mind. But that which obtains expression in the two sorts of case will be widely different; and so will be the significance of the product.

On Looking Below the Surface

I call my paper 'On looking below the surface', because I wish to make some remarks on the rights and wrongs of an endeavour to probe behind the literal or historical sense of sacred documents.

Calida in juventa—in my hotheaded youth—I unwisely wrote some studies in the typological interpretation of Scripture, and still more unwisely published them. And had it not been that some of my friends, yet more unwisely still, had read them, I would not trouble you with second thoughts on this sort of writing. But as it is, Miss Helen Gardner[1] has not only read me, but lectured upon me, and so I am moved to consider whether what she has said is well said, or not. The text I have to examine is the second of her Riddell Lectures. The three lectures were published as a pamphlet in 1956, and have now appeared in book form, bound up with an earlier series, 'The Profession of a Critic'; the whole composite work bearing the title *The Business of Criticism*. The Riddell Lectures had a more precise title 'The Limits of Literary Criticism', Miss Gardner's purpose being to see how far the critic and expositor, whether of divine Scripture or of secular poetry, could usefully go beyond the evident literal sense and visibly presented shape of his author's work. Now Miss Gardner would not have selected such a butterfly as me to break upon her wheel, but for the circumstance that I had happened to call attention to the parallel between the typological exegesis of Scripture and the sort of poetry-criticism which Mr Empson and in some places Charles Williams and other writers had endeavoured. As this parallel was the very subject of Miss Gardner's lectures, she made me, who had talked of it, her example, rather than other more solid writers who had been too wise to talk in any such strain—Dr Robert Lightfoot, for instance, whose presence used to be such an ornament to this society.

No analogies are more than partial, and all parallels, if we

Presidential Address to the Oxford Society of Historical Theology 22 October 1959, reprinted from the *Proceedings* of the Society, 1959-60.

allow ourselves to be misled by them, are misleading. St Mark's Gospel (let us say) is neither a poem nor a play, and it has to be interpreted as what it is, not as what it is not. Any comparison between Gospel exegesis and Shakespearian criticism will be no better than it happens to be; and to argue that, because something is true of Shakespeare, something similar must be true of St Mark, would be merely ludicrous. Yet, when all is said and done, comparisons are illuminating, and they often give rise to suggestions which we are able to test on more direct evidence. Logicians may talk themselves hoarse in demonstrating that all analogical syllogisms have an ambiguous middle term, and are therefore without formal validity; we shall nevertheless go on cheerfully treating everything in heaven and earth as a parable of everything else, so long as the parable helps us. How good a parable poetical (and let us say Shakespearian) criticism may be of Gospel exegesis, is what we shall have to determine by sense and judgement as we proceed.

Now with regard to the parallel, such as it is, between Bible exegesis and literary criticism, it is fair to say that Miss Gardner has her own special stand-point and interest. She is a literary critic, not a biblical exegete, and though profoundly and widely learned in the literature of other centuries, she shows herself in these lectures specially concerned with English writers of the seventeenth century. She knows of course, and cannot possibly wish to deny, that, at various times and by various writers, double senses and wilful ambiguities have been cultivated, and whole works written or conceived on partially concealed symbolical patterns. It is useless to stick to the plain moral or narrative sense and avert your eyes from piercing beneath the surface when you are travelling through a medieval masterpiece such as Dante's *Divine Comedy*. It would be a facile generalization indeed to make type and allegory simply characteristic of the Middle Ages; and Miss Gardner rightly insists on how much ordinary down-to-earth human interest medieval work exhibits. Nevertheless, there was an awful lot of the spiritual sense in medieval art, far too much for most of us to stomach; and though the writers of the later Renaissance still had the medieval inheritance on their backs, what is mainly characteristic of them is their turning towards human values and literal statements. Miss Gardner is able to illustrate such a movement of thought from Dr

John Donne's explicit remarks; and it seems highly plausible to say of Shakespeare himself, that the figurative or theological in his writing, even where it can be felt, is a starting-point from which he works away rather than the goal of his interest or the life of his thought. Thus the allegorizing or thematic interpretation of Shakespeare may be represented with much plausibility as a swimming backwards against the tide of history, and a concentration on what is of least concern. We should be attending to what his characters do and say, and how they break out of their traditional or symbolic attitudes, rather than to the symbolism from which they effect their happy escape.

But it is not clear that the position of the evangelists was at all the same as Shakespeare's or that they were facing out of symbolism in the direction of human and moral values. Indeed, it would be plausible to suppose the reverse; and to bring out the point, I will put up a monstrous piece of diagrammatization, which must scandalize any historical mind. Let us talk about the tableland of Christian symbolism (if you take a high view of it) or the tunnel of Christian symbolism (if you take a low) as extending from the end of the first century to somewhere in the sixteenth. Then it may seem that the evangelists and Shakespeare are unlikely to be doing both the same thing. If Shakespeare is emerging from the tunnel, they were plunging into it; if he is descending from the plateau, they were climbing on to it. To see the evangelists as pointing forward through the patristic into the middle age may be reasonable: to see Shakespeare as pointing back into it may be absurd. So the unhelpfulness of a certain exposition when applied to Shakespeare may be no ground for denying its helpfulness when applied to St Mark. And Miss Gardner's interest in the seventeenth century may disorientate her rather than otherwise for understanding the first. But, in its reflection on Miss Gardner, our remark is unjust. After all, it was we, not she, who brought forward the comparison between the evangelists and the great early modern poets. So all she has done, perhaps, is to show us how little good the comparison does us, and if so, I suppose it serves us right.

To summarize Miss Gardner's judgement upon the Shakespearian and so-forth critics who interpret by means of hidden patterns, undisclosed allusions, or wilful ambiguities, she thinks first, that they have overdone their part, and second, that they have largely exhausted their usefulness, so that we should now serve literary studies best by calling the public off in an opposite direction. But in the biblical field, it is not clear that the method she criticizes has so limited a scope of proper use; and it is still less clear that the time has come when we ought to be calling a halt to its activities. When she tells us that the world of Bible scholarship is now all too prone to seek after types and to elaborate allusions, it makes me rub my eyes and wonder if I am awake. Has not Miss Gardner noticed, that, in matters of literary or scholarly fashion, theology is always a quarter of a century behind the times? We are not just due to recover from the typological measles: we are only beginning to come out in spots. And many of the most solid and flourishing exegetes have resisted the infection altogether.

Karl Barth called his theology corrective—that is to say, it was admittedly one-sided, but on the side most needing emphasis at the time, and in most danger of being neglected. All schools of criticism or of exegesis have this character in greater or less degree, and are corrective in Barth's sense. It is then always possible to attack any such school on two counts: (*a*) that it fails to give expression to the side of the truth it does not emphasize, (*b*) that it emphasizes the side which for the present least calls for emphasizing. Thus we might complain of Barth himself, either that he failed to do justice to the immanence of the divine, or that his thumping of the transcendentalist drum was then inopportune. The first type of criticism (that a corrective movement is one-sided) is surely irrelevant in any case; how could it help being so? The second type of criticism, (that the corrective emphasis is thrown on the wrong side) may or may not be justified, according to the circumstances. We should wish to plead that the corrective emphasis offered by typological interpretation was and is still needed; but admittedly the matter is open to argument. When, however, we are taken to task for not talking about what we do not talk about or for failing to do justice to the wholeness of Scripture truth, we offer no defence because no defence is required. Typological studies deal with typological symbolism in so far as it is present in the sacred texts. A student of typology is not a preacher put up to deliver in one sermon the whole counsel of God. By suggesting that he is, or should be, you can place him in an unfavourable light: how shocking that a theologian should miss the heart of the gospel. Perhaps he would miss it if he tried to hit it, not being much of a theologian or much of a Christian; but anyhow he is not trying to hit it in his special studies, he is talking of something else. We can raise odium against political economists for failing to do justice to the noblest aspirations of the human heart; and yet high ethical reflections would be no true adornment to economic treatises. And so the remark that typological studies make an impression of frivolity or irrelevance will not move us. If they are offered as expositions of the saving gospel, they fairly might be held to make such an impression. But they are offered in answer to particular questions, which in any case theologians and exegetes are not going to let alone, whether they typologize or not:—for example, why St Mark put several paragraphs in the order in which he placed them, or what continuity of thought he exhibits as between one part of his book and another. If Miss Gardner wants, as she seems to want, a plain biographical answer to such questions, all one can say is, that she is asking for the impossible. It might be agreeable to return to the days before Schmidt and Dibelius, if it could be done, but it cannot; of that method of exegesis we must say, *Conclamatum est*. There are, no doubt, other methods of tackling the unity and order of a synoptic Gospel beside that of typology and of a somewhat riddling symbolism. But plain historical biography is not among these alternative methods, and to suggest that the typological approach is displacing the historical is misleading.

Some of the considerations Miss Gardner advances are surprising, and, in point of logical bearing on the issue, not altogether clear. For example, she quotes the opinion of a learned man to the effect that the simple realism of a narrative about Peter's denial in Mark 14 is, for its period, most striking, if not unique. The fact is apparently taken to be embarrassing to the typological exegete. But on what supposition? Only on the supposition that he denies the whole historical content of St Mark's Gospel, and declares every line in it to be a tissue of typological allusion. But where is this wild interpreter? Is there anyone who wishes to deny that St Mark, when he had a plain unvarnished tale to tell, could tell it, anyhow to the extent of a single anecdote or episode? What, in fact, would a typologist wish to say about St Peter's denial? He might wish to say, I think, that the scheme of typology we have to consider here is not one of allusion to the Old Testament so much as a system of prefiguration and fulfilment interior to the Gospel itself. The denial of Peter stands most plainly on the double background of the confession of Peter in chapter 8 and the prophecy of Peter's denial in the beginning of 14; here, indeed, is an example of the prefiguration scheme which the greatest enemy of typologizing can scarcely deny. But a typologist would show his peculiar art (or betray his peculiar folly, as you view it) by pointing out how the story of Peter's confession has been embedded by the evangelist in discourse material giving an explicit prediction of that rejection and passion of Jesus, in which, when literally fulfilled, the story of Peter's denial will be found to be embedded. The typologist might go on to remark that the prediction of the passion given in connection with Peter's confession lays the greatest and most exclusive emphasis of any Marcan passion-prophecy on that rejection by the elders, high-priests, and scribes, which proves in the event the occasion of Peter's denial. 'The Son of Man must suffer many things and be rejected by the elders, high-priests, and scribes and killed, and after three days rise.'

There is no end to what can be said about the confession, and about the admittedly curious arrangement of the surrounding material. But enough has been said to illustrate the prefiguredness, or antitypical significance, of Peter's denial as we might view it on such a background, and to show how little this is likely to detract from an acceptance of the plain historical sense of Peter cursing and swearing and then weeping tears of shame among the crowing cocks. On the contrary, it might be said that the background prepared in our minds for this event as we read the earlier pages of the Gospel sharpens our attention to the literal detail when it comes. And so I do not know why the plain realism of this scene should be thrown up against us. We may go further. You might say that the religious and philosophical writers of St Mark's time were much inclined to improve the occasion, point the moral, and write up their episodes. St Mark himself (we may suggest) shares this propensity, and often brings out the lesson of an anecdote by appending a word of Christ, the reaction of the crowd, or the like. If he is able to present the denial of Peter, and other episodes of the passion, with a narrative bareness which may satisfy even the readers of tough guy novels, is it not because the prefigurative structure of his earlier chapters has provided beforehand all the moral we shall need?

I shall now pass to another of Miss Gardner's remarks of which the logical bearing (as I have confessed) puzzles me. She admits our plea that the New Testament writers manifestly believed Old Testament types to be fulfilled in the saving mysteries of the gospel, because they quite often say so in so many words. But, says Miss Gardner, so far from explicit typological references in our authors being a warrant for our suspecting the presence of implicit typological allusion, the very reverse is the case. Why should they ever be content with the obscurity of allusion, if they frequently employ the plainness of citation? How little force there is in this argument may be shown by the simple device of turning the matter the other way round. Some writers (as Miss Gardner knows) have employed veiled allusion or undisclosed symbolism; there is no denying, then, that the thing happens. But, to speak generally, in what authors would it be most reasonable to look for it? In authors who sometimes anyhow betray an allusive or symbolical bent, by the use of open citation and declared symbolism; or in those in whom no such visible evidences of that propensity are to be found? Is not the answer obvious? The authors who are in places openly allusive or symbolical are those likely to be disguisedly so elsewhere; as we see in Dante or in Spenser. It looks as though any suggestion whatever of concealed allusion in any author will receive short shrift from Miss Gardner. For she can ask us whether our author openly plays upon the same sort of allusions elsewhere. Whatever we answer we are sunk. If that he does not, she can tell us that there is no indisputable evidence that our author's mind ever moved in the way we allege it to have done. If that he does, she can ask us why a man who knew how to make explicit citations or references should elsewhere have been content with half-disclosed allusions. Now when we meet a Morton's-Fork argument of this sort, we have reason to suspect that something is wrong.

We may pursue the point by taking up another of Miss Gardner's remarks. She says that explorations of undisclosed symbolism or patterns seldom help her to understand the meaning of an author: what pays is the careful examination of the thing he directly says. It is difficult to assess this statement. If discussions of concealed symbolism are seldom helpful, it may not be because few texts call for illumination by such methods but that the greater part of what has been attempted by symbolizing exegetes has been rank folly. It might still remain that many texts call for exposition of this kind, and that such exposition can help us to the author's meaning. There is not much we can do to establish the point, except by citing examples and suggesting that they are typical of many others. In fact, I shall cite one example. In Romans 7.9, St Paul writes thus: 'I was alive once, without any law incumbent upon me. But when the commandment came, sin came to life, and I fell into death.' Now according to Miss Gardner's precept, we should attend to the literal sense since there is no indication of any other. St Paul is writing autobiography, it would appear; the circumstances of his moral history had been such as to make the surprising expressions he uses appropriate. But it is very generally supposed by interpreters that the choice of expressions is dictated by St Paul's seeing himself in Adam, or in the type of Adam. Adam had lived, with the full immortal life of one freshly created in the very similitude of God; and so far he had no command incumbent upon him. But when God said to him, 'Thou shalt not eat of the tree in the midst of the garden', resentment of the prohibition quickly led to transgression, and transgression to death; for it was said to him, 'In the day that thou eatest thou shalt die.' How was it then (since God cannot lie) that Adam did not die in the day he ate? He did die—in a certain sense; though he continued to drag his mortal body, it was dead to goodness; though he might now approve of God's law in his mind, he found an anti-law in his body, preventing it from being alive to God. And so St Paul, as a child of Adam, exclaims, 'Who shall deliver me from the body of this death?' That is, of the death Adam died on the day he ate; and he replies, 'I thank God, through Jesus Christ our Lord'—through union, that is, with his death and resurrection, the 'body of death' is abolished, and true life regained.

Now supposing the Adamic interpretation of Romans 7 is right, does it do nothing for us, towards the understanding of what St Paul is telling us about himself? He is describing his own predicament, with great intensity of language; he is saying, with passion, that the Adam-predicament is (or was) his predicament.

But does it cast no light on what he is saying about himself, to realize that it is an applying of the type of Adam, and not a free psychological or moral analysis?

I will not take other examples, for one is enough. You can judge for yourselves how typical a case this is, and how many other New Testament texts are illuminated by the same sort of exegesis. It may seem very much a matter of chance that the name of Adam does not anywhere occur in Romans 7—it might have slipped in, without disturbing the balance of the passage—and yet the possibility and, as it has chanced, the actuality of its absence is surely symptomatic of something. Miss Gardner quotes, as an example of that explicit typology which we might expect to be general, St Paul's allegory on Sarah and Hagar in Galatians. If we compare the character and purpose of Galatians 4 and of Romans 7. 7 ff, perhaps we shall be able to see why the typology is explicit in the one passage, and inexplicit in the other. In Galatians 4. 21, St Paul writes: 'Tell me, you who want to be under the law, do not you hear what it says? Abraham had two sons, one by his maid, and one by his wife', and so forth. The apostle is forcing a scriptural argument on those who, as he says, accept scriptural authority, but who need to be convinced of the truth he proposes to deduce from it. Nothing plainly will serve his purpose but to produce his scriptural evidence and to draw out the typological application. In Romans 7 the situation is quite different. There is no question there of proving something to be true about the predicament of St Paul, because his situation is antitypical to that of Adam. That all men are first in Adam, then in Christ, has already been explicitly set forth in Romans 5. What is on hand in the seventh chapter is the application of Adam-language to the illumination of the human predicament, as instanced in St Paul himself. Nothing would be more useless or distracting here than the 'As in Adam, so in us' formula. 'Oh, bother Adam!' we should exclaim, 'Get on with telling us about that Adam who is Paul.'

Perhaps we may advance, on the strength of the comparison we have made, to reconsider the case of St Mark. What is he trying to do in such typological applications as he makes (for I suppose no one will utterly deny that he ever makes any)? Is he for the most part trying to prove that this and that had to happen to Christ because it had been written of Elijah or Moses or David or some other. Or is he, for the most part, taking the typological argument of the Church for granted, and on the basis of an admitted prefigurement, using Elijah language or Moses language, or whatever language it be, to illuminate and directly to present the figure of that greater Elijah or greater Moses who is Christ? If he is arguing a typological case, then of course it is very careless of him to omit his evidence; but if he is painting a typological picture, then for heaven's sake let him get on with laying the colours, and not keep putting the brush down while he lectures us on the provenance and composition of the pigments.

The parable is, of course, not wholly just; because the colours laid on the canvas make their effect, irrespective of our appreciation of their chemistry; whereas the typological colours in a Gospel narrative derive much of their distinctive tint as typological, that is, as Mosaic or Elianic, from our recognition of their sources. St Paul's use of undisclosed Adamic typology in Romans 7 is made possible by the background offered in the explicit Adam typology of Romans 5; of which, however, it is not a mere and direct continuation, the thread having been broken by the introduction of detailed law-symbolism (status of slaves and status of wives) in 6.15—7.6. Nevertheless, we may well say that the Adam argument is still sufficiently in mind to afford a reasonable clue for the interpretation of 7.7 following. Now St Paul is writing an epistle, a mixed piece in which argument alternates with descriptive presentation, not to mention exhortation, laudation, and vituperation. And the argumentative passages are natural occasions for an explicit typology which is then available for allusive application in passages of another kind. St Mark's Gospel is a different sort of book. The evangelist is not going to come forward *in propria persona* and argue his typology; and so, perhaps, he has not such a natural occasion as St Paul has in Romans for putting the clue into our hands. Nevertheless, St Mark does *report* discussions, and some of these are typological and may serve the same purpose. Already in chapter 2.25 he reports a discussion between Jesus and the Pharisees in which he compares himself with King David during the days of his persecution and concealment. In 6.14 he reports a sort of discussion between Herod and the Galilean public; is Jesus Elias or John Baptist Redivivus? The same suggestions are repeated and summarized in a discussion between Jesus and his disciples in 8.28. The relation of Christ to David is discussed again between Jesus and the scribes in 12.35. But of course St Mark has other methods for giving us our clues. The figures of Moses and Elijah appear in visionary glory; the voice from heaven echoes Scripture. And the general principle of what we are to expect is given to us in the very exordium of the Gospel.

'The beginning of the *blessed message* concerning Jesus Christ, according to the text of Isaiah the prophet: See, I send my *messenger*. . . .' Out of this text the advent of the Baptist is written; but it is an imperceptive reader, surely, who supposes that the Christ of the blessed message springs out of Scripture any less evidently than his messenger does. A word is enough to the wise; St Mark is not going to burden his story with continual citatory asides. Are we then to say that St Matthew either lacked this point of literary discretion or depended less on the wit of his audience? But we must remember St Matthew's different position. He was working up St Mark's book in which the prophecy bearing on the Baptist's advent already stood. St Matthew, however, was not content with making this the beginning of the gospel of Jesus Christ; he was going to prefix the infancy narrative. Under these circumstances, the text about John Baptist could not serve to show how the whole gospel of Jesus Christ springs out of Scripture. What was St Matthew to do? He might have done many things, but what he has done is to let the prophecy about the Baptist fall into place in a whole series of prophetic citations concerning the advent of Jesus—a series, however, which peters gradually out after the Baptist has duly appeared, St Matthew having no more intention, after all, than St Mark had, to supply his readers with a running prophetic commentary spoken in his own voice.

We are turning aside into matters of detail, and chasing attractive hares, not to say rank red-herrings, which are liable to carry us off the scent of the argument. What we have wished to do is to work out a parallel which Miss Gardner herself proposes between the handling of typic allusion in St Paul and the handling of it in St Mark. And we hope that the parallel will have cast some light, as it ought to do, being an argument *a clariore ad obscurius*—it is more evident how the apostle handles his typic themes in an argumentative Epistle, than how St Mark does in a perhaps wilfully enigmatic Gospel.

I have done my best, in this paper, to dissolve those of Miss Gardner's arguments which appear to undermine the charter of an exegesis I believe in and wish to see practised. But I am well aware that even if I have succeeded in my immediate aim, I have not broken the force of her criticism, anyhow in so far as it bears upon my own work. It was not good enough; it did not convince her; and so it discredited in her eyes the innocent assumptions and principles on which it proceeded. Bad practice should not discredit an art, but it commonly does; and I must take the blame. It is not, in fact, Miss Gardner's arguments which teach me the lesson I require to learn; it is her standards. I read her critical work in her own field with admiration and delight. I see intellectual and imaginative sympathy chastened by candour and restraint. In whatever field exposition is to be exercised, these are the qualities.

---

[1] Now Dame Helen Gardner, Merton Professor of English Literature at Oxford University.

CREED

The Christian Doctrine of Man

To define against heresy is a well-known task of the theologian; all our positive credal statements, serene and timeless as they now appear, are but the crystallized deposit of such defensive definitions in the past. When some heresy is in the field, we have to draw a line and say: 'the Christian Verity is to be found on this side, not that, of such-and-such a boundary.' This much theology *must* do: it is her life-and-death concern; and, whether we like it or not, we are bound in so far to dogmatize because it concerns man's salvation that we should.

But when, within such necessary boundaries, the theologian is called upon to state the Christian truth in positive terms, what is he to do? Our Lord, faced with a similar question out of the blue, replied: 'Thou knowest the Commandments.' We, following that example, may be tempted simply to refer inquirers to the divine gospel and the living Church. But, it will be said, surely we are not irrationalists: it is the business of the theologian to systematize as best he can the revealed truth in the light of natural knowledge. Very well; but such speculative systems are tentative and private. Who can venture to put his own forward as *the* Christian doctrine of man?

We become even more alarmed about the task laid upon us, when we realize that the Christian doctrine of man is being laid down as the foundation on which practical conclusions are to be built, referring to the social and political spheres. This doctrine, then, is to be some sort of bridge between the faith of the gospel and its practical application. Now it might very well be suspected that no such a bridge exists or can exist. Perhaps, after all, there is only the Word of God on the one hand, and on the other the Church's consciousness which, responding thereto, arrives at convictions about certain particular things which ought to be done. The preacher proclaims Christ: in responsibility towards the Christ proclaimed and in view of the situation before him, the

Reprinted from *The Christian Understanding of Man*, 1938.

Christian man of practical vision sees what he thinks should be done; the Christian scholar adds the guidance of precedent from the Church's former acts; the critical theologian judges the proposed decisions by the standards of faith. The series is complete: nowhere does there intervene a constructive theologian with a theory of man from which the practical decision needs to be deduced.

'Well but,' it may be protested, 'the practical and moral judgements of Christians are not chaotic, not unconnected by any thread of common principle. From the Church's moral experience generalizations can be drawn; and these might well be called a Christian doctrine of man.' They might indeed: but then they are reflective, and subsequent to the action which is the primary response to the gospel; and, being generalizations from the past, they share the unsatisfactoriness of all such generalizations—the practical light they shed on new situations is dim and equivocal, and those who expect from such a doctrine clear deductions about the desirable direction for new forms of state activity will probably be disappointed. The only theologian who can help much there is the theologian who feels inspired to prophesy. Let those that have it exercise the gift.

It looks as though the Christian doctrine of man will fall apart into two halves—a generalization from the Christian practical conscience, and the gospel itself viewed from its human end. The essay which follows will deal with the relations between these two doctrines of man—the doctrine revealed from Heaven and the doctrine which springs from the enlightened conscience. Then, by an inevitable transition, we shall find ourselves led to deal with the relation between the conscience enlightened by revelation and the conscience not thus enlightened, between the practical ideal for man within Christianity and that which is to be found outside it.

What is meant by a Christian doctrine of man?

The reflections we have so far made seem to be confirmed when we examine the attempts of philosophers or theologians to arrive at an account of man's substance. Their real object, we quickly discover, is to answer the question: 'What ought man to be and do?' But it seems natural to attempt first the apparently prior question: 'What is man?' For if man be a spiritual organism so constituted as to perform a certain function, observe the structure of the organism and you will be able to infer the function's nature; proceed, therefore, with your analytic exposition of man's constitution.

But when we examine the analyses that have been made, we find that they consist in the enumeration of 'active properties'. Elasticity is an active property in a ball; and if the ball has this property, it is capable of an elastic rebound. But in attributing to it this property, we are merely attributing to it a quality x, such that it will rebound in suitable circumstances. And our only evidence for its doing so, and therefore for its possession of the quality, is the observed fact of its rebounding.

Similarly, we may be told that man has spirit in his make-up. Either this means nothing relevant to our purpose or it means he is capable of what are called spiritual activities, of which the types could be roughly enumerated. But we can only know this by having observed such activities in exercise; and all we shall then know is that various men in various observed degrees have shown themselves capable of these activities. We cannot proceed to the universal 'man has spirituality', nor even if we could to the conclusion 'and therefore he ought to behave thus and thus'.

It appears vain, therefore, to construct a wholly invisible substance which all men are, in order to explain why a certain pattern of activities is what they ought to practise. Our primary certainties, if we have any, are about this pattern itself: we may claim that a certain configuration of it is good, or the good, for man, and this may be the only doctrine of man worth having.

If we do make such statements, we must be assuming that the relation between man's life or realized perfection on the one hand, and on the other his determinate substantial being *qua* man, is certainly not fixed. He must be capable of various patterns of life, or it would be needless to inquire which is best. His pattern must be alterable; but no doubt there are limits to that alterability. Perhaps it is here that an examination of what man *is*, of his actual 'nature', may come in: we may try by observation to arrive at the probable limits of his variations. And so we do, if we are psychologists or physiologists: we gain an ever-increasing body of evidence as to what tunes can and cannot be played on the human instrument without material damage to it.

Even this evidence is no surer or wider than the instances from which it has been generalized: it does not rule out the possibility of a fundamental change in man or in some men, falling completely outside its generalizations. But let us ignore this point and accept the sciences as they stand. Still, they only tell us what will not work. Among the various lives that will work—for there are many—we have still to make our choice, and Christian theology claims to be able to assist us.

Theology can but point to the data of revelation; but these, whatever it is that they give us, do not supply a system of ethics and sociology, nor yet do they give us a doctrine of man's substantial composition from which these things could be deduced.

It is true, no doubt, that Scripture gives some account of man's substance in terms of body, soul, spirit, and other such conceptions. This language is primitive, inadequate, and confused. The Scripture was not given to teach us psychology. One need not deny that such terminology was accurate enough for the purposes of Scripture; that is, for referring to the human pole of the relation with God which God brings about. But that only shows how completely Scripture is concerned with the relation, and how little with the human pole considered apart from the relation. If the terminology has any merit, it is the merit of infancy as compared with maturity. Maturity in becoming determinate and effective excludes many possibilities that still seemed to lie open to childhood. So human thought in becoming mature becomes accurate indeed and systematic, but narrowed by its very definiteness; and a glance back to the childhood of the human mind may convey to us vague and undifferentiated suggestions of a wider truth than can be expressed in our current philosophy or science. That might mean for us the reform of our present conceptions, certainly not a return to their primitive counterparts.

Revelation, then, does not set out to answer for us the question 'What is man?' but to tell us how God made him but little lower than the angels, how he regards and visits him, and crowns him with glory and honour. Here we have primarily acts of God, but no doubt secondarily activities also of man in response thereto. Since these activities of man are the appropriate responses to the objects set him by God's acts, they make up what is the true pattern of man's life according to the Christian revelation, and to know this pattern would be to know, if not a Christian doctrine *of* man, at least the Christian doctrine *for* man. We may indeed study the pattern direct in the lives of those who have worthily pursued the God-given objects, but even so, the objects were determinant for them and the primary matter of Revelation. For piety, in a Christian view, is just whatever a man does in conforming himself to the self-revealed God, and to infer the revelation from the response is in the strictest sense preposterous.

This is not of course to say that we begin with the revealed knowledge of what God is, simply in himself. Of such knowledge we are not capable recipients. What is revealed is his actions, and himself only as the agent of them; and what he does is to create, call, redeem, promise; that is, to determine our existence and not his own. And yet these determinations do not reveal to us what we are, but give us the objects we must pursue.

It would not do to say that the relations of man with God which Revelation displays are simply external to man, as they are external to God. The relations which come into existence between the creature and the Creator do not affect the Creator's being: the creature's they not only affect but effect, since both our nature and our existence are pure effects of his will. That is true of the order of being; but in the order of knowing it is otherwise. As knowers we begin by taking ourselves for granted. Then we learn, in this case from Revelation, the relations in which we stand to our environment—in this case, our supernatural environment which is God himself, and next, the claims that this environment has upon our activity. And so Revelation is primarily of God's acts and the relations to him which they create for us; and it is through the knowledge of these things that we come to the knowledge of the sort of life we ought to live in response to them, and so to the Christian doctrine of man.

How the relations of man to God make possible the idea of a doctrine of man

We can only attempt to show here how the very notion of a true nature of man, which he ought to and in some cases is destined to realize, is, for the Christian, bound up with those relations to God in which revelation sets him. Of these relations we may specify:

1. Man's relation to God as his Creator and Sustainer.
2. His relation to the end intended by the Creator.
3. The correspondence or non-correspondence of his present course with the steps divinely intended to lead him to that end.
4. His relation to the gracious intervention of God which is to restore that correspondence when lost.

To the Christian it appears that the very conception of a true or natural pattern for human existence depends on the first two of these relations. If we take man apart from God, why suppose one end or goal for mankind at all? Men are many, and they are various. It is true that they have, in general outline, the same biological basis, being of one animal species. But there seems no reason why they should not go as many ways as their common species allows them to go, or as their herd instincts allow them to desire. But if what appears to phenomenal observation as the evolution of man is in its reality the creative act of God, then a Maker may have a purpose, and a Maker of many a common purpose for all, and this 'idea' subsisting in the Divine Intention is the true exemplar of the true doctrine of man—that is, indeed, where the true nature of man truly *is*, and only secondarily in anything that man may be observed to be, or to be tending towards, or aspiring after in fact.

It is this intention of man's Creator that imposes on him an absolute obligation—that of acting in correspondence with it; and failure to correspond makes his state one of sin. How great the lack of correspondence, and how complete the inability of man to recover it, is known by revelation alone; and that revelation takes the form of the divine intervention itself which recovers it to him. For it was in the act of God's recovering man that man saw how low he had fallen. The revelation of a depth implies the revelation of a height, and both were revealed by the act which lifted man from the one to the other.

If it is true that the first two relations specified above give us the bare possibility of conceiving a true and unitary 'nature' for men, it is the second two which afford the possibility of filling that conception with any content. Words about our final consummation or true end would bear no sense unless they bore analogy to present experience. And so the actual reception of grace, as being a foretaste of our end, is our key to the conception of it. If our end is to attain unto God, then the entry of God into the world in Christ, and our being by the Spirit enabled to know him there, is the actual revelation of our end; and it is from our end that we know our true 'nature'. By our redemption we are already in some measure in reception of God, and therefore able to attach some sense to the teaching that promises us an increase both of our capacity to receive and of its satisfaction up to such a point, that any further increase would destroy our determinate nature as creatures of a certain kind.

The notion of such a fixed point might suggest an arbitrary limit, as though we might be destined to fret for all eternity against a barrier we may not pass. There is no need to think anything of the kind. If we are to receive God up to the limit of our capacity, and that capacity finds its measure in our very nature as men, then we should presumably feel no barrier, for who can feel a barrier in the absolute fulfilment of himself? To desire more would be to desire extinction, by absorption into the very being of God himself. Absorption is a misleading word; it suggests that something remains of what is absorbed. But God realizes in himself the full possibilities of the divine nature: there is no room for more gods but One, or in the One for any addition; and the deification of the creature is exactly its annihilation. By this path also, then, we are led back to the same point—that the Christian doctrine of man's end and consummation itself implies that the Creator has assigned to man a determinate nature, which can be perfectly fulfilled but not passed beyond.

That does not mean that the present pattern of our nature is eternally unalterable; for who can determine exactly which aspects of manhood as we know it belong to the conditions of its ultimate perfectibility and which to the state of earthly existence? Grace, then, may perform upon us marvels that we cannot conceive, but still in perfecting, not superseding, our nature—a nature which is a datum for grace and imposes a measure on what grace may effect: just what measure we cannot know.

Our ignorance is not removed by the revelation of God in Christ. There indeed we see divine perfection measured or limited by the capacity of human nature, yet not of the nature we shall ultimately be, but only of the possibilities of its perfection under the conditions of this life. To know the other we should have to have direct knowledge of Christ in glory, which we have not, so far as regards his manner of being. We have some knowledge of him in the days of his flesh; and there we see him clothed in certain elements of our nature as we know it here, which we assume, therefore, to belong at least to the raw material of our perfection, and not to the dross of perversions which grace will simply purge away.

If in the man Christ Jesus we have a man in perfect response to the acts of God through which we are related to him, then in the same Christ we have in actual and perfect expression the human pole of the relation between God and man, as redemption restores it under the conditions of our present life; and to know this would be to know the Christian doctrine of man in the only way possible to us here.

The status of non-Christian doctrines about man

We have so far attempted to show that while it is not possible to begin with the knowledge of a human substance simply given, it is possible to conceive a true nature of man—true with the truth of correspondence to a divine exemplar, as artistic expression can be true in corresponding to the artist's thought. We have hoped to show the possibility of such a conception within the framework of Christian revelation. We proceed to consider whether there can be any conception of it outside that framework; and if so, what it is that revelation adds to a knowledge obtainable without it.

To maintain that apart from the one Revelation there is no conception of man's nature or pattern of life is nothing more nor less than an attempt to silence good evidence by hard swearing, though some appear not to have shrunk from it. It is evident that all philosophies, religions, or views of the world, excluding those that are purely sceptical and including most that pretend to be so, have something to say about the true type of human life. It is equally plain that the subject matter about which they try to speak is the same as that about which the Christian doctrine does speak—equally plain that while all are, by the Christian standard, more or less wrong, all are more or less right as well.

That is the evidence, and our difficulties do not begin till we launch into dogmatic explanations of it—which admittedly we are bound to try to find. Could we say, for example, that before Revelation a certain area of the rational conscience was indefectible and uncorrupt, a certain set of moral propositions clear, while those other truths remained in the dark which revelation was later given to illuminate? Such a suggestion remains plausible only so long as we abstain from trying to enumerate these truths of reason.

If, then, we cannot maintain in this sense a residual but reliable reason left over by the 'fall', are we to go into the other camp and assert 'total depravity'? That depends on what we mean by 'total depravity'. If we are adopting an eschatological view and taking our stand at the final consummation of the world, then no doubt it is proper to say that everything in the world is totally depraved, if it is turned so crooked as not to be following a line which will bring it to its God-intended consummation. If a creature is so behaving as to lead to its becoming a final and total loss, then there is a good sense in saying that it is totally off the right line.

If, on the other hand, we consider any creature as it is at any moment of its progress towards its end, however lamentable that end is to be, and ask what it now is in itself, then to say that it has no correspondence of any kind with the nature intended by its Creator does not make sense. So long as a creature continues to exist, its existence cannot fall wholly outside the nature intended by its Creator; that is the charter of its being, and by passing outside its terms it would either cease to exist or become something else. Human nature totally depraved in this sense would be totally denatured and dehumanized. We might accept that description of the totally insane so far as their life is manifested to us, but hardly of mankind as a whole before Revelation.

Corruption is a real and terrible thing; but it is distributed partially over man's whole moral nature and is not the total extinction of any particular elements in it. There is only one thing that is definitely and simply 'lost'—a sure, true and objective vision of God. That vision, and the relation to God founded upon it, may well be the very head in the body or organism of man's spiritual nature, the very keystone to the arch. But this head being lost, the members do not simply mortify and perish; if they did, there would be nothing left for redemption to redeem. They have a certain vitality which causes them to struggle against their own corruption—not, we may well say, with such success that they ever unaided shake it off, or attain a mastery which is the earnest of final victory and final perseverance, yet vigorously enough to maintain their own existence, to be still holding out when grace comes to give the triumph they cannot themselves attain.

But in nature's unaided struggle it is absurd to draw lines she cannot, in this and that instance, overpass. There is no specific human virtue or social attitude of which we could dare to say that it is not to be found in those untouched by the Christian dispensation. In perfection, no doubt not: but we might look in vain for that among the elect who have not perfection but only the earnest of it. And even their having that is a matter of faith.

Man, then, apart from revelation and grace, is still man and the creature of God; and though corrupt in his spiritual nature to an undefinable extent, still has, as is evident, the power of reflecting on his true nature and obtaining some impression of the pattern of it intended by God. He may not even be aware that God is, but that does not prevent his having some sense of a goal set before him, because man as a spiritual being is essentially an aspirant, and an aspirant must have an object of his aspiration; so that in being aware of himself in any wise, man is aware, however confusedly, of a pattern of true nature; and, once again, we can draw no line that his unaided moral reflection is incapable of passing. There is no single moral conviction that nature may not arrive at for herself, so long as we are speaking of man's ideal for his own life on earth, or for his relations with his neighbour.

In saying this, we are not going back on our original denial that man has a substantial being which can be objectively defined in such a way that his true end could be inferred from it. What the pagan philosopher does is not this at all, even if it is what he thinks he is doing. He is, in fact, becoming vaguely aware—*sub quadam confusione*, says St Thomas—of the exemplar which is actually in the divine mind and nowhere else. The persistence of man's moral nature even under corruption means the persistence of actual aspiration towards the divinely appointed end, and that implies a certain vision of that end, however confused and however dissociated from all ideas of theology. It is sufficient here to state the fact, without asking through what channels this confused conception of the divine purpose reaches the 'natural reason'.

We will pause to refute a heresy, partly because it is pernicious, partly because the refutation of it will cast further light on the relation between revelation and 'natural reason'. This heresy attempts to prove, in the teeth of all evidence, that certain vital spiritual attitudes and convictions about the human side of human life are impossible without faith in Revelation, or at least in God.

The heretical argument builds on the propositions asserted above, that a right conscious relation to God is the keystone to the structure of human life or head to its organism. For in an existence ordered towards God the various elements belonging to the true pattern of our life are seen to find their reasonable and organic place, and to co-operate harmoniously in subserving the one supreme end. Remove the governing principle, and the harmony and completeness to which Christian eyes are accustomed will no longer be found. But the now headless members of our moral nature—the various elements of interest, desire, and aspiration, social or self-regarding—are unwilling to fall into complete dissociation and dissolution. Having lost their king they elect a president, and tend to reunite themselves under some makeshift principle or another when they find themselves deprived of their proper head; and so arise various philosophies, whether formulated or unconscious.

The Christian dialectician takes these various substitute highest principles of action. One may be self-realization, another the good of the totality of mankind, another the attainment of a certain list of 'values'. About all these he proceeds to demonstrate that they are inadequate for the role they have undertaken. Treat any one of them as your supreme motive and it becomes impossible to regard some one or other of the Christian virtues—it may be absolute chastity, it may be true neighbourly love—as means that you would naturally adopt in order to compass that end. Either the end fails to provide a place for the Christian virtue at all, or else, in adopting it, more or less seriously distorts it.

The Christian dialectician may further claim to show that even though you may have true neighbourly love as derived not from your false first principle of action but from some independent source—e.g. from the example of Christians—then still the false first principle, if it has any serious influence on your thoughts and acts, is bound to cramp its exercise. If you really treat the friendship you show to your neighbour as means to your own self-realization or as a contribution to the well-being of an abstract totality called mankind or the state, the quality of your neighbourliness will not remain unimpaired.

All this may very well be true; but it is at the next step in the argument that error arises: i.e. when the theologian goes on to draw the conclusion that so long as you have the false first principle, you cannot exhibit true neighbourly love at all, nor possess the notion of it, nor admit the claim of it. This conclusion is false. The only true conclusion would be: 'You cannot *logically*, so long as you pretend that all your morality is to be deduced from your false first principle.' But even if men do seriously pretend this, how many of them are logical in its practical application? It is very implausible to maintain that men are so single-minded and logical in their aims: all are in practice pluralists to a greater or less extent, and follow many uncoordinated values; and, therefore, though the possession of a false first principle and the loss of the true may make impossible the realization of the full true pattern of human nature in the ordered Kingdom of Ends, it remains possible for any single human virtue or worthy aim to flourish illogically under the makeshift republic.

If men who have lost a true conscious relation with God could not patch together the consequent disunion of their aims and of their life with some sort of substitute general principle, their minds would fall into extreme disorder. But equally, if they could not set up such a patched unity without the substitute first principle's imposing an absolute dictatorship and *Gleichschaltung* upon all the elements it patches together, men would become completely dehumanized. We see the process going a good way in certain fanatics: but if it goes all the way, the man is mad. In the ordinary case, it is the essence of the situation that the patch remains a patch, and so in more or less disharmony with what it patches. Only the true first principle can be anything else. And this no doubt is the reason for the world's profound suspicion of philosophy whenever it proposes to take itself too seriously, and a similar suspicion of Christianity, with those who do not know what it is. If one gave God an inch, he might so easily take an ell!

But, it is said, apart from the love of God we have at least one purely human disability: we cannot love humanity. No: but then the love of humanity is not a human possibility at all, because humanity is nothing but an idea in the mind of God, and we can only love the idea by loving the mind and desiring the fulfilment of that mind's purposes. Otherwise, humanity is merely a general description of such men as we may be in direct and indirect relations with, and to love humanity can only mean to entertain the resolve to take up a friendly attitude to any men we may have to do with from time to time.

The paragraphs which have preceded might be welcome to a humanist as a plea on behalf of natural goodness, a suggestion that man is not so very bad after all and in need of supernatural grace only to add the last touches to his perfection. Any such interpretation must be far from the mind of the Christian theologian. Our object has been merely to show that what corruption fastens on is human goodness. A parasite cannot be parasitic on nothing, nor can corruption prey upon itself. But the terrible nature of the disease is only heightened by the worth of what it undermines and will at length destroy. A stinking fungus in the woods may be offensive to sense; but to the mind it is infinitely less distressing than a cancer in the human throat.

From the point of view also of our responsibility for evil—a topic on which we shall later have more to say—the same thing appears. The shining excellences that are in mankind themselves create the blackness of a sin which can turn from a realized spiritual beauty to feed on garbage. Every such act is guilt which cannot be weighed, much less atoned, by man. Had his present condition simply dropped to that of some baser creature, then whatever the guilt of his ancestors, his own would be small. The type of sin is not the serpent considered according to its natural kind, but the rebellious angel who chose to crawl the dust.

It is in this spirit that we have maintained the roots of all the human virtues to be in natural man. And it is none the less only by supernatural aid that they can at last be saved alive, not to say brought to perfection.

Whence the content of the Christian doctrine of man is derived

There might at first sight appear to be a contradiction between the last two sections of this essay. In the former, the very idea of a doctrine of man was said to spring from that of the relations in which man stands to God. In the latter, men, quite unaware of any relation to God, were admitted to have some sound notions about the true nature of man. Now we did attempt to cover this contradiction by the statement that the unbeliever is actually apprehending the effect of a divine relation without realizing it. But this naturally suggests the rejoinder: 'But cannot the Christian do the same? When the Christian sees some aspect of the good for man, does he necessarily see it as the consequence of a relation to God?'

We must answer that it is obvious that the Christian's conscience can function without the awareness of theological principles just as anyone else's can. It is only on philosophical reflection that the very notion of a 'true good for man' hangs upon theology. The particular content of that notion may be given not by awareness that man is made in God's image but by the functioning of that image in man.

The Christian's human virtues are not all dictated from Heaven, nor are they inferred by mere hard reasoning as logical consequences from the relations in which he learns himself to stand towards God. They are not a mere conformity to principles imposed by his theology, but spring naturally in his human consciousness as faith towards God completes the pattern of his nature. They are natural and not supernatural to him; but in order to attain their proper perfection they need their true setting, and that setting is itself partly supernatural, being in this aspect nothing else but those relations to God of which we have spoken. This setting being given, nature has her true efflorescence, like a plant that has obtained soil, sunlight, and air.

This does not mean that it is impossible to enforce the detail of ethics by theological considerations. For all these parts of the pattern once it is finished—both the supernatural setting and the microcosm of nature—are interrelated in a true order, in which the various elements are felt to imply one another, so that men can be told to love as brethren because they have one Father, or to purify themselves even as he is pure. But it remains true all the same that human duties are duties because they are human, because God created man that he might realize his manhood; and what that is, is known to the Christian by redeemed nature's own response to God—doubtless not the nature of the isolated individual alone, but human nature all the same.

This matter is somewhat complicated by the fact that Christians have in the life and ethical maxims of Christ a standard of the truly human; and it is a usual way of speaking to call this standard a matter of revelation, which in a sense, no doubt, it is. But if we carry consideration a step further back, we shall say that the humanity of Christ, in human activities and relations, is itself human nature perfectly actualized in its true setting, that of absolute rightness of relation towards God. And so what happens in him is what happens, however imperfectly, in believers.

We have attempted to reconcile these two propositions: 'The Christian doctrine of man is just the human conscience come fully to itself', and 'The Christian doctrine of man essentially presupposes the Christian revelation of God in Christ'. And this coming to itself of the human conscience we take to include the stabilizing of it. But now how far is this stabilization a fact? No doubt there is more agreement between Christians who claim to obey the authority of the once-given revelation than there is in the rest of mankind beside. But there is disagreement also, and that is not hard to explain.

In the Christ of the Gospels we believe that the true self-awareness of humanity is found pure. There is the true man truly responding to the true God with true humanity. But Christ's acts and words do not give us a complete guide to life, and what they do give us may be misinterpreted in being applied to new circumstances, nor can any mere logical accuracy eliminate such misinterpretation. An element of fresh spiritual judgement is involved and our judgement may be impure.

Both for interpretation, therefore, and for supplementation we are forced to call in the Christian consciousness outside our Lord, a consciousness liable to an indeterminable degree of perversion and error, and yet the best that we have. We shall look for it where we suppose it to be purest or most surely guided. To raise the question as to where that is would be to compare the claims of Churches to their authority, and of saints to their aureoles. This is not the place to do it, nor is it the place to discuss how much weight is to be attached to precedent, even the best, or how far the individual has to make new decisions for himself in responsibility towards God. It will be sufficient to state that everyone respects some authority in practice; or if not, then he must deny any expressible Christian doctrine of man at all.

The content of the Christian doctrine of man

From what precedes it must follow that the content of the Christian doctrine of man is the whole deliverance of the true Christian conscience, in unity with our Lord's, concerning the good for man in this life. To attempt an expression of this would be to attempt a complete system of ethics. We can here go no further than the most bare generalizations and arid platitudes, mentioning only these principles—the hierarchy and balance of activities, sociality, liberty, and spirituality.

Quite apart from all questions of duty to his neighbour, the Christian sets certain activities before others: other things being equal, feeding should yield to philosophy and pushpin to poetry. But this principle of hierarchy does not exclude the principle of balance. There is a time for philosophizing, but a time also to refrain from philosophy, and some kind of balance is to be observed, though only in broad principle. It is absurd to think one can write a prescription for the employment of everyman's leisure, or demand that every example of *homo sapiens* should be an example of *homo rotundus*, that mythical species, the all-round man. Yet however absurd we become in attempting too much exactness in their application, the principles of hierarchy and balance of activities are perfectly binding as far as they go, and form a man's absolute duty, so far as that duty can be considered apart from duty to his neighbour.

The preservation of such balance and order requires discipline, not merely the resolute choice of the right activity when the inappropriate one is bewitching, but the systematic hardening of oneself in habits conducive to right choices. For we are creatures of habit and cannot trust habits to look entirely after themselves.

In his respect for these things, the Christian need be in no way singular. Although it is unlikely that his hierarchy and system of activities will correspond exactly with that of the non-Christian in detail, the non-Christian may recognize these principles in general, and have many details too in common with him, and be as absolute in his sense of duty.

But now there are certain activities which will be peculiar to the Christian. For his conscious response to God, in acts of understanding and love, is not indeed itself human activity, nor subject matter of ethics, but demands and uses human activities none the less. These religious practices will have their place in the scheme of life, and will carry with them further and peculiar developments of self-discipline. For now this is valued not merely for the formation of useful habit but for creating the state of life conducive to the contemplation of God.

But once again, religious practice and the religious discipline that goes with it are not peculiar to the Christian alone: other followers of other religions know them. Yet here we have something in which the Christian is more directly determined in his conduct by revealed truth—religious practice does not spring simply in the human conscience, but is a direct opening of oneself to God according as one believes in him. As the beliefs differ, so will the practices and the estimation in which they are held, and it is the less to be expected that the Christian will coincide with others in this field. The source and value of non-Christian religious ideas is a question which we must refuse to consider here.

It is odd that the duties of sociality should have been sometimes treated as the chief matter of the Christian revelation. Sociality is part of the true nature of man as man, and so recognized by the most considerable non-Christian thinkers. It is part of what we are from the start, it is a datum for grace when it comes, and lays down lines along which grace will have to proceed if its action is not to dehumanize us. The plurality of men belongs as much to our existence as the unity of God does to his, and the end of man must be a social one. That this involves the absolute and universal obligation of justice and loving-kindness is a possible piece of moral knowledge apart from revelation, however much it may be stabilized and enforced by the theological consideration that other men are as much objects for God as we ourselves, so that to love him means to adopt his purpose for them.

Justice means impartiality in all men's minds, and loving-kindness means wishing them well and giving them friendly assistance in the defence and attainment of their good. There is much more agreement about these definitions than there is about the goods that we have to be impartial in allotting if we are to be just, and that we have to wish and strive to obtain for others if we are to be loving. Thus while two of us may coincide exactly in our definitions of these great social virtues, our views of their practical application may be poles asunder, in so far as we differ in our estimation of the goods to be distributed by justice or sought by loving-kindness. So the practical meaning of our social morality will depend on our individual morality—on our opinion about the hierarchy and balance of activities, but also on our belief in supernatural goods, which though they do not form the subject matter of this essay, cannot be excluded here. The Christian in wishing well to his brother and acting on his wish, will desire for him a right relation with God in response to divine grace, expressed in contemplation as well as obedience, and supported by a self-discipline conducive thereto.

It is in its content, then, rather than in its form that Christian altruism is peculiar: the Christian is not singular in exercising sympathy, but in sympathizing with his neighbour's position as a soul living in the sight of God. If loving-kindness is to be defined as sympathetic co-operation with others in the attainment of whatever aims they happen to adopt, then the Christian must be confessed to be not more, but less, loving than other men. True, he has sympathy for error, or rather for the man that has fallen into it, but to support him in the recovery of the right path, and not in the attainment of his erroneously chosen goal.

This aspect of the Christian's social conscience gives a peculiar turn to his version of the principle of liberty, the third of those we proposed to consider. That principle is not a Christian monopoly. It may be stated in the form, that men's attainment of their good must come through the exercise of their own choice and will. But now the Christian, together with some other moralists, will have a particular temptation to interfere with the liberty of others, because he thinks it important that they should pursue the right goods and not the wrong. This may lead him to adopt the line of conduct which has been euphemistically but nonsensically described as 'forcing them to be free', i.e. *driving* them into the right channels of endeavour.

But then on the other hand he has an equally strong interest in leaving them to act for themselves, since the chief of those 'right goods' that he wishes for them is a right standing in the presence of God, and that can only consist of a right attitude of the autonomous will. Our wills are ours to make them God's, and it cannot be done by proxy.

The Christian's respect for liberty, then, will be something of his own. He will appear to others to be inclined to unwarranted interference; but he will claim that his so-called interference is intended to create the very condition of the true exercise of liberty. For liberty is the voluntary choice of the good. But the good cannot be chosen unless it has been seen. The interference of the Christian, then, will consist in that effective presentation of the good which makes possible for another the choice of it.

Needless to say that, other things being equal, the Christian sympathizes and co-operates with his neighbour in the attainment of immediate and natural desires, and that the obligation to do so is absolute.

Under the last head, spirituality, comes the problem suggested by an earlier section of this essay, when we touched on the subject of the bounds set by our earthly condition to the progress of our nature, under the impulse of grace, towards its ultimate perfection. What, in fact, are these bounds? Ought we to push them back as far as possible and follow the Aristotelian maxim which bids us live the life of immortals even here, as far as in us lies? Since certain things, for example, in Christ's words, marrying and giving in marriage, and every pleasure of sense, seem to belong to our present condition rather than to our ultimate perfectibility, can we anticipate paradise by mortifying them?

This question is partly a practical one—how far can it be done, without cutting our life off from the roots of its natural energy, and so frustrating our object by starving the higher activities themselves? To mortify the 'body of flesh' is not to enter into immediate possession of the resurrection-body: we cannot hope to live in the flesh and out of the flesh at the same time. But partly too it is a social question—how far can it in fact be done without irresponsibility towards the rest of mankind, from whom we are not free to dissociate ourselves?

The answer then depends on practical considerations, and has been solved for the few by the admission of a social and regulated monasticism as a specialized function of society in general, which those who are called into this life help more in this way than they would in any other. For the many, infinite varieties and degrees in otherworldliness have to be recommended according to the vocation and opportunity of each.

Our conclusion is that the Christian doctrine of the good for man is no more than a pure and stabilized form of the human conscience about it. This is so, in so far as human goods and relationships are concerned. But those supernatural goods which Christianity adds are no mere addition, nor merely the cause of the purity and stability of the Christian's view of the rest. For the life of man's spirit is not an agglomerate but an organism, and of that organism we have called his conscious relation with God the head. The whole is more than the sum of its parts, and the natural goods become transmuted in entering into the supernatural good by becoming the field of man's service to God. For the Christian, there can be no mere morality. His moral judgements may agree with other men's but his obedience to them is obedience to God, and a means of appropriating the supreme good.

The freedom of man and the image of God

We have said something about man's nature in its relation to God, and something about its content in itself. We must turn to man's nature in its relation to man. For the paradox of human existence is that man becomes an object to himself; he is concerned with realizing what he is: this is the mystery of the will.

Man's nature has appeared in the double role of goal and limit to his aspiration. It is a certain measure of the divine perfection, and, therefore, the object of his striving; but again it is only a certain measure of it, and, therefore, a limit to his pursuit of perfection itself. But neither a goal nor a limit to aspiration would have any meaning unless man were an aspirant and, therefore, a free creature: if he had not a power to aspire after his end and to conform his actions to his aspirations.

That man's will is free—that it is a will, in fact, and not something else—is certainly Christian doctrine, however many views have been taken by Christians about the scope of his freedom; and it seems best here not to attempt to take sides with any school, but rather to express the minimum doctrine of human liberty which must be held if our religion is to make sense.

We need not assert, then, an arbitrary freedom of choice—that man is able to will anything that could ever come into his head. But we must assert the freedom of effort. Let it be granted that a man can recognize an aspiration as the highest he has—either the highest absolutely, or the highest that applies to these or those given circumstances with which he is today confronted. He *can* recognize it, but only if he makes the effort of sincere reflection. He may or may not make that effort; here lies his freedom. But again, when he has recognized it, he may or may not make the effort required to bring his action into line with his aspiration; and here is freedom again.

It does not seem necessary to assert that a man could always have reflected honestly or acted virtuously on each given occasion. Past failures may have incapacitated him; there may be impediments in the physical or psychic constitution he has inherited. It is enough to assert that he has *some* freedom, however narrow its scope; for then there is something to which the moralist can address himself, and some field in which the will can be exercised.

Christians are not singular in the assertion of free will; it is really acknowledged, though often with much confusion by most religious and moral systems. It does not require Christian faith to bring the acknowledgement of absolute obligation to use all the liberty one has in the pursuit of his best aspirations. Nor need the non-Christian's sanction be a selfish one. The atheist may ask no other motive than the duty of bringing good into existence, whether that good consists of his own activities and states, or those of others, or material conditions productive of these.

The success of a man in actually following his best aspiration depends upon two factors: first, the clarity, force, and unity with which the object of aspiration presents itself to his mind, and second, the effort he actually makes in concentrating attention and activity upon it. No man will be a hero in the service of an ideal he has but faintly seen, nor in that of the most luminous vision, if his will-power is slight.

On both accounts the Christian claims supreme advantage. First, the object of aspiration is not a mere multitude of particular human goods, but the will of the Creator, the one highest good, so far as that can be imparted, and is imparted, to the created universe—an object, therefore, which has a natural power to move the will out of all proportion to any other. And it is the very work of revelation to make this object effectively known to man, that is, in such fashion as to command his desire. Second, the Christian hopes to have received in the grace of the Holy Spirit a power to conform his act to this supreme aspiration.

Kant thought that if I am to recognize the highest good as highest, when presented to me by revelation, I must already have the pattern of it in my heart to recognize it by. In that case I already know what is 'revealed'. That is an error. The faculty of judgement is a faculty of recognizing which is better of two objects or more. In order to acknowledge *Hamlet* as the best of plays I do not need an innate knowledge of *Hamlet* but only a power of comparing it with other works. The same is true of my recognition of the true good when presented; I had no knowledge of it before—except *sub quadam confusione*—but when I really see it, I can know it to be superior to all else I know. The object itself instructs us. But in the case of the highest good, I am not, in fact, free to recognize this. Good can only be apprehended as such with the co-operation of desire. Mine is warped so that I cannot see it to begin with, and therefore the presentation of the good objectively is only possible if it is accompanied by the subjective correction of aspiration. This is the work of the Holy Spirit, and there is no longer any sense in talking of a 'capacity' I have for his action upon me. The only capacity I need is that I should be a mind in order that there may be something there for revelation to illumine. There must be a mind to use light when it has come, there must be desire and will to be clothed with the love of God shed abroad in the heart, otherwise God would not be redeeming but creating anew; but there need be no other innate power beyond these faculties existing in a more or less degree of perversion. Their freedom before grace need be only such that they *exist*, not such that they are capable of response to God apart from God's enabling action. For discovering the various degrees of perversion and perfection before grace, there is nothing like the observation of instances.

If we speak of the supreme good as our supreme motive, it may appear that we are depersonalizing the relation between us and God, and this has led some to prefer to interpret the claim of the Divine Will upon us as 'an absolute personal claim' rather than as the duty to realize intrinsic good. But 'an absolute personal claim' is difficult to understand if taken alone. No person has any claim upon us that we should further his purposes unless these purposes are good, either intrinsically or as a means to other good, so that a personal claim itself needs the sanction of intrinsic goodness. We may say in another sense that all persons have an absolute claim on us because they are all creatures of God, and doubtless God has a good to be realized through them, which good we are bound to try to discover and to foster—not because they now actively desire it, but because it is good. Our duty to God is the opposite—an absolute duty to promote his actual purposes, for they are simply good: none at all to promote the realization of good in him, for he has and is it all.

The sanction, then, of our obedience is the supreme and sole independent worth of his existence, which he extends to others according to the capacity he assigns them. But his existence is life and spirit, and, therefore, it is true enough that in subjecting ourselves to his activity and aspiring after him we are moved by emotions of reaction to a person and not a principle—and that, no doubt, is the substance of the contention that we have been criticizing.

Aspiration after true good, and the loyalty of the will thereto constitutes the spirituality of man and the realizing in him of God's image. It is the co-operation of his whole self, and not his abstract intellect alone, with reason, in the sense not of a mere ratiocinative power, but of the faculty for grasping truth. So the man becomes, and not merely possesses, rationality. God, in willing his own existence, wills absolute good. Man is the image of God in so far as he both has a will and wills the supreme good according to his ability. To will one's self as God wills himself would be to realize not the image but the parody and blasphemy of God.

Such an actualizing of true humanity has its true pattern completed in faith towards God through Christ. But there exists much aspiration after the true good in ignorance of its true nature, and much loyalty of will in seconding it. In men that are sane, such active rationality is never quite extinct, and there, just in such proportion as it is found, is a vestige of the image of God. But once again, as we said above of total depravity, if we wish to adopt the eschatological point of view, we may say that the image of God is lost in those that are lost—in those whose apprehension of good is insufficient to bring them to the attainment of final and immovable rationality, that is, an absolute dwelling of their desire upon God. But if we speak not of the lost but of those that are being lost, then we must speak also of those that *are losing* the image of God.

In conclusion we will return to our beginning. Christianity asserts indeed that there is a true nature of man, for that is the Creator's intention, actual in the divine mind and never wholly unactualized in men if they are men at all. Of this true human nature men can and do become aware, not through speculative deduction, but piecemeal in the recognition of what is good for man. For such recognition the favouring conditions are sensible reflection, honest intention, and a right relation with God.

Christianity, therefore, does not come before the world with an ideology about man, the rival to several others. Those others it must condemn as forms of idolatry, but not by substituting an idol of its own. The Church's first mission is to re-create the right relation with God, or rather to be the instrument of God for such a work. Concerning the gospel of redemption, others have written eloquently, and it would be superfluous to repeat what they have said about man's fall and its divine remedy.

But the Church has a second mission besides. She knows the humanity as well as the deity of Christ; she exhibits the good for man shown forth in his conscience and life, and in the life and conscience of the saints ever since; and this supplies in part a guide to action, and on the basis of it she must utter the divine law in such detail as her vision allows or men's need demands. We have suggested some of the heads under which the distinctively Christian teaching is likely to fall. But the codified experience of the true conscience in Christ cannot be treated as an oracle which will answer all questions. History does not wholly repeat itself, and a new situation will require a new decision which cannot be deduced simply from established principles. Such a decision, if it is right, cannot indeed be out of harmony with the mind of the Church hitherto; but harmony is a difficult thing to dogmatize upon: it cannot be settled by syllogizing.

But however difficult the process of forming judgements, the Church must judge whenever she thinks that a judgement, either vital or valuable, can be given; and she must judge, among other

THE CHRISTIAN DOCTRINE OF MAN

things, the state. Her judgements in this sphere will (on the evidence of what proceeds) differ from those of others only in being more purely ethical. She must refuse every assumption of the unquestioned value of any political aim: everything must be judged according to the part it can play in the realization of true human nature in the many, according to the Church's vision of what that nature is.

State action must always present itself to the Church in a double aspect. Every deliberate human act can be regarded as a mere event, likely to lead to consequences good, bad, or indifferent. But equally it can be regarded as language more effective than words, the eloquent expression of the agent's mind. So every act of the state is an event likely to produce consequences by the ordinary sequence of cause and effect; but also it is the expression of a doctrine in the minds of those who stand behind it. A measure for physical education is an instrument by which the bodies of the educable will be affected; it is also an expression of the value attached by its authors to bodily welfare. It may be purely beneficial in the first regard, but in the second be put forward in such a way as to preach materialism.

The Church *qua* Church is perhaps more concerned with the second aspect than the first, if, indeed, any comparison can be drawn. For the doctrine of life, silently preached by state action, may be to the Christian simply false. It is less often that he can judge the probable effect of measures to be simply deleterious or demonstrably unjust. For he does not suppose that state action can realize the ideal without defect. No state measure will be perfectly just or unmixedly useful to all inhabitants of a partly unregenerate world. It is a matter of finding the least bad alternative.

Moreover, the Church *qua* Church is concerned first with spiritual truth, and, therefore, with combating the practical expression of falsehood by all the means in her power. It is much harder for her to judge, through channels of ecclesiastical organization, what practical tendency the maintenance or change of any institution will have towards promoting or hindering her ideal for human life, except, indeed, when it is a question of her own freedom of spiritual action being extended or diminished.

This is the inevitable misery of the Church: she must fight for the right to judge not only principles and doctrines expressed in the state, but also the ethical expediency of measures and institutions. And yet she cannot expect often to be either inwardly united or practically wise in judging the expediencies of the moment. But neither can she fall back on established precedent alone, and treat new situations as cases of old rules. She will often, then, cut a foolish figure; but she will be at least illustrating in act the ethical and spiritual judgement of state affairs, and that is more important sometimes than the prestige of ecclesiastical infallibility. If we have any belief, however dim, in our guidance by the divine reason, we must suppose that Christians uttering and comparing their reflections on the ethical expediency of politics will be contributing towards the formation of a right judgement in the end, whatever the ineptitude or disunion of their first suggestions.

Justification

1. Justification would never have been heard of as a doctrine, but for St Paul's controversy with the Judaizers. Even then the idea did not continue to play any part in the life of the Church. Augustine revived it as a rod for the backs of Pelagians. It belonged to controversial or 'corrective' theology. Only in more recent times the attempt has been made to nourish the Christian soul upon it.

2. More lately still, attention has been called to the fact that in the Old Testament 'righteousness' or 'justification' often means 'God-given victory'. In this use of the word, God is still seen as judge, but in an antique sense. He is not the judge who establishes the fact of guilt or innocence, but the judge invoked by the oppressed against the manifest oppressor. His justice is more like that of the knight errant than of the King's justiciar.

This fact, true in itself, is a red herring so far as the exposition of St Paul is concerned. For St Paul was arguing on rabbinic ground, and must therefore start from the rabbinic idea of justification as acquittal before the Throne of Judgement. The different language of the Old Testament may occasionally lend colour to the Christian paradoxes in which St Paul involves the rabbinic notion. It can cast no light on his starting-point.

3. In considering any biblical doctrine we ought to start from the vision of God, or of the Act of God, with which it is concerned. For the substance of biblical doctrine is not to be found in concepts, but in images. Behind all the discussion of justification in St Paul stands the image which breaks through in Romans 2.15–16; 8.31–9; cf. Revelation 12.9–12. There is the Great Throne, before which men are arraigned. According to the Rabbis, God has mercifully published a tariff of 'works of Torah', and promised acquittal to those whose fulfilments of

Written on the reverse side of *A Rebirth of Images* manuscript, published in 1949.

them exceed their failures to fulfil. Moreover he has allowed that breaches may be compensated by supererogatory good works. According to St Paul, only Christ has merited the World to Come by his good works: but God, in sending him to fulfil all righteousness, pledged himself to acquit us for his sake; and in case this should be forgotten, Christ is at the Judge's side, our prevailing advocate. Indeed, we are so one with Christ, so inseparable from his love, that we are on the judge's side of the bar ourselves. The accuser pleads against us in vain. This is the paradox for justification.

4. The image of the Throne is eschatological: yet there was no eschatological image in which the principle of anticipation was more regularly applied. According to Judaism, God caused the human race to file like soldiers before his judgement-throne between New Year and Atonement (Tishri 1—10). We are always coming under that judgement. What we call our conscience, if it has any truth in it, is but a mirror of it. So St Paul, in a passage of which the obvious sense is traditionally evaded by printer's tricks, says of the Gentiles: 'They are law to themselves, in that they show the work of the law written on their hearts, their conscience [i.e. feeling of guilt or innocence] acting as witness to it, and their reasonings pleading for or against [i.e. as prosecution or defence] in that session ['day', cf. 1 Cor. 4.3] at which God judges the secrets of men through Jesus Christ—as my gospel proclaims' (Rom. 2.14–16). Those who are acquitted in this court, he says in the same place, are 'justified' (v. 13).

All anticipations of the Last Things are anticipations and no more, and this is as true of justification as of anything else. Thus, we were saved in God's eternal decree, we were saved in Christ's work, we were saved when we were baptized into Christ; we are being saved daily through the Spirit; we shall be saved on the last day. As with salvation, so with justification. In Galatians 5. 4–5 St Paul contrasts with the legalist the true Christian as a man for whom justification is the object of *hope*: 'Ye are undone from Christ, who *are justifying* yourselves by law; ye have fallen out of grace. For we, in Spirit and from faith, *look forward to the hope of justification.*' (Here the antithesis makes it intolerable to render δικαιοσύνη as 'righteousness' in the sense of 'attained perfection'.)

There is no scriptural warrant at all for making 'justification' something once for all accorded to us, any more than 'sanctification'. (We *were hallowed*, by Christ's death, or in our baptism, just as much as we *were justified*.) And we have still to face the Throne of Judgement: and that will be no joke.

5. It was correctly urged by the Protestants that 'justification' means 'acquittal' and not 'making good'. That is to say, that in the whole and inseparable unity of God's saving act, it is the aspect of acquittal to which this word refers. But there is no substantial divine act which is an act of acquittal and nothing else. It belongs to the feebleness of human power, that the act of decreeing acquittal is separate from the act of rewarding the acquitted with freedom and compensation. God gives no decisions which consist simply of making marks in books. God's acquitting is the turning of his favour upon us; it is the beginning of our sanctification by the infusion of charity. So long as God is sanctifying us, he is acquitting us. If the sanctification is suspended, so is the acquittal; and the acquittal is not absolute until the sanctification is absolute.

It may be proper for theologians to distinguish between a basic justification which remains while we commit venial sin, and a divine approval which is withheld from us until we have repented. In this sense justification is once for all given, unless it is destroyed by sin which is equivalent to apostasy. Such a distinction is surely proper enough but the same distinction must be made in sanctification. There is an actual hallowing of the deepest springs of the will, which remains through the abiding presence of the Holy Ghost, when the surface and visible action of our mind is not 'hallowed', but profaned by sin.

To conclude: there is no divine act upon us which is simply, or primarily, our justification. Justification is an aspect of our redemption or incorporation.

6. What was it, then, that called the 'justification' aspect of our redemption into prominence? It was opposition to the Pharisaic doctrine, that a man must 'earn his World to Come'. To say that St Paul rejected 'justification by works' is false, unless 'works' be given the special sense of 'wage-service', 'paid labour'. To 'work' ($\dot{\epsilon}\rho\gamma\dot{\alpha}\zeta\epsilon\sigma\theta\alpha\iota$) means equally 'to earn'. St Paul did not

teach that man is saved by an inward act (believing) rather than an outward act (doing). He taught that man is saved, not by earning salvation, but by adhering to him who is salvation. This adherence is faith, and it is actualized by deeds rather than by states of mind, or by words pronounced within the mind.

In so far as a man's justification lies in himself at all, it lies in faith or adherence. But adherence is conditioned by inherence: it is only because Christ has taken us into himself that we can adhere to him. It is far more profitable, and more important, for Christians to meditate upon their God-given inherence than upon their responsive adherence. For to meditate gratefully upon inherence is, in fact, to adhere: the reverse is not the case.

7. Since justification is God's saving act under one particular aspect, it is fair enough for Protestants to describe the saving act by the name of justification. There may be such an abstract idea as 'the idea of mere justification', but there is no such reality as 'the act of mere justification'. This being so, it follows that no light is cast upon the nature of the saving act by meditating on 'justification'. Whatever the saving act is, it justifies. That is common ground. We get no further by suggesting that the saving act essentially is, or begins with, justification.

It seems probable, on the contrary, that Protestants have talked of salvation under the name of justification, because St Paul was discussing it under this name and aspect when he was contending that the human condition of salvation is faith. It is the doctrine of faith that is important.

8. Pharisaism taught salvation by (*a*) status (*b*) merit, and the Protestants found a great deal of debased Catholicism which amounted to precisely this combination. (*a*) The baptized Christian—as long as he fulfils his sacramental duties, submits to discipline, and does not positively disbelieve—is in the way of salvation. (*b*) In so far as he incurs disciplinary penalties expiable in purgatory, he can diminish or get rid of them by performing acts on a certain tariff to which indulgences are attached. Against this the Protestants set justification by faith. A man is a Christian because he is awakened to lively faith, not because of status; and no acts can assist his salvation, except as expressions or fruits of faith. (The controversy whether we are saved on the basis of faith

or love was a red herring, except in so far as the Catholics used, or were suspected of using, *caritas* to describe acts formally charitable, but not animated by a voluntary adherence to the love of God.)

9. The truth of Protestantism is that salvation demands full voluntary adherence. But to what do we adhere? Not just to God (for then Christ died in vain) but to the saving mystery. In a true Catholicism, the Church and the sacraments are parts of the saving mystery to which we adhere: they are not substitutes for our adherence to it. I must believe, by lively faith, in the Christ who died for me on the Cross, regenerated me in the font, and unites me in his mystical body. None of this divine action is a consequence of my faith: still less is it a substitute for my faith: it is the object of my faith. The crassest Transubstantiationism is surely no excuse for supposing that the reception of the sacrament is a substitute for faith. So awful and immediate a Presence must be believed and loved above all.

10. In so far as membership in Christ's mystical body was debased into mere status in a *Heilsanstalt* (i.e. a 'salvation-factory'), lively faith tended to turn into other channels, and to concern itself with an exterior and personal relation with Christ, as with one who had died for us, and whom we were bound to follow. And in many Protestant minds, it is an axiom that lively faith is concerned with 'personal relation', i.e. with that aspect of our relation to Christ which is most closely comparable with our natural relation to another human person; any religion which takes the *inherence in Christ* as primary, or even as on an equal footing with 'personal relation', is accused of being 'physical rather than personal' and therefore 'sub-Christian'. But it is obvious to Catholics that the Christ who has caused us to inhere in himself is as proper an object of lively faith as the Christ who has suffered *on our behalf* and called us to follow him. Whether we talk about inherence or personal relation, we are talking about will and act. If Christ makes us to inhere in him, he makes our will and action to inhere in his, at a deep and hidden level of our voluntary being.

There is no more reason to think of justification as Christ's persuading us that he has paid our score, than as his making us to inhere in him through his sacrifice, previous to any merit or even response on our part.

Mary, Scripture and Tradition

The intention of this essay will be critical rather than purely theological. I do not propose, for the most part, to argue from accepted notions or beliefs, as is done when, presuming a faith in the incarnation of the Son of God, we ask what such a faith implies, as to the part played by a human parent in the coming-about of such a mystery. I propose instead to ask what evidence we have about Mary, and how the ecclesiastical interpretations of that evidence can (when and if they can) be justified.

When we think of Mary, or of any saint departed this life, we are thinking of an actual citizen of Paradise. So we may be tempted to speculate about the structure of the heavenly kingdom, and of her place in it. The society of heaven is centred on the Heavenly Man, Jesus, in whom, and as who, the godhead is personally present. Surely his mother's seat must be next to his throne. Perhaps, if the King of Heaven has a mother. By an *a priori* speculation on the heavenly kingdom one would not know that he had; or that if he had, she was more specially related to him than his human father. Her heavenly place must be a deduction from what we know of her earthly place in relation to Jesus. So we come down to Mary's history and our knowledge of her history. Apart from that basis of fact we have nothing to build upon.

The earliest and most copious of apostolic writers, St Paul, tells us not a word about her history. There is, however, a passage in his Epistle to the Galatians (3.23—4.7) which contains all the essential themes of the doctrine of virginal birth. God is our Father, and (though he had placed us under nursery governors and stewards) has now promoted us to the status of free sons. He has done this by adopting us into the condition and privileges of his own Son, whom he sent to deliver us through first sharing our bondage—born of a woman, born under the law.

Reprinted from *The Blessed Virgin Mary: Essays by Anglican Writers*, 1963.

By becoming fellow-heirs with Christ we become children of Abraham.

According to this passage, though St Paul uses of his fellow-Christians a metaphor which implies that they are naturally Sons of God (the Father puts his own children under nursery governors and stewards), he presently takes back the implication: the admission to the status of adult sons is really *an adoption.* So we are the children of our human parents, adopted as Sons of God. But this is possible because Christ, the real Son of God, is sent to share our condition, and to share his with us: the Son of God is born of a human mother. But, by being so born (it appears) he becomes *the* promised Seed of Abraham, and we (by union with him through faith) became seed-of-Abraham too, whether we be Israelites or not.

It follows that Christ has one Mother (a woman), but two Fathers (the descendant of Abraham who directly fathered him and God). The parts of the divine and human Fathers have somehow to be accommodated to one another. If we read the text as it stands, it appears that God, by sending forth his Son, sprung of a woman, is presenting the family of Abraham with an heir. He cannot do this through the female line, for that way (in Jewish and biblical thought) no one inherits. It lies very close to the pattern of ideas in this passage to conclude that as the children of earthly fathers are adopted into God's inheritance, so (reciprocally) the Son of God was adopted into Abraham's. It is of course clear that, from the point of view of human inheritance, Christ is 'seed of Abraham', and so 'of David's seed'. When the apostle takes his start (as in Galatians he does) from Christ's divine sonship, he thinks of a change in his status which is his being placed in human 'bondage', born of a woman, under the stewardship of the Law. When, as in Romans 1.3, he takes his start from Christ's human condition, as 'a member of the human family of David', he thinks of that change in his status which is his being 'declared Son of God in the realm of Spirit, through the miracle of resurrection', a change which is prototypic of our own adoption and the breaking of our bondage. The Romans text tells us no more about the way in which God's Son became a member of David's family than the Galatians text tells us of the way in which he became a member of Abraham's.

It would, indeed, be possible to suppose that the Galatians

passage theologizes the story of Bethlehem without detailed historical reference, just as so many other Pauline texts theologize the story of Calvary with the same absence of historical detail. But there are two obvious difficulties in the way of such a supposition. The first is that St Paul does many times roundly declare that Christ died on the cross, and rose again. He nowhere states that he was born of a virgin. The second difficulty lies in his manner of applying the type of Abraham. According to Galatians it is an error to think that the blessings attached to Abrahamic inheritance go by mere physical descent. It is no accident that they come through Isaac, who would never have been conceived or born but through the supernatural effect of a divine promise. The mere physical descendants of Abraham, though they may trace their descent from Isaac, have no more right than his descendants through Ishmael's line. The blessings are still attached to the seed of supernatural promise, that is to say, to Christ and to those who by faith and baptism have part in him. Now to anyone with the Bethlehem story in his mind it would seem natural to think of Jesus as the child of promise in the same way as Isaac was, only in a higher degree. But for God's promise to Abraham, Isaac would not have been conceived; nor Jesus, but for his promise to Mary. In the one case the power of the promise endows a father with a fertility he had lost; in the other case dispensing with the action of a father altogether. So far, however, from making this application, St Paul speaks of Christ's being born of a woman at all as a circumstance of bondage, placing him (by condescension) in the Ishmael-condition of Israel-after-the-flesh. That of which Isaac, the 'child of promise', is the type is a wholly spiritual begetting, by which Christ has his essential being, and into which that fleshly being he took upon him in the family of David is manifestly taken up when he dies on the cross and is raised from the dead.

In Romans 4 Abraham, in begetting Isaac according to God's promise, is seen as performing an act typically equivalent to faith in Christ. Once again a writer with the Bethlehem story in mind might be expected to see faith in the possibility of Isaac's generation, despite parental infertility, as typical of faith in a Christ generated without any human begetter at all. Not so St Paul. The *deadness* of the generative powers in Isaac's parents is for the apostle typical of the death out of which God raised his Son on Easter morning.

It is fair to conclude that St Paul sees Christ as being made *a* son of Abraham by his condescension in being born of a woman into David's family; but sees him revealed as *the* Son of Abraham, the more-than-Isaac, by translation into the spiritual world through resurrection. How Christ became a member of David's family, he does not tell us, except that he was 'born of woman'. If St Paul knew of Christ as virginally conceived, he still did not (it would seem) attach to the virginal conception a positive value as revealing a heavenly Son grafted on earthly stock. What is most obvious about St Paul's argument whether in Galatians or in Romans is the constant concern with the central object of faith. Faith is directed upon the regeneration of man through death and resurrection. If Abraham's faith is typical of saving faith, then it must be typical of *this* faith and of no other. Supposing that the mystery of the virginal birth could have played a positive part in St Paul's argument, it would have been as itself a type and a foreshowing of rebirth from the Easter sepulchre.

The synoptic evangelists may be seen as developing the Pauline inheritance in their several ways. St Mark is the most negative of the three. He mentions Mary twice, though he names her only once. His object is to show that the new covenant is not tied within racial or hereditary limits. And this he does, not by exhibiting Christ's strange birth as a breach in physical descent, but by recalling that Christ found the nucleus of his fellowship not in his family at all, but in the apostolic company which he himself created out of such as received his word. After a brief mention of John the Baptist's preaching and Christ's consequent baptism, he associates the beginning of the ministry with the call of individual disciples. From these and from others Jesus creates the body of the Twelve 'to be with him' and to go on his missions. The immediate sequel is that Jesus goes home—that is, to his present place of abode at Peter's in Capernaum—but cannot get a meal because of the people crowding in there to hear him. Having news of this, his home people—that is, his family from Nazareth—come to fetch him away, saying that he is *distraught*.[1] (St Mark turns aside here to report how Christ refuted this accusation in the much graver form the Jerusalem rabbis gave it when they said he was *possessed*.) When it was reported to Jesus that his mother and his brethren were at the door, calling for him, he cried, 'Who is my mother? Or my brethren? See, my mother and my brethren'—turning his eyes on the circle of his hearers. 'Whoever does the will of God is my brother or sister or mother.' The story goes straight on to tell how, in the parable of the Sower, Christ set forth the method by which the New Israel is gathered. The seed is thrown broadcast: those in whom it strikes root, and who persevere, make up the divine harvest. The other seed-parables follow, and an account of three 'mighty works' which Jesus did in connection with the journey he made, when he sailed across the lake and back, in the very boat which had been the pulpit of his parable-discourse. Then follows the visit to Christ's native town, where they could not allow him the honour of a prophet. 'Is not this the carpenter,' they said, 'the son of Mary, the brother of James, Joses, Judah and Simon? And are not his sisters here with us?' In comment Jesus said: 'The only company in which a prophet goes unhonoured is in his native place, his kindred and his home.' And leaving Nazareth he began touring the Galilean villages.

The comment of Jesus appears to associate his family with his townsmen. The family had shown their attitude in their untimely anxiety about his mental and physical health; his townsmen show theirs by doubting if anything much can come of a member in a commonplace local family. St Mark's account of Christ's mother and brethren is no more and no less unfavourable than his account of the apostles. The family cannot understand his strange way of living in a new home at Capernaum, which is virtually the first Christian church. The Twelve, called as his associates in this new pattern of life, cannot understand the entire break with official Israel, which involves his passion. St Mark knows, but hardly tells us, that the apostles returned to their faith and to their obedience after the resurrection. He must similarly have known that the family adhered to the Church, for there sat James the Lord's brother presiding in the church at Jerusalem.

St Mark does not trouble to distinguish, as St John later does, between the attitude of Mary, tempted to indiscreet maternal interference, and the attitude of the brethren, at first downright unbelievers in Christ. He shows no sign of attaching a personal value to her function as mother of the Lord; but it is noticeable that he says nothing (according to the text which is surely correct) of Christ's having a human father. No Christian writer in fact mentions Joseph, who does not also refer to the virginal conception. It is easy enough to explain the absence of Joseph's name from Mark 6 by the supposition that he was no longer a familiar figure in Nazareth, having died years ago. But that is hypothesis, and not entirely convincing in view of the Jewish habit of using patronymics. What we should expect would be: 'Is not this Joseph's son? Is not his mother Mary still with us, and his brethren. . . ?' Both St Luke and St Matthew in rehandling the episode mention the Lord's legal father.[2]

When we come to the Gospel according to St Matthew, we find, of course, an explicit account of the virginal conception, but scarcely more personal a valuation of Mary's part. As though taking up St Paul's thoughts in Galatians and Romans, the evangelist begins his Gospel with a derivation of Christ from Abraham through David. He gives us a succession of 'correct' fathers, but reminds us how often they obtained their heirs 'incorrectly', by mentioning certain mothers—Tamar from whom Judah got Perez by a sort of incest;[3] Rahab, a non-Israelite and a harlot from the doomed city of Jericho; Ruth, a Moabitess; Bethsheba, adulterously married by David. The next in series is 'Joseph, thou *Son of David*, fear not to take to thee Mary thy wife: for that which is conceived in her is of the Holy Ghost.' The moral is drawn by the first preacher to appear on the scene. 'Begin not to say to yourselves', says the Baptist to the orthodox, 'we have Abraham for father. I tell you, of these very stones God can raise up children to Abraham.' There had been much irregular grafting on Abraham's stock, approved by God's election; now there was a supernatural grafting. So plain it is that the promises do not go by right of natural inheritance but by the will of God. Christ's wholly supernatural birth cuts off the physical entail and prepares the way for Gentile Christianity: the Magi come to hail the 'light of the Gentiles'.

Though the mother of Jesus is introduced as the non-bride of Joseph and as a cause of scandal, it is nevertheless made clear that the scandal is only apparent; her conception is 'by the Holy Ghost'. But St Matthew's readers, recalling the many and various effects attributed in ancient Scripture to the Spirit of God, are not to know whether Mary's conceiving is simply 'by divine miracle' or also 'by divine inspiration'. On the second view something like St Luke's annunciation-narrative is supposed; on the first it can be imagined that Mary finds herself inexplicably pregnant, and simply allows herself to be informed and guided by Joseph—an inspired dreamer like his great namesake. The highest positive value St Matthew visibly assigns to her virginal conceiving is as a predicted sign: 'This whole happening was in fulfilment of the word spoken by the Lord through the prophet, behold a virgin shall conceive. . . .'

In the sequel St Matthew softens a little the Marcan picture of Christ's family in the time of his ministry, but no more than he softens the picture of Christ's apostles. Christ's comments remain, scarcely modified 'Who is my mother, who my brethren? Behold my mother and my brethren! Whoso doeth the will of my Father in heaven, the same is my brother. . . .' And again, 'A prophet lacks not honour, save in his country *and in his home.*' He suppresses the indiscretion of the family in coming to fetch him because he is 'distraught' and neglects his food. But by so doing he leaves the Lord's comments to look causeless or even harsh. Why, on the mere occasion of his family's desiring to have speech with him, should he say, 'Who is my mother. . . ?' St Matthew patches the awkwardness by giving the Lord's saying more the air of a universal truth: by doing the will of Christ's heavenly *Father*, all men may become his (spiritual) *brethren.*

Such a rehandling of the Marcan story scarcely allows us to affirm St Matthew's belief in a truly personal participation of Mary in the mystery of Christ's birth: it seems fairest to say that the question did not enter into his views one way or another. We may think that, holding the secret of her Son's origin, she could have no reserves about accepting his own way of developing his messianic mission. But St Matthew sets before us the example of Peter, blessed for the Father's revelation to him of Christ's divine Sonship (16. 16; cf. 11. 27) and yet presently rebuked as Satan for being man-minded, not God-minded, about Christ's passion.

St Luke approached the Gospel-story with a firm grasp on the sequel which would form the subject of his second book. Christ's family joined hands with his apostles in the Church of Pentecost. It was natural that he should cast back for the origins of such a development in Mary's first introduction into the divine history. And so perhaps he sought out, or more seriously valued, what the

Lord's brethren had to report as coming from Mary.[4] We have no means of identifying his sources of information. What we can see, is the strong doctrinal or typological themes which have moulded his narrative.

He too, as befits a good disciple of St Paul, takes up the inheritance of Pauline ideas and begins from Abraham. The miracle of Isaac's birth, which had so much occupied St Paul's attention, is exactly reproduced in the miracle of John the Baptist's. But it is immediately made the type, not (as with St Paul) of Christ's resurrection, but of his virginal birth. It is as though the miracle which began the Old Dispensation were brought back on the stage in the ending of it, that it might be presently transcended by the greater miracle which inaugurates the New. By being brought forward into this position the miracle of Isaac (or rather, of John Baptist) is able to serve as a verifiable sign that the promised miracle of Christ will be fulfilled. Will Mary indeed conceive? Yes: for first, the Holy Ghost will come upon her; second, her cousin Elizabeth is six months gone with child, a fact of which Mary hastens to make herself the personal witness.

St Luke contrasts Zacharias and Mary, not only in respect of the supernaturality of what is promised them, but also in respect of their degree of faith. There is a close parallelism between the two annunciation-stories. Zacharias's response is, 'By what token am I to know this? I am an old man, and my wife advanced in years.' Mary's is, 'How is this to be? I know not a man.' 'How is this to be?' does not so explicitly ask for confirmation of statement as 'By what token shall I know it?', but the difference is fine and we should not notice it, perhaps, but for the difference in Gabriel's rejoinder on the two occasions. Zacharias is immediately told of the temporary dumbness which would avenge his disbelief; Mary's question is answered in its literal sense: 'How? Why, by the illapse of the Holy Ghost', Elizabeth's conception being added as a sign of the power of God's word to achieve its own fulfilment. So Mary has the opportunity of a second answer, denied to Zacharias by his dumbness; she makes her submission: 'Behold the handmaid of the Lord: be it to me according to thy word.'

While it is true that St Luke allows the merit of Mary's faith to appear, this is by no means the only concern he has on hand, as may be seen by comparing the dovetailed revelations to Zacharias and to Mary with the similarly dovetailed revelations to Saul and to Ananias, to Cornelius and to Peter. The conversion of the apostle to the Gentiles and the conversion of the first Gentile rest on divine revelations having the same form as the revelation of Christ's birth. Single visions are of no certain authority: independent visions, mutually confirming one another, give assurance. A vision strikes Saul blind, as a vision struck Zacharias dumb. Ananias is vouchsafed a vision, before he knows anything of Saul's, directing him to a line of action which will bring him to the knowledge of Saul's complementary vision. Saul's disbelief in Christ, and Ananias's in the possibility of Saul's true conversion, need both to be overcome. The general pattern of the Cornelius episode is the same, the detailed parallel with the first chapter of the Gospel less close. In fact we may say that the three episodes of double visions are in natural series with one another: the second modelled on the first, and the third on the second. For the Cornelius episode takes up from the Saul episode a feature not found in Luke 1, namely, a Christian brother (Ananias, Peter) to whom the second of the paired visions is given, and who needs to be convinced of the possibility of the admission of an unlikely convert (the Jewish enemy, the Gentile 'sinner').

These simple reflections on St Luke's narrative-construction may suffice to show us that a main concern of his in the annunciation-story is to show with what objective certainty God has assured Mary (and through her, the Church) of her Son's divine messiahship. It belongs to her position in the double-vision story that she can be given the effect of the previous vision as a confirmatory sign; it is so also with Ananias. There is no such sign for Zacharias (any more than for Saul) other than the sheer stroke of divine power breaking his resistance.

Nevertheless, it is not to be denied that St Luke places Mary's faith in antitype to Abraham's, and Abraham's faith is the type of a faith which justifies. In accordance with this valuation of Mary's part is the attribution to her of a religious thoughtfulness. 'While all who heard wondered at the things told them by the shepherds, Mary kept all these sayings, pondering them in her heart.' And much the same is said in conclusion to the Finding of Jesus in the Temple.

The Finding in the Temple is perhaps felt by St Luke to illustrate in a less distressing way than the story in Mark 3 the lesson which Jesus's family had to learn about him. Mary reproaches the twelve year old Jesus for causing his parents to search about for him in agony of mind. He replies, 'Why search about for me? Did you not know that I am bound to be among my Father's things?' In similar words, the futility of the search for Jesus in Mark 3. 21,32 might have been rebuked. As he could be nowhere but in the Temple at Jerusalem, so he could be nowhere but in Peter's 'church'-house at Capernaum. The action of Mary and Joseph in Luke 2 is more obviously excusable because Jesus is then only just ceasing to be a child; and indeed, on his return to Nazareth, he submits to parental authority. However this may be, St Luke follows St Matthew in making the occasion of the saying about Christ's true 'mother and brethren' a mere and unexplained desire on the part of Mary and his kinsmen to see him when crowds stood in the way (Luke 8. 19-21). A similar word of the Lord is reported at 11. 27-8; 'Nay rather, blessed are they who hear the word of God and observe it': this in answer to a woman's cry, 'Blessed the womb that bare thee, and the paps that thou hast sucked!' However much St Luke may desire to write appreciatively of Mary (or of the apostles), he does nothing to weaken the Lord's own teaching, which separates a saving relation to himself, or to his work, from any question of physical kinship.

For the rest, St Luke records old Symeon's prophecy that Mary would feel the sword in her heart; he does not mention her in his narrative of the passion. He tells us that she and the Lord's brethren joined the company of the apostles after the ascension, in prayerful waiting for Pentecost. And that is all.

St John's Gospel adds little that is positive to Mariology. What it does contain is best viewed as a balanced reflection on the previous tradition, a sort of synthesis of St Paul, St Luke, and St Mark. This Gospel follows Marcan form in concentrating on the ministry and passion, with John Baptist's preaching as the first historical episode. The first mention of the Baptist is embedded, however, in a theological preface, which describes the incarnation of the Word in a manner most naturally taken to imply a knowledge of Christ's virginal conception and to interpret what is physically true of Christ as being mystically true of Christians.

Those who believe in his name receive the right to be called Sons of God—'they who were begotten not of blood, nor of the will of flesh, nor of the will of a man [husband], but of God. And the Word was made flesh, and dwelt among us.' In 6. 42 St John repeats the 'synoptic' objection to Christ's claims, 'Is not this the Son of Joseph?' He gives it fresh point by relating it to Christ's declaration that he is a 'bread' descending from heaven. St John's text is most easily interpreted as 'tragic irony'; he and his readers know how Christ's 'descent from heaven' was made compatible with the legal paternity of Joseph.[5] The discourse with Nicodemus takes up the theme of a Christian's supernatural birth, through the Spirit. The thought of Christ's conception by the Holy Ghost may supply the background, but the discourse leads us in a Pauline direction; it goes on to link the regeneration of man with Christ's death and resurrection (3. 14).

The episode of Cana (2. 1-11) contains, among many other themes, St John's picture of Mary learning not to rule her Son but to be ruled by him. The behaviour of the Lord's brethren in 7. 3ff is presented in conscious contrast. Both the mother in 2 and the brethren in 7 move Jesus to act in advance of the 'hour' or the 'moment' marked by the divine will. But whereas the brethren are said to be, and are left, in a state of disbelief, the Lord's mother accepts correction. The advice she gives the servants can be compared with her submission to Gabriel, according to St Luke. 'Behold the handmaid of the Lord; be it unto me according to thy word.'—'Whatsoever he saith unto you, do it.' Her previous remark, 'They have no wine', may be similarly compared with 'I know not a man'. Each saying presents the difficulty which lies in a lack of physical means.

The mention of Mary's presence at the crucifixion does justice to Symeon's prophesy of the sword in her heart, according to St Luke. The dying Christ's action in willing Mary to his beloved disciple, and the disciple to Mary, shows how the passion and its sequel brought Mary into fellowship with the apostolic group, where we find her immediately after the ascension according to Acts 1. 14.

We have summarized the evidence. What are we to say of it? The best-attested fact about Mary is that she remained outside the action of Christ's mission; and that she made common cause with his family in trying to bring him back home, if only for rest and refreshment. St Luke's statement that she was in the Church after the resurrection is almost equally well-founded, in view of independent evidence about the early adherence of the family (I Cor. 15. 7; 9. 5; Gal. 2. 9). In judging the bearing of these facts we have to remember the dependent position of a Jewish woman at that time. Jesus has left home: Mary remains one of the family, and very likely is their housekeeper.

The virginal conception rests on the testimony of St Matthew and St Luke, perhaps of St John. It is obvious from what we have written that a critic uninfluenced by motives of faith is free to conclude that the belief grew out of doctrinal considerations, of which the seeds can be found already in St Paul. The Church, that is, judged Christ to have been virginally conceived because they thought he must have been, not because they had evidence that he was. The late appearance of the story—say eighty years after the alleged event—will be cited as negative evidence; and though, on the orthodox hypothesis, explanations for the lateness of the written testimony can be found, they cannot give the hypothesis itself the support which early evidence could give. The evidence for any active or spiritual participation of Mary in the acceptance of her virginal motherhood lies in St Luke alone. A critic who will go no further, but only so far as to allow a simple genuine tradition of Mary's virginity, variously overlaid by St Matthew and St Luke with typological decoration, will have no *historical* ground whatever for the Catholic valuation of Mary's sanctity.

The most believing of us cannot fail to mark a notable difference between the evidence for the virginal conception of Christ, and the evidence for his resurrection. Whatever attempt we make to find coherent sense in the events following the crucifixion and issuing in the emergence of the Church, we shall admit that something strange and powerful happened to the disciples to make them proclaim Christ risen from the dead. Because we share their faith and are touched by their inspiration, we accept their account of the fundamental nature of their experiences. But if we did not, we should still give some account of it, though it was no more than to say that they suffered vivid hallucinations; or that they took a man who had recovered his injuries for a man who had conquered his death; or that they mistook one man for another. Whereas in the case of the virginal conception, there will, on the infidel hypothesis, be nothing that requires explanation of any kind. How did Mary come to conceive? St Matthew is at pains to explain to us why St Joseph had not taken her to wife. All the infidel need do is dispense with St Matthew's explanations.

How different, again, in the two cases is the time interval between fact and testimony to fact! St Paul, the preacher of the resurrection, is converted to a Church already proclaiming it within some three years of the event. St Matthew's infancy narrative may be eighty years after the nativity. It is perfectly easy to explain the late appearance of familiarity with the facts of Christ's birth if we first make the hypothesis that the facts were as our evangelists report them. But such an explanation merely removes a difficulty; it does nothing to establish the hypothesis.

Well, but the Church received the Gospels of St Matthew and St Luke with all acceptance; and before any creed was formulated, the virginal conception had the virtual status of a credal belief. The fact on which our faith reposes is not the fact of Christ's history alone, it is the double fact of that history taken together with the existence of the Spirit-filled Church, which proclaimed that history and lived by its fruits. And the Church accepted the virginal conception as a harmonious part of the sacred story; once it had been set forth it could not be thought away; it belonged so absolutely in its place. Inspired authority established the belief; Ignatius and Irenaeus make it a kernel of orthodoxy.

There is much matter for reflection here. What limits shall we set to the Church's function of inspired teaching? She is inspired to proclaim facts, and to interpret facts; but not to create facts: nothing can create a fact but its occurrence. A fact created by a subsequent declaration about it is false by definition. (True facts of a sort can be created by declaration—for example, you declare me your deputy and I am. But this sort of fact-creation has obviously no bearing on the case.)

It is too simple, however, to say that facts are first acknowledged, then interpreted. The whole of philosophical wisdom is opposed to so black-and-white a distinction. Facts, in their objective existence, are just occurrences; and occurrences occur, whatever we think or do not think. But no fact enters into human reckoning without receiving some initial interpretation from us, however immediate, however instinctive. And in cases where occurrence of the fact is open to doubt, our belief or disbelief will be conditioned by our ability or our willingness to interpret. You tell me that, passing a certain field in the dark, you saw an elephant at some distance. I can interpret the presence of the elephant if I *know* that a circus-menagerie is camping there: I may be *willing* so to interpret the elephant's presence by supposing something of the sort out of deference to your accuracy of observation, though I have no such knowledge. If I have no such knowledge and no such willingness, I shall suppose you to have been mistaken. There was no elephant.

Now the Christian mind approaches historical evidence with what it takes to be a certain knowledge, and also with a certain willingness; and both are relevant to the interpretation of that evidence. What we take to be our knowledge is of God's dealings with mankind, whether in ancient Israel or in modern Christendom. This gives us a basis for interpreting events as divine interpositions and for judging in which direction such interpositions point. And faith is a willingness to trust God's (seeming) actions in the Christian dispensation and to take them for what they seem to be. Those who lack the knowledge of religious instruction, or the willingness of faith, will disbelieve the account of a divine interposition suddenly thrown at them without context. So no one can fail to see that interpretation not only values facts once acknowledged; it also contributes to making them acknowledged as facts. All this is mere commonplace; but when we come to theology, or rather, to sacred history, we touch upon a subtler point. The fact of sacred history receives not one interpretation but two interpretations on two different levels. Physically speaking, Mary conceives unaided, as happens often in the females of certain lower species; perhaps we should add that in her case the event is psychologically conditioned; a vision convinces her of her power so to conceive before she does. Theologically speaking, her conception is a special act of God, whereby the divine Son makes a beginning of incarnate existence. The subtle question is how the physical and the theological interpretations of the event are, or ought to be, related. We may state three possible positions.

First, it may be held that no physical fact can be established except through a physical, or at least a natural, interpretation. That is to say, I can only accept the virginal conception of Christ if I have physical, or psychophysical knowledge encouraging me to interpret the literary evidence as historical fact; or at least a willingness to stretch whatever physical analogy there is to cover such a case. On this view theology can only come in afterwards, when the physical question has been settled on its merits. Only then is theology free to consider how the physical fact is related to the will and act of God.

Second, it may be held that theological interpretation will suffice alone in the entire absence of physical interpretation. Suppose, that is, that we can offer no natural interpretation whatever of Mary's conceiving; we may be content to be ignorant so long as it seems in the line of God's saving purposes that she should conceive without a male partner. The context, that is, which makes the physical event credible need not be a physical context at all, but the context of God's dealings with his people.

A third position would be that of compromise between the first two. Theological interpretation will not suffice, there must be some degree of natural interpretation. Nevertheless, the two can act together in making the alleged physical fact acceptable. This will mean in practice that the physical interpretation fails to decide us for belief; the theological interpretation turns the scale.

If we look at these three positions, we shall perhaps be likely to agree that they reduce to two; for there is no practical difference between the second and the third. Every physical event must receive *some* degree of natural interpretation, must be fitted into the continuous context of natural happenings, or it simply would not have the value to us of a physical event at all. We shall at least suppose that conception and embryonic growth proceed in the production of the Christ-child as they do in that of other children. Even for the unique beginning of the process St Luke suggests natural analogies. John Baptist's conception suggests that Christ's is something like the case of a child produced by old parents, through a surprising spurt of vitality, when they seemed to have lost the power. Here at least is analogy for conception taking place outside the scope of the usual rules. Again, the attribution of the effect to the action of the Holy Spirit, and its connection with Mary's vision, tacitly invokes the analogy of people acquiring or revealing physical powers they did not appear to possess, under the influence of 'inspiration'—which, on its psychological side, is perceptible as strong religious emotion or conviction. Nevertheless, it is evident that the decisive interpretative context for St Luke, and that which makes the event credible to him, is the context of God's ways with Israel, his continued action in Christ, and his action through the Spirit in the Church.

We are left, then, with two positions to consider. According to the first, no physical event can be accepted as credible except by a stern application of physical or at least natural criteria: theological or supernatural interpretation cannot be applied except to an independently established natural belief. According to the second, we may accept as Christians what as mere naturalists we might reject.

The way to argue for the first position is to show what a floodgate to superstition will be opened if we once depart from it. The way to argue for the second is to point out that an interpretation of Christianity in terms of the first is totally unreal. The whole supernatural story of the gospel never was believed on natural evidence: it was accepted by men who, catching the apostolic preacher's attitude, believed that God had come to them and had shaped natural facts in such fashion as his merciful purpose required. And the way for the upholders of the second position to meet the 'flood-gates' argument is to point out that there is such a thing as Christian common sense, and that it operates in perfectly describable ways. The Christian mind may have a normal defence-mechanism against the supernatural, such as not to give way except under overwhelming pressures.

Without going further into the argument, we may venture to conclude that any Christianity other than the most radical and iconoclastic modernism must be committed to the second position. If, then, it is the function of the Paraclete in the apostolic Church to interpret the facts of the gospel by however theological or supernatural an interpretation, it is on that very account his function to make credible and accepted the gospel facts themselves, even the physical facts. And the extreme case of a fact made credible in this way is the fact of Christ's virginal conception; for not only is the fact physically improbable, the evidence for it lies in testimonies both late and (though capable of harmonization) not *prima facie* harmonious.

Nevertheless, the post-apostolic Church accepted the testimony and put the fact in the Creed—Conceived by Holy Ghost, born of Mary in her virginity. If we say that the Church, or her hierarchy, was *inspired* to acknowledge the virginity of Mary, by using that word we do not excuse ourselves from logical considerations. What the Paraclete inspires is an activity of feeling, thinking, or judging; he sustains it, and sends it divinely right. The inspired process of mind, being itself human, should be either visible or inferable, and its divine rightness should be appreciable, anyhow after the event. What sort of right-judging, then, did the inspired Church do? Surely, in this case, it was not so much that she judged the testimony to rest on sound historical evidences, as that she judged the fact testified to be absolutely fitting, and therefore presumed the soundness of the testimony. That is, the Church accepted on other grounds the resurrection, eternal kingdom, and divine sonship of Jesus; and when told by the first and third evangelists that he came into the world by virginal conception, she said 'Yes, that is how he came into the world; how else?' It was thus that the general credit due to these evangelists' histories was readily extended to cover their infancy narratives. Such men would not write carelessly about so important a point; and there was no reason to think they had done so, for the testimony they bore was worthy of God and of his Christ.

'It was fitting, and so it was the fact'; *decuit, ergo factum est.* Put like that, the formula awakens the deepest misgivings. Surely the human mind, assisted or unassisted by the Spirit of God, does not validly infer from theological fittingness to fact of history. What God does is not what we expect: it is paradoxical, surprising to us; only after the event are we inspired to see that it was divinely best. If we trust our inspirations about what God must have done, we shall err with Peter, when he judged that God *could not have* destined his Son to suffer. So long as Peter confined himself to putting a value on what God had visibly done, in Jesus's ministry and mighty works, his inspiration took him right. This was the Christ; flesh and blood had not revealed it to him, but the Father in Heaven. He began to speculate and he was lost.

The objection is just. But in fact the formula is ambiguous. 'It is fitting, and so it was the fact' may be acceptable or unacceptable, according to the sort of thing that 'It' stands for. 'It' may be 'our conjecture' or it may be 'these men's professedly historical account'. If the first, then the formula is unacceptable.

If the second, it is acceptable. For it is commonly through someone's testimony that we are informed of those paradoxically right acts of God, which we see to be fitting once we have digested our surprise. (St Matthew insists on the paradox, or scandal, of the virgin birth itself. It involved a domestic disgrace and it meant that the destined Son of David had not a drop of David's blood.)

Thus, though a pure historian might judge the literary testimony for Christ's virginal conception to be weak or indecisive, it is essential that there should be such testimony, and that it should be at least open to us to view it as resting on a real tradition. Christ was first known in his manhood, and preached as risen and ascended; the Gospel-story took form from the known facts, and found its beginning in the prophesying of John Baptist. The Palestinian church (we can suppose if we wish) became presently acquainted also with family traditions about Jesus's wonderful birth, but even then it was some while before the set form of Gospel-story was stretched to include them. Were it, on the other hand, impossible to see by what genuine channels our evangelists could have received their story, were the silence of St Mark and St Paul decisive, then we should be in the greatest difficulty about admitting that the post-apostolic Church was truly inspired to make the virginal conception into a credal belief. As it is, there is a *datum* for the Spirit to interpret; and in confirming the belief he leads us to give a favourable account of the transmission of the tradition to our evangelists.

We have said that revelation is effected by the concordant testimony of Gospel fact and inspired Church; and where, as in the case before us, belief must lean so heavily on the side of the Paraclete, our sense of dependence on the Church must be proportionately greater. I myself, let me hope, enter into the credal faith and appreciate the divine rightness and heavenly meaning of the virginal birth. Yet I would not trust my judgement unaided in such a matter. I should scarcely come to the decision of positive belief but for the massive consent of the primitive Church and of so many subsequent Catholic ages, confirmed by authoritative declarations, themselves in turn confirmed by Catholic consent.

Having defined the position we wish to commend, we may look briefly at tenets which lie to the left and to the right of it. On the one hand we have the man who, however willing to accept the Church's interpretative authority, cannot persuade himself that the historical evidence really amounts to anything at all, and concludes that, as there is nothing there for the Church to interpret, there is no fact for him to believe. On the other hand we have the position of the Roman Church, which, on the face of it at least, appears to claim for authoritative interpretation the power to establish facts which are vouched for by no historical testimony at all.

To take the former case first. We confine ourselves to the man who is in other respects orthodox and whose disbelief in Christ's virginal birth is simply forced on him by what he judges to be the inadmissability of the historical evidence. (His is the interesting case. Who does not know that there are negative heretics in all degrees, maintaining the name of Christian and, indeed, true lovers of Christ?) His orthodoxy, then, will incline him to accept the inspired guidance of the ancient and universal Church in a matter of credal belief. The Church was inspired to think rightly and Christianly about the evidence before her, so far as the common science of the time enabled her to understand it. What inspiration did not do was to equip her with an art of historical criticism and a science of natural fact, which have been the lesson to mankind of more recent centuries. And so, in matter of fact, she erred. What value, then, can be attached to that inspiration which enabled her to theologize correctly over evidence which our orthodox modernist judges to have been unsound?

He will observe how the Fathers reasoned. The conception of Christ by the Virgin was taken as evidence of a double truth. Christ was both divine son and a real member of the human race. Our orthodox modernist agrees; and he accepts the infancy-narratives as symbolical stories, or myths, enshrining and protecting these truths for an age which, perhaps, could not have grasped them otherwise. For himself, he is able to believe that the eternally begotten Son of God took flesh of man from two human parents, not from one only.

Shall we say that the man is fundamentally orthodox in intention if he can say *Decuisset, si factum esset*, 'It would have been fitting, had it been the fact', and really heretical if he says, *Nec factum est, nec factum decuisset*, 'It neither happened in fact, nor was it fitting it should'? No, we can scarcely distinguish in such terms as these. For it cannot be orthodox to say that it would have been fitting for God to have done otherwise than he did; there cannot have been a better way for him to enter into our condition than that which he chose (whatever it was). Indeed we may be sure that our orthodox modernist will feel that a completely natural fashion of birth most perfectly secures and expresses the entirety of Christ's manhood; a virginal birth would, in the long run, set him too much apart from us. In the short run, however, he may allow that it was otherwise. It would not have been fitting for Christ to have been virginally conceived, but it was fitting that the primitive Church should have projected her understanding of his divine humanity in mythic terms, the only terms, perhaps, in which she could have grasped the fundamental truth of his Person. By contrast it will be fundamentally heretical to say that the Church was misguided to formulate the credal belief, because, *in the terms of that day*, it was theologically misleading, and indeed more so than a denial of the virginal conception would have been.

One cannot but sympathize with the modernist *malgré lui,* whom plain honesty of mind, and historical conscience, cuts off from fullness of communion with the Church's credal faith. He loses the dearest of saints from his calendar. For, apart from the drama of Christ's conception, birth, and childhood, there is nothing to give any features to the mother of Christ.

We will turn now to the opposite case. Romanists appear to us to accept traditions about Mary, supported at certain points by an ecclesiastical authority claimed as infallible, but for which no historical testimony in the ordinary sense can be found. On the face of it, the acceptance of such traditions requires some justification and it may be of interest barely to list several positions that might be taken.

First, it might be said that, in so far as the approved mariological traditions state facts about Mary's historical existence, they must have obtained credence on historical evidence after all. There really was an oral tradition extending in unbroken and unperverted continuity from apostolic times to the Dark Ages, though it was only in the Dark Ages that these matters came to light. The subsequent massive acceptance of the traditions in the Church, confirmed by the seal of papal authority, is sufficient to assure the Catholic believer that the chain of historical testimony, though now perfectly invisible, was sound in every link.

What this amounts to is the extension of the *decuit ergo factum* argument from the history of the thing believed to the evidence for the belief. Not only must it have happened; there must also have been a chain of testimony to tell us that it did. The principle of argument is surely vicious; but that is not the worst of it. The allegation about the chain of testimony is liable to collide with historical probability at any point. We may have to admit that the vocal part of Christendom at any given period was not only silent as to the alleged belief but talked as though they believed otherwise.

A second position possible is to admit that there is no distinct testimony to matter-of-fact other than that contained in Scripture itself or in other genuinely historical sources, and to claim that the substance of the tradition you defend is reasonably educible from the known historical evidence. All, in fact, that the Church has been inspired to do is to draw out or interpret the sense. (We say that the *substance* of the traditions is educible from the evidence. Of course we shall have to admit the currency of pious legends embodying truth in tales.)

This line of defence is sound in itself if only it will stretch to cover the case. Its applicability is likely to depend very much on the view you take of biblical inspiration. Was St Luke guided to record inerrantly the very words Gabriel spoke, as it were out of the mouth of God? And was St Jerome guided to give a Latin translation valid in itself? '*Ave, plena gratia!*' It has been divinely said, then, that Mary has fullness of grace; and so the whole theology of grace as worked out from Augustine to Aquinas may be brought to bear, and we may boldly describe Mary's existence from the moment of her conception as one from which no grace was withheld, which God and the Schoolmen know how to give. But if we feel obliged to fall back on St Luke's Greek, we find this charming play on words, χαῖρε κεχαριτωμένη (a word-play, because χάρις and χαρά are different notions). Puns cannot be translated: 'Good day to you, since God's so good to you!' gives the general effect. The suggestion is that a newly granted favour from heaven makes her day, or, to stick to the Greek, gives her reason to be glad. What the angel brings is news. So Mary is dumbfounded and wonders what the news is.

But perhaps Gabriel did not speak in Greek either;[6] and perhaps the most we have the right to expect of St Luke is that he should express in good old biblical style and image what St James said Mary had said about an overwhelming experience.

Tacitly yielding to such modern considerations as these, the Catholic theologian will no longer rely on possessing a divine utterance which virtually informs him that Mary was conceived immaculate. Her having been so conceived must be made to depend on what is presupposed in her playing the part that she does. But no sooner is this said than the logic of the case is altered. The eduction of implications from (guaranteed) statements is one thing; the inference to antecedents from the occurrence of events, is another. And the possibility of doing it with any confidence is in direct proportion to the commonplaceness of the event. 'Kettles never boil, unless they have been heated.'—'A man never writes a poem of outstanding merit, unless he has. . . .' Well, unless he has *what*? And the composition of poetical masterpieces is itself a commonplace event compared with that of experiencing and accepting a call to become virgin mother of the Son of God.

If God has not (implicitly) told us that Mary was conceived immaculate, then it seems that we are involved in the presumption of inferring from one unique divine act another unique divine act. 'It was fitting that the God who did thus should also have done thus, and so no doubt he did': *decuit, ergo factum est.* If such reasoning is vicious, it will not have been divinely supported or inspired; and if Catholics in the mass have thought thus, it reveals a common infirmity of the human mind. The difficulty is not met by pointing out that such events as the immaculate conception and the assumption (anyhow in the most refined and theologized version of that mystery) are by their nature invisible happenings and therefore no parts of the history for which historical testimony is either demanded or forthcoming. For it does not lessen the presumption of inferring what God must have done, that there is not merely no evidence that he did it, but no possibility even that there should be any. It is not a less impertinence to tell a man what he says to himself in solitude than to give him an unevidenced account of what he must have said in the market-place. God's invisible acts are only known if he reveals them in perceptible effects.

I incline to judge that the best defence for the believer in the papal dogmas is a counterattack against the absoluteness of the canon we have just laid down. It is presumption to argue '*decuit, ergo factum*' of the ways of God. Nevertheless, no one can think of the continuous action of God through a whole train of events without filling in a few gaps in the evidence. We cannot argue, 'This is the *proper* thing for God to have done, so he did it.' But we cannot help supposing that the path of God's will from one revealed action to another, when the two are in series, was continuous; nor can we withhold ourselves from conceiving the bridge, or transition, between the two. And the Church, we might hold, has been supported and directed by the divine Spirit in thinking such transitions.

The defence may be allowed in general. It might apply to the transition between the death on the cross and the resurrection. 'He descended into hades'; the transition was through the state of being dead, Christ touched the bottom of our condition. The fact was not visible; the Church learned to think it. If the transition from God's dealing with old Israel to the incarnation of the Word could be charted with the same sort of reason as passing through the immaculate conception, I might believe that the Church had been guided to think so. And, presumably, if I were a willing subject of the Pope, I should take it on his authority that such a charting of the divine path was reasonably and Christianly drawn.

However that may be, devotion to Mary does not need such extraordinary justifications. If she is loved, it is because she is; she has her place in the Body of Christ and it is a place no other creature can share. Christ is worshipped for what he uniquely is in each of his sainted members; the relation of Mary to Jesus is an endless subject of fruitful contemplation, and her will is a handle to take hold of the will of God. Her glory is that she is the virgin mother of God; what more can be added to it?

Mary appears in Scripture as a glorified figure only in the vision of the Apocalypse (Rev. 12), and the reference of even this passage to Mary has been disputed—mistakenly, indeed. How could St John write of a new Eve who bears the Messiah to crush the old serpent without even thinking of Mary? Still, the figure is not primarily the figure of Mary nor, indeed, of a *new* Eve. It is the figure of Eve, that is, of woman, attaining the fulfilment of the promise implicit in the curse laid upon her in Eden. In one sense of the promise and the curse, woman (let us say, Eve) has always been bringing forth her children in sorrow, and they have always been at odds with the serpent. But in another sense, her travail is fruitless until she brings forth the man-child who bruises the serpent's head; and this she does in the person of the ecclesia of God, and more narrowly, in the person of Mary. Even this account is simpler than St John's picture; for what he sees is not just the literal birth of the earthly Christ at Bethlehem, but the birth of the heavenly Man who now reigns and will come to judge. The event of the heavenly Man's birth is in fact earthly, for he is threatened by the serpent and needs to be caught up into the throne by his ascension before the failure of the serpent's lying-in-wait becomes evident. Yet since it is the birth of the heavenly Man rather than the incarnation of the Son of God that St John sees, it has all the dignity of a heavenly birth, and the mother becomes a heavenly figure.

What sort of glorification of Mary is involved in this picture? The ecclesia of God is glorified, or celestialized, by association with the heavenly Man she is privileged to bring forth; and this she does in Mary. It is through the person of Mary that she becomes the Mother of Christ. But only in the moment of the birth. When St John goes on to recount the Woman's further history, her flight from the serpent and the persecution of 'the rest of her seed' by the serpent's seed (Antichrist), we have no right to suppose that he is thinking of Mary, or making her the mother of Christians, or the mystical substance of the Church. For the figure of the vision is Eve, not Mary; she does her childbearing at Bethlehem in her Mary-phase, she travails in the sorrow of Christ's disciples (says St John's Gospel, 16. 20-2) over his 'birth' from the Easter sepulchre into the light of heaven; she bears her other children, the brethren of Messiah, in her role of Ecclesia.

Mary, then, according to this vision is not seen as the foundation-member, or archetype, or universal matrix of the Church. The relation is exactly opposite: the Church comes first, that is, the people of God under the womanly guise of mother to the children of God. Mary is glorified by being taken up into this function in a unique way; she is the embodiment of the

Community in the physical bearing of *the* Child of God, the fruit of all Eve's travail.

NOTES

[1] ἐξέστη It is impossible to give a precise meaning to this word. It describes any condition, whether trance, strong emotion, madness, or intense preoccupation, which suspends normal attention to present circumstances.
[2] St Matthew's correction is conservative. For 'Is not this the carpenter?' he writes: 'Is not this the carpenter's son?' St Luke says roundly: 'Is not this Joseph's son?'
[3] He also mentions Perez's brother Zerah, who should have been the elder twin: but Perez thrust out before him (Gen. 38. 29).
[4] Whatever we may choose piously to think, there is no difficulty whatever in supposing that Mary's story (if she disclosed it) was doubted in the family until after the resurrection, especially if Joseph, who might have confirmed it, was dead.
[5] There is a further point of irony, however. What can be more appropriate to a son of *Joseph* than to feed a starving world with bread?
[6] In Semitic speech he would need a pun: 'Peace, daughter of peace!' would do it.

Very God and Very Man

When I was asked to name a title to this paper, I chose the dogmatic phrase 'very God and very man', for a simple reason. My arguments (I said to myself) will be ineffective and my expositions unintelligible—but my title may have a chance of being remembered. At least someone will go away saying to himself: Dear me! the Christian faith holds that Jesus Christ is very God and very man. The emphasis, of course, is on the adjectives: 'very God and very man'. Not a man who was really rather divine nor God being really rather human, but a genuine coincidence of undiminished opposites—God and man—each word being used in its true or proper sense. Rather as though I were to say about any man that he is both a rational person and an animal, and were to insist that neither description diminished or weakened the force of the other. Not an animal with some of the characteristics of a rational person, nor a rational person with some of the characteristics of an animal, but each absolutely. An animal, generated, born, growing, feeding, breathing, and destined to putrefy everlastingly; a rational person responsible to the throne of eternal Reason. Whereas Christ is both God—the eternal Reason himself—and man, a common or garden rational animal like you or me. When I say that, I am merely putting into my own words the assertions of that unpopular document, the Athanasian Creed: God complete and Man complete of reasonable mind and human flesh subsisting. Who, though he be God and man, is nevertheless not two but one Christ; for as reasonable mind and flesh are one man, in like manner God and man are one Christ.

But why talk like this? And perhaps you think my answer ought to take the form: because the history of Jesus Christ obliges us to talk like this; because the person historically established by the Gospel records was nothing less than what the Athanasian Creed defines. Well, all right; only we must avoid being caught

Written on the reverse side of *The Crown of the Year* manuscript, published in 1952.

out by the ludicrous ambiguity of the word 'history'. Christians of course believe that the Athanasian definition applies to the actual and historical person whose doings and sayings are reflected in the Gospels; it is the historical reality that deserves the dogmatic description, and not some fancy being in the sky. But it is quite another thing to say that the approved methods of historical inquiry establish the presence in Galilee and at Jerusalem round about the year thirty of God Almighty present in human flesh, or that an unbelieving historian with no other considerations before him than the Gospel texts is being simply pigheaded not to admit that divine presence. When I say that 'history' is a ludicrously ambiguous term, this is the ambiguity I wish to unmask. History can mean (*a*) what really happened and (*b*) a certain technique for discovering what happened. Now history (*b*), the technique of inquiry, is like any other technique of inquiry. It is a net with its own sort of meshes let down into the ocean of total fact and gathering whatever harvest of fishes that sort of net will catch. No net will catch all the living matter in the water and no historical method will fish up the whole of live historical reality, unless we give to 'historical reality' the tautological sense of 'what our historical method fishes up'. There is plenty of history which will forever elude historical inquiry and it is pretty obvious that the supernatural being of Jesus Christ is some of that. The Christian faith is not believed on historical grounds alone, that is, on grounds which unaided history can establish: it is believed on living testimony of a special kind. The disciples were encountered by God in Jesus Christ and called on others to encounter him there. The second generation made this encounter partly indirectly, through the faith of the first, partly in the formulated tradition which, when it was written down, became the Gospels, partly in living and praying, and partly in the ever new examples of Christ's work in the saints. Historical inquiry of the scientific sort can, obviously, test some of the links of the evidence. What did the first witnesses actually assert about Christ? Will their story fit into the secular history of the time in so far as known to us? This is all, obviously, important, but it is no more than a check.

So, if we ask '*Why* say, very God and very man?' the answer is not 'because no other formula can be squared with facts established by naked history and evident to unbelievers'. The answer must take another form: we say 'very God and very man' because the words most properly describe the object with which Christian existence is bound up. It is not either an obstructive piece of misdescription, or a rhetorical paradox for those who get a kick out of rhetorical paradoxes, or an adulatory hyperbole expressing inexact emotion like the things Spenser said about Queen Elizabeth and Goebbels said about Adolf Hitler: none of these things, but an illumination of our fundamental belief. A Christian, for example, may recite to himself a very well known formula: Blessed be God, blessed be his holy Name. Blessed be Jesus Christ, very God and very man—and there he may break off and seriously endeavour to plumb the depths of that equation: to think of Godhead dealing so humanely with us as to come in an actual human being; or again, to think of human existence so rooted and grounded in God's will and action as to be the personal life of God himself, under the self-imposed conditions of a particular human destiny. And (my meditative Christian will go on to reflect) this person is not what *was*, but what *is*, alive in the one universe of life with us on earth, and with the saints departed; the core and pivot of a spiritual community, with every member of which he is present by his care and by his intercession, so that by association with him we are continually drawn into the life of God. But I am sure this is a very improper place to describe the movements of a Christian mind at prayer. I only strayed into so improper an exhibition because I wanted to illustrate the fact that *very God and very Man* is what Christianity is about.

Look here: the longer I go on trying to tell you about this the more I become convinced that the job that really wants doing is to expound the formula rather than to justify it; or, anyhow, that the justification required is identical with exposition. So let's get on with that.

The other day a colleague of mine, hearing a supposedly historical discussion about certain Gospel statements, was observed to mutter and to shake his head. 'The whole discussion is a logical mistake', he said. 'Jesus wasn't a man, he was just a god.' That remark was what is sometimes called a 'priceless' remark, that is to say, a remark in which every word is packed with erroneous meaning. It is perfect in its way: one couldn't change a syllable without losing something. Jesus was '*a* god', one of a class of gods, it seems, or why the indefinite article? A God like Attis, or Osiris (see the *Golden Bough*). And if such a god, then *just* a god, a *mere* god, that is to say, no part of flesh-and-blood humanity at all, but a phantom of religious devotion, not intersecting with the historical plane, but hovering above it. And so, not a man at all: therefore, to discuss his person or acts as a problem of history is a logical error, the application of the wrong category. We talk about what sort of thing happened under Pontius Pilate's regime when we ought to be talking about the sort of things that mythical saviours 'have' to do in order to satisfy certain religious cravings.

Well now, those who first acknowledged the claims of Jesus did not see in him '*a*' god but '*a*' man, for they were Jews and they rejected the sort of god to whom the indefinite article can be applied as being utterly puerile and superstitious. If Jesus was 'an' anything, he was a man; indeed, 'a' Jew, 'a' Galilean, 'a' self-taught rabbi and spiritual healer. There wasn't 'a' God like Attis or Hercules for him to be: there was just the infinite Godhead.

Now this means that our formula 'very God and very man' is in a manner deceptive: the verbal antithesis is neater than the real fact. We are not talking about the paradoxical identity between two examples of finite and determinate being, as when we say *a* green expanse which is also *a* triangular area (which is not paradoxical, indeed) or, a square which is also a circle (and that is a paradox, and in fact a flat contradiction). Now what we have here is not a mere point of chopped logic but the heart of the whole matter. 'A' god could not also be 'a' man, any more than a dog could be a cat. One personal subject, one species: you have got to make up your mind which. We might have 'a' god letting on to be 'a' man, like a fairy godmother letting on to be an old hag, in which case he is really a god all the time and not a man at all: his mind, action, and being remain of the divine variety. Or, I suppose, we might have a god who turned himself, or got turned, into a man so effectively that he just was a man, and couldn't help it, as the companions of Ulysses, perhaps, are to be taken to have become real pigs under the influence of Circe's wand. In that case all we could say would be that he had once been a god, and, perhaps, hoped to be one again soon; but for the present he was just a man. To take another possibility, we might try a composite solution: a god so possessing or indwelling in man that the man's mind remains but is heavily under the divine influence. And in this way, the primitive Christians naively thought about the unfortunate man possessed by *an* evil spirit, but they never so thought of God in Christ, because God, though he was spirit, was not *a* spirit.

To explain better what I mean I must turn to the doctrine of creation. God's creative will takes effect in every creature's becoming of its own sort; every creature is, so to speak, handed a limited charter of privileges and a limited set of rules to which it has to work: that's what makes it the creature it is, and in being that creature it can be no other. But God himself, the creator, is not subject to any such limitation or particularity of sphere or of kind: he is the sheer creative energy from which all such limitations proceed. To talk about 'divine nature' and 'human nature' as though God's nature were one of the ways of being alongside the human way is sheer paganism.

Thus 'very God and very man' is not the botching together of two ways of being, the divine way and the human way. No: it says something more like this. The infinite energy who creates the human Jesus fortifies and redoubles his creative act in living, or being, that man by personal identification. And God, infinite God, no more ceases to be God by thus being Jesus than he ceases to be God by making Jesus. But neither, on its side, is the humanity of Jesus forced, altered, or overborne. For God's incarnation consists precisely in being the man Jesus and not in being anything else. God, becoming incarnate, does not first become a non-human angelic form and then go and force that form on Jesus. Jesus is the form his incarnation takes, and Jesus is a man.

What, then, is the formula? 'Infinite God living the existence of one of his creatures, through self-limitation to a particular created destiny'? There, perhaps, is an acceptable set of words, but does it mean anything?

Suppose I had never heard of Jesus Christ; suppose, for example, I were a little African boy being instructed by a missionary who was so stupid as to begin with the abstract doctrine of incarnation and only afterwards go on to historical fact. Suppose, then, that the missionary says to me, 'Infinite God living the existence of one of his creatures, through self-limitation to a particular created destiny. 'Now, my boy, what sort of a person would you expect this incarnation of Godhead to be?' We will suppose that the boy is as phenomenally intelligent as the missionary is phenomenally stupid, and furthermore that he has been fortified with all sorts of philosophical techniques and cautions—in fact, he is a surprisingly mature, sophisticated, and learned child, except in the one particular of Jewish history, on which his mind is a perfect blank. What, then, will the boy reply? 'Father,' he says, 'I do not think it will be a baboon or a crocodile, I think it will be a man. It will be a good man, a wise man; a man full of the power of Spirit. But not like you, Father. You are full of the power of the Spirit: you get him by going into the prayer hut and asking. He will not do that. Who would he pray to? He is God. He will not pray to himself. He will say to the others, Come and pray to me. I give you what is good for you. I tell you all the answers.'

'Oh dear', says the missionary to himself, 'this instruction isn't going at all as I intended. This was the point when I was going to whip the Gospel out of my cassock-pocket and say, "Exactly! Here is the man. Go away and read about him." But as it is, that would never do. He will say: "That is not God. He prays to his Father in Heaven; and says: 'One only is God. Keep his commandments and thou shalt live.' He says: 'of that day and that hour none knows, not the angels in heaven, nor the Son, but the Father alone.' " '.

'I have muffed it again', says the stupid missionary to himself. 'I know what it is: I left out the piece about the Trinity—or anyhow, about the Binity; the doctrine of the third person will keep for another day.'

So the missionary clears his throat, and starts again like this: 'My child, I have put you on the wrong track. It is not just Godhead that becomes incarnate, it is Godhead in the special form or person of Sonship. Divine Son becomes incarnate: and since Divine Son draws his whole person and being from the divine fatherhood anyhow, quite apart from his incarnation, when he becomes incarnate he does not cease to do so. He goes into the prayer hut, he goes out into the hills, he talks with his Father, he draws the Spirit of the Father into him, he opens himself to receive the power and the will. But, you will say, what is this about Divine Son? Are there two Gods? My child, I know you are clever when you want to be. Now concentrate, and I will tell you. My child, what do we know about God? What but that he is the cause of all? An infinite energy of making, giving, self-outpouring; a bounty that has no limit; a life that ceaselessly mirrors himself in the faces of living things. The golden bounty splashes down, the creatures catch it in a million little cups, and still it overflows. The living spirit is mirrored in a million faces: in yours, my child, and mine, and doubly so when we go into the prayer hut and look back into the divine countenance and throw back his own light upon himself and the beam dances between us full of angels. But how little, cracked, and dusty a mirror in you or me to give God back the light of his countenance; and how confused and splintered a reflection does he receive from all the variety of creatures taken together? Is there nowhere a face to look into his eyes with equal eyes, nowhere a bowl to catch and treasure and contain the whole overflow of infinite bounty? My child, do you believe God is almighty? Do you believe that there lacks anything to his perfection, or his joy? Then tell me: does he or does he not, from all eternity and always, give himself a son?'

'Now what can we say of this Son? He is utterly receptive, wholly derived; in fact, a Son. But he is also infinite: all that his Father is, for his Father has withheld from him none of what he is himself; and he has the capacity to receive all that the Father gives. But these are not two Gods operating independently or even forming an amicable and voluntary alliance. They are the two persons of one divine life which could not exist at all otherwise than in them. For the Father, the source of Godhead, is an overflowing bounty; a giver, a cause, and he is all this in being the Father of this Son continually.'

'Yes,' says the boy, 'I suppose so. But have you not taken away from us the love of God? If this is the Son in whom he is content, why will he trouble with us? He does not need us. He . . . Oh, excuse me, Father . . .' The boy broke off to recapture a little furry animal which had jumped out of his pocket. It was soon comfortable between his hands and he looked at it with manifest benevolence.

'What's that?' said the missionary.

The boy laughed. 'He's my little friend.'

'Rather a small friend', said the missionary. 'Haven't you any bigger ones?'

'Yes, you know: the boy Azarias. Why d'you ask?'

'Never mind,' said that tiresome and didactic priest, obviously improving the occasion. 'Now concentrate: think. If we had just had animals, no fellow men, each of us alone in a patch of forest, would we ever have called the animals our friends, or made friends of them?'

'No,' said the boy, 'I think not. No other man, no friendship: no talk, no give and take, no anything.'

'Still,' said the priest, 'now you have got Azarias and the others, you make a little friend of the squirrel.'

'Yes,' says the boy, 'I put the friendship on him, I talk to him, I pretend he understands.'

'But is it all pretending? Does he understand nothing?'

The boy laughed again. 'He's a very clever squirrel. He understands about ten different things. And I think he really likes me a bit.'

'Well then,' said the missionary, 'and what about God? God is not just a fairly loving person. He is just love, that's what the book says. Now do you think he could be the love he is if he had only us? Do you not think that the Love the Father is loves his Son, and then his love overflows on to little creatures like us, so that, as you said about you and your squirrel, he puts the friendship on us and treats us as though we were his Son? And not content with that, he sends his Son into the world to associate us with that Son, and make us resemble him, and, as far as possible, parts of that Son, so that his love for us might be part of his love for his Son. That association is called the mystical body of Christ.'

The missionary's hand returned to his cassock-pocket and he brought out his Gospel-book with an air of chastened triumph. 'There,' he said, 'go and read how the Divine Son came into the world, in which he still remains.'

I must apologize for this nineteenth-century missionary idyll, which is hardly, I fear, to the taste of the present day; but the thing ran away with me and I have no time to rewrite. Oh, how awful! I see that there is going to be another scene of it.

A day or two later the missionary came upon the boy sitting with his nose in the book and a frown of intense concentration. 'How are you getting on with it?' he asked.

'Very nice', said the boy. 'This man, he does the work, he

speaks the words of the Son of God. But he doesn't know who he is himself, he has to find out. He is thirty years old and he still doesn't know. He comes to a man called John who is baptizing the people to make them clean and ready for someone called Messiah, someone very great, to come. Jesus is baptized too, and then bang! the sky splits, down comes the dove, down comes the voice, You are that Messiah, you are my beloved Son. He goes away into the bush to think. The bad spirit comes to him and bothers him plenty, "*If* you really are the Son of God" he keeps saying to Jesus in his mind. And even to the very end he never says just like you told me, "I am the Son of God who is God too." It is a funny thing if Divine Son has to find out that he is Divine Son and never quite manages it. He comes as a man:—all right; that is, he hides himself from the others. But does he hide himself from himself? I mean like this. Divine Son is divine Son because of his thought, not because of his hands, feet, lungs, heart; for those are just like anyone's. But if divine Son doesn't think he is divine Son, how can he be divine Son because of his thought?'

'My boy,' said the missionary, 'did you ever see a picture of President Eisenhower?'

'Yes, plenty . . . with a grin from ear to ear.'

'Yes, I know: they teach them to do that in America. But did you ever see a picture without a grin?'

'Yes, once. Him taking the oath.'

'Good. Well, there is a man rather like that in my native country: he is not top man in politics like Eisenhower, he's top man at thinking. He's called Gilbert Ryle. And he says. . .'

At this moment there was a blood-curdling roar. In jumped a lion, and ate the missionary. The boy ran screaming out, and was eaten by a leopard. So now we have got rid of these tiresome characters and can proceed in our own way.

I want to apply Ryle's famous distinction between *knowing how* and *knowing that* to the mystery of the incarnate consciousness. The little African rightly said that the divine Son could not be in Jesus otherwise than as mind; and rightly, too, that mind must be expressed in knowing, or what is it? But the little African, like so many victims of Ryle's criticism, assumes that 'knowing' means *knowing that*, knowing clear factual truths; for example, in this case, that the thinker is very God of very

God, begotten not made, consubstantial with the Father, and mediator of the whole creative process. But such a supposition not only conflicts (as the little African objects) with the evidence in the Gospels, it conflicts no less with the very possibility of genuine incarnation. Christ is very God, indeed, but also very man; and an omniscient being who knows all the answers before he thinks and all the future before he acts is not a man at all, he has escaped the human predicament. And (not to speak of omniscience in general, but to restrict ourselves to the single point of self-knowledge) how can a person who knows his unique metaphysical status with more than Aristotelian exactitude be a largely self-taught Galilean village boy whose store of ideas derived from the Synagogue? How, moreover, can he be tempted at all times like as we are, or fight a lifelong battle of faith, and suffer seeming dereliction on the cross?

On the other hand, he *knows how* to be Son of God in the several situations of his gradually unfolding destiny, and in the way appropriate to each. He is tempted to depart from that knowledge, but he resists the temptation. And that suffices for the incarnation to be real. For 'being the Son of God' is the exercise of a sort of life; and in order to exercise it he must know how to exercise that life: it is a question of practical knowledge. A theoretical knowledge about the nature of the life he lives is unnecessary, it suffices that he should live it. 'I would rather know how to repent than know the definition of repentance' is an ancient saying; and it was enough for Jesus to exercise the personal existence of the Second Person in the Trinity: he might leave to schoolmen the definition of the Trinity, especially in view of the fact that it cannot be verbally defined. There is, indeed, something shocking and absurd about the thought of the divine person talking divinity, as Alexander Pope says in criticising the bathos of Milton's heavenly scenes: 'And God the Father turns a school-divine.'

God is that life which schoolmen falter to express, and which an eternity of exploration will not exhaust; but it will be ever new to those deemed worthy of that blessedness.

And God the Son on earth is a fullness of holy life within the limit of mortality; it is for him to be, and for theologians endlessly and never sufficiently, to define.

But *knowing how* commonly involves elements of *knowing*

that; for example, knowing how to set a broken leg involves knowing what is the form and function of the bones and muscles you are handling. And knowing how to be Divine Son in earthly flesh doubtless involved knowledge of the realities with which the existence of that Son is concerned and especially a practical and contemplative and, shall we say, a mystical, knowledge of the Father. If it is true that the saint knows God, it is true that Jesus knew his Father, and in a surpassing degree, so that God was absolutely and continually real to him and he drew his whole life and action with simplicity of heart out of that blessed fountain. To *be* the Son was to *know* the Father, not for the Son to know himself. What is the profit of real knowledge? How happy we should be if we could forget ourselves, especially when we pray.

I will, in closing, confide to you, for what it is worth, a speculation, which is, as I see it, a probable consequence of the 'knowing-how' view of the consciousness of the Son of God. It is this. His knowledge of his unique Sonship will be largely negative. It will be the sad and progressive discovery that other men have not the Sonship he has—they are not all pure incarnations of divine Sonship; indeed none of them is that. For, as the divine Child grows, he lives a life filially divine, because, after all, that is the way for him to live and be; he seizes all that his religious training, or the works of nature, offer him wherewith to think the thought and conceive the image of his Father and God and lives in perfect faith. How does he know that other children, other men, are not so? He discovers it in living. Sin is not an occasional breakdown, but a state; irreligion not an occasional distraction but a dominant attitude; wilfulness not a flourish of play but the set-direction of existence. The experiment was not complete until his countrymen had crucified him and his disciples ran from him.

There are many questions concerning the powers and acts of God incarnate besides the question of his knowledge on which alone I have touched. But I must bring this desultory paper to an end and, since desultory it has been, I will conclude with a summary of the points I have made.

1. Why we should say 'very God and very man' of Christ is not a matter of mere historical inquiry because Christians do not

pretend to know about the divine Christ by mere history but through testimony, faith, and life. So what we are asking is whether the formula properly describes the reality with which Christians believe themselves to have to do.

2. The combination of God and Man in Christ is not the combination of two determinate sorts of being, the divine and the human, either compatible with one another or incompatible. It is the act of the Infinite Godhead finitizing his personal action in a unique way, and so that he is purely divine in being purely human.

3. We cannot understand the incarnation without the Trinity. What becomes incarnate is not just the Godhead but the divine Sonship in the Godhead. That is what is translated into human terms, for that is what we are adopted into by association: the sonship is spread to embrace us.

4. The incarnation is not just an accepting of the formal conditions of humanity in general, it is the becoming an actual, particular man in the limitation of his circumstances and his knowledge. The divine infallibility of Christ's knowledge as Son of God is concerned with knowing how to play his divine part rather than with knowing that his part was, in a metaphysical sense, divine.

5. It is an apparent corollary of this that his sense of his uniqueness would be arrived at negatively by the discovery that other men lacked what he was. It was, indeed, a function of his divine compassion for us sinners.

There: that is all I have said. I have really done no more than define and explain a few of the things which the Christian Church teaches and believes. I have proved nothing.

Gnosticism

I must begin by wishing fervently that I have my audience in a frivolous frame of mind and ready to indulge a theologian in amusing himself with the absurd and curious by-ways of his subject. I suppose that every branch of learning has its oddities: I have been told that in certain high and exclusive mathematical societies one of the initiated utters a row of algebraic symbols and the rest collapse with mirth. If the curiosities of theology were as recondite, I would not be troubling you with them; my hope is, indeed, that you can taste them as well as I.

Anyhow, be it understood that we are looking for curiosity: Basilides, Valentine, Simon Magus, these men no doubt were men, grappling as well as they could with the riddles of existence; and their efforts have a pathetic and sometimes a noble aspect. But it is their vagaries that I propose to consider, and hope I shall be pardoned for neglecting their souls; these people were so far away that they cease to be men to us.

They are usually known as gnostics: I have called them theosophists because the name is more familiar. The Theosophical Society, we all know, was founded in 1875 by a certain Madame Blavatsky, than whom few women have been more remarkable for the power of making solid objects fade into thin air among the mountains of India, and crystallize back to physical solidity in the middle of English drawing-room cushions, thence to be hacked out with scissors by delighted seekers after truth. With her began the theosophic name, but not the thing, as I hope presently to convince you. For there are few parallels more exact in the history of thought than that of nineteenth-century theosophy and second-century gnosis: it is not something *like*, it is the thing. That a coherent system should recur in time, no one need marvel, for what man has thought man may think again. But that an elaborate tissue of contradictions, a centaur and chimera of speculation, should twice appear the same, is something of a

Date and occasion unknown.

miracle in nature. It is *gnosis*, knowledge, *sophia*, wisdom, something universal, rational, and freed from the narrowness of the great historic religions; and yet it attaches itself to the most obscure and esoteric religious traditions, claiming a secret ancestry through magicians, Rosicrucians, alchemists, Freemasons, I don't know what, driving the roots of its invisible tradition back into the immemorial and barbarous past. It is philosophical and scientific, it makes a parade of logic and free inquiry; and yet it is occult and visionary, it accepts dreams for evidence of fact, it traffics in spookery, magic, and abnormal psychic states. It claims to be spiritual and condemns the rest of us for earthly-mindedness, it reveals a mighty spiritual hierarchy of being to which the world of our common experience is as a drop in the bucket; and yet it is helplessly materialistic, its spirits are only refined invisible matter, fiery or ethereal. You and I, the theosophist tells us, have astral selves, constituting a psychic aura which projects two inches beyond the outline of our visible body, and is somewhat egglike in shape. Do some Higher Thought exercises, and look at yourself in the mirror and you may see your ovoid super-self; and if you are one of the elect, it will appear as of a rosy hue. One last contradiction: it is anti-dogmatic, it claims to have sucked the pure juice of spiritual principle from the religions of mankind and to have rejected the inessential mythologic mind; and yet it is immensely elaborate. Its system of angels and reincarnations and its divisions of the soul's anatomy leave the work of medieval scholastics to look simple and meagre by comparison. Now all these features are common to gnosis and theosophy—the pretence of science and the actuality of superstition; the contempt of authoritative dogma, yet the pride in fantastic speculation, materialistic spiritualism and esoteric universalism. Both believe in an impersonal god who both is and is not distinct from the hierarchy of spirits which emanates from his being; both believe in the pre-existence and divinity of the human soul and its salvation through knowledge. One could carry the comparison further; but it is certainly time that we turned to the gnostics themselves.

First, the origin of gnosis. The ancient religions of the nearer East, in Egypt, Syria, and Palestine, not to mention Mesopotamia and India, tended to produce a learned priesthood, treasuring the ancient traditions of their faith. Now the time was bound to come—in India it came very early—when the learned became discontented with the mere repetition of sacred histories, the mere elaboration and reapplication of a fixed rule of ritual and conduct. It was inevitable that reflection should begin; that an attempt should be made to extract the living principles from the anomalous mass of legend and of law. It was no longer enough that this or that had been handed down; one must see the sense of it, one must find ideas which appeared to be their own evidence.

Well, you may say, and a very proper development; men cannot forever believe merely because their grandfathers said that their grandfathers had said that their grandfathers had said it. Is not that the road from superstition to philosophy? Yes, no doubt; but philosophy takes some doing, you have to get the trick of it. The Greeks were lucky enough to stumble on the method; other peoples were less fortunate. The Greeks, having detached thinkable ideas from their religious and moral tradition, managed to remain masters of the ideas. But ideas are dangerous things; while they remain tied and bound by the tribal traditions, at least they stay put—'there's a great deal to be said for being dead'—but once they get loose in a speculative brain they can breed like rabbits, till before we know where we are the poor man is quite overrun with them. The Greeks, I suppose, without noticing it, hit upon the blessed principle of economy—that ideas are not to be multiplied beyond what is necessary. The gnostics thought no such thing and succumbed to the awful fertility of their own notions.

We ourselves, perhaps, when we cannot get the fully trained mind, are inclined to prefer the simple rustic traditionalist, because, if he does not think, at least he does not think nonsense; and the tradition, to have survived so long, must have some relevance to reality—it cannot be a hopelessly bad guide to life. But the half-baked, the half-educated, are our despair; here are people who will insist on reasoning and finding reasons, yet whose thought-processes appear to us to have nothing rational about them: they gallop through a riot of false analogy. That is the intellectual stage represented by gnosticism; every parish curate knows it well, it meets him in the small tradesman and the intelligent artisan.

Well, this process of philosophy-gone-wrong sprang up as a side-shoot in several of the old historic religions; and no doubt its growth was fostered by the spread of cheap culture at the beginning of our era and by the intermingling of religions, both factors which tended to leave men discontented with their traditional faith. We can follow the development fairly clearly in Judaism, in spite of the efforts of an ultimately triumphant Pharisaic orthodoxy to obliterate the traces. But now, once your Jewish or Egyptian sage has distilled from his religion a quintessence of pure ideas, and let it breed a system in his head, 'Here', he cried, 'I have the soul of all religion'; all religious ordinances everywhere are types and shadows of it, to be read by the clue of allegory. And so, wherever he started from, whether from Jewry or from Egypt, he was soon all over the world, raking together scraps from every source; and so gnosticism becomes international, even though Jewish, Egyptian, and Syrian gnosis continued to bear the dominant characteristics of their origin. Now obviously the gnostic was claiming to be a man who *sees*; the simple believer took things on trust, but he, the gnostic, saw the truth. But since, unlike Descartes, he lacked a criterion of what is intellectual or spiritual vision, he was liable to mistake every kind of hallucination and self-deception for it; and fell into an abyss of dream-ecstasies and nonsense, all solemnly accepted, recorded, and codified, because it was experienced; because it had been seen.

About the middle of the second century flourished the Egyptian Greek, Valentine. To him there had come down an ancient speculation of the Egyptian priests—we find it in documents of a thousand years before—concerning the number of the gods. Faced with the problem of why eight chief deities were known in their district of Egypt, while yet the Godhead seemed to be one, the priests of Thoth had produced a barbarous piece of theology. Thoth, they said, had once been alone; but then had projected from himself a second god, who immediately doubled himself into a pair and bred two more. These pairs each bred another pair; and so there was constituted a blessed ogdoad or set of eight gods, who joining up again with Thoth their begetter became his two hands, his two eyes, his two feet, and so forth, a rounded and perfect body of deity which in one aspect was the complete and perfect Thoth, in another the company of Thoth and his children.

This is already typical gnosticism; but Valentine gnosticized it further: it must be made more spiritual; and one must rename and rearrange the divine ogdoad so as to show a semblance of reason why it developed as it did. It must supply a real solution for the problem πῶς τὸ ἓν πολλὰ γίγνεται : how the primal unit propagated itself into the whole multiplicity of the world. And then, *on ne s'arrête pas dans un si beau chemin*: why stop at eight? Why not expand the system to explain the origin of evil, and of matter, and of human life; and what will befall the soul hereafter? Well, this is what Valentine produced.

In the beginning was *Bythus*, the infinite abyss of being. He was alone just pure 'itness' and 'thereness', till reflecting on himself, he saw the notion of himself in the form of the absolute Silence: *Sige*, which is what he was himself indeed. But the word *sige* happens fortunately to be feminine; and so in reflecting on his own silence he begot the act of understanding, *Nous*, a second god, the only first-begotten. But Nous is by nature a twin: understanding cannot be without its object, and so along with him was born his consort *Aletheia*, truth, a word which, again, by good luck, is feminine. But understanding, having intercourse with truth, produced in turn a son, that is, rational discourse, or *Logos*: but he, too, is a twin, for discursive thought involves movement and life; so here we have little *Zoe*, or life, as the twin and consort of Logos. But rational discourse and life naturally wished to express themselves in the form of some definite creature, and produced Man; but Man is incomplete, being by nature social, as Aristotle had observed, and so required a consort and twin-sister, Community; and how lucky that that, too, is feminine, *Ecclesia*. And that is the first and blessed ogdoad of Valentine the Gnostic: infinity and silence; understanding and truth; discourse and life; man and community; eitht gods, yet one God; abstract ideas, yet persons; verbal logic, and yet family history.

Well, anyhow, you may say with relief, here we are; we started from infinity and we have got to man in four hops; and so presumably we are home: we have bridged the process of reality from start to finish. Don't you think it. This man is the pure, spiritual, prototypic, ideal man; he is the type of what manhood should be, but, alas, is not. We know only too well that we are not part of the blessed ogdoad, you and I: on earth, manhood is broken into a multitude of atoms, each inclosed in a separate body. Being burdened by the flesh, we groan: how did this deplorable state of affairs come about? Why is our pure spiritual part incarnate, as the pure bubbles of air are entangled in the slimy structure of the sponge and sunk to the bottom of the bath? How did this entangling sponge of matter come to be? And how did our souls get into it? How can the world-sponge be squeezed so as to allow our bubble-souls to escape upward and join their native air, the divine life of the holy *Pleroma* above this visible sky?

So Valentine starts again.

The blessed and inviolable ogdoad did not, after all, exhaust the fertility of the divine being. Discourse and Life had a fresh family and propagated a decad of ten emanations, while Man and Community produced a dodecad of twelve. To provide these also with names in male and female pairs, Valentine ransacked the stock of Greek abstract nouns, but I am sorry to say that he became lazy and took no pains to arrange them in an order which suggests why one pair should have given rise to the next, as he had done with the ogdoad. Anyhow, the ogdoad, decad, and dodecad, being added, came to thirty, which is a nice round number; and these thirty make up the complete manifestation of the divinity technically known as the *Pleroma*, or fullness, and constituting, as it were, the President, Fellows, and Scholars of the College of Eternity.

But now an element of human interest comes into this story. The youngest scholar on the foundation, the female spirit *Sophia*, is the heroine of it. She became dissatisfied with the intellectual converse of her twin and consort, *Theletus*, and conceived the impious and frantic desire to penetrate to the origin and father of all, the first god, Bythus. But he is unknowable except to Nous, his immediate son; and poor Sophia, vainly struggling to reach with her little bucket of understanding to the bottom of the well of infinity, fell into disordered passions of misery, despair, and frenetic hope. These corroded her pure spiritual being with a kind of impure rust, which weighted her down and would have sunk her forever below the floor of the divine world had not the other spirits intervened to save her. They separated from her this rust of passion, a formless, impure lump; and, so purified, restored to the embraces of her rightful consort a sadder but a wiser Sophia.

But what of the abortion? Separated from its parent, the evil stuff of passion still remained something, and there were fragments and seeds of spirit within it. And so the gods, unwilling to leave it there rolling chaotically to and fro, intervened to give it form, and made it a world. From poor Sophia's tears they made the sea and all things wet; from her wild laughter the light and fire; from her consternation and bewilderment all things opaque and hard. (The church father Irenaeus is not content with this. What, he says, about her sweat?)

The finest elements of spirit—to cut a very long story short—became the souls of men; the grosser became *daemones*, who were entrusted with the running of the world-machine, and who were stupid and unspiritual rather than bad. They turn the heavenly spheres and control our physical destinies; only our souls are free, if we can but realize it. It is our part, armed with this spiritual knowledge, aware of the divine origin of our spirits and of the essential irrelevancy of our bodies, to live as much like pure spirits as we can, in contemplation of these heavenly truths, and contempt of the flesh. Then, when the last day comes and the sponge of the world is squeezed, we shall be airy and pure enough to fly up to the heavenly *Pleroma*, while the sponge of matter, emptied of all spiritual content, will cease to have any *raison d'être*, collapse, and become as though it had never been.

Such is a highly simplified version of the gnosis of Valentine, the most intelligent and intelligible of the great systems.

The materialism of the system is noticeable: Matter is only a grossened form of spirit, and Spirit a purer form of matter, so that the one can give rise to the other by degeneration, and the lower hold down the higher by imprisoning it. It is noticeable also that there are no adjectives, but only things, in this odd philosophy. Evil and good are not alternative qualities that may belong to substantial things capable of being either better or worse; evil is a stuff called Matter and good is a stuff called Spirit. The gnostic contemplated the universe as one of those puzzles under glass that you solve by shaking, just a jumble of black and white balls. If only these were sorted out, he said, it would be grand; and when all the white elements have got worked along into their own compartment, the puzzle is finished and the world is saved.

Another oddity one notices is the eroticism of it all: the *Pleroma* is a system of marriages, and poor Sophia's misfortune was a kind of spiritual adultery. This erotic element could have curious consequences; we will mention the case of Simon Magus. This biblical villain appears in the text of the Acts as nothing but a Samaritan magician, who, having attempted to buy from the apostles the power of the Holy Ghost, became the victim of St Peter's severity and the prototype of all ecclesiastical corruption. In fact he was an historic figure of some importance. The bitterness of St Luke against him is to be explained by his having indeed attempted to steal the apostle's thunder by grafting Christian elements into his Samaritan-gnostic misbelief. The Samaritans, as St Luke quite accurately remarks, said of him, 'This man is the Power of God which is called the Great.' Now this is pure gnostic language: a Power is an emanation—the Valentinian ogdoad is a system of Powers. Simon was claiming indeed to be the incarnation of the chief power in the *Pleroma* of God's being, descended to earth to rescue the elect from their spiritual prison by teaching them Gnosis. The Church Father Hippolytus knew disciples of his school who possessed writings attributed to the Master himself, and a lively tradition about him. Well, the great Simon came to earth not only to teach the elect, but to rescue his heavenly consort whose fall, like Sophia's, had started all the trouble, and her he found in a back street of Tyre, following the least respectable of the female professions. Her name was Helen, or else he called her that; and declared her to be spiritually identical with Helen of Troy, whose history is symbolical of the winning back of the fallen female Power from her corrupt estate. Well, Simon taught her Gnosis and reunited her to himself, and so the redemption of the world was wrought. What became of Simon? According to St Hippolytus, he came to a bad end while trying to stage his own resurrection; but of that I wouldn't be so sure; it sounds like Catholic malice. He probably died in his bed. But the Helen story rings true and has better evidence.

This note of eroticism brings us to the general question of the morals of the gnostics, a subject over which their enemies, the Church Fathers, are inclined to linger lovingly; and it is not without its amusing aspect. For, if you take for your grand premiss the doctrine that the true gnostic *is* his spiritual soul, and his body is irrelevant, two opposite practical conclusions could be, and were, drawn. 'Treat the body with contempt'—that was common ground; but there were two interpretations of the phrase—asceticism and licence. The ascetic said, 'Despise your body by mortifying it'; the libertine said, 'Despise your body by letting it do exactly what it likes; it is not worth your attention—asceticism is the worst form of body-preoccupation. Let your passions work themselves off, for the body will perish, and concentrate your attention on your immortal spirit.' This second view is nonsense of course because the mind and the senses are not in fact separable, and to talk of 'letting your body do what it likes' is a form of self-deception. If I let my body take a walk to Beckley when I might else be reading in my room, well then *I* walk to Beckley and *I* fail to read, and if at Beckley I let my body eat too much cheese for me and pickles which no man can digest, with a couple of pints of beer, it will be in vain for me to pretend that the spiritual and intellective 'I' remains transcendently calm and meditatively unaffected; still more vain, if I fall in love with the barmaid.

To do them justice, most of the gnostics appear to have grasped this elementary and practical truth: the sects of the libertines were much the smaller, though naturally the Catholic Fathers make the best they can of them and their hideous enormities.

The system of Valentine illustrates another aspect of gnosticism—the magic of names. We all know this primitive superstition; we all know about the African savage whose 'real' name is buried and never known for fear that by knowledge of it his enemies could work him woe. The name he is called by is not, so to speak, his christening name, but a fiction. The true name is the person, somehow; and conversely the persons of Valentine's heaven are nothing but their names: the names breed one another in the gnostic's head, and accordingly the Powers breed one another in the heavenly *Pleroma*. Obviously the Valentinian adept who did not know the names would know nothing, for the spiritual universe *is* a tangle of bad Greek.

This name-magic gets a particular development in the doctrine of the Soul's Flight. Our souls, as we have seen, are entangled in the material universe like bubbles in a sponge, and the business is to get loose. By asceticism and Higher Thought we keep them pure, dry, and buoyant. The moment of death arrives; up shoots the gnostic soul and bumps against the first sky-sphere. For, by a barbarous interpretation of the Ptolemaic astronomy, the universe is like an onion of pure glass. In the middle is the earth and the air; and for each planet, for sun, moon, and fixed stars there is a separate and complete glassy skin, the nine unbreakable walls of the prison of destiny. In each there is a single gate, where the planetary spirit stands to bar our passage. The buoyant soul circulates till she finds the gate; but does she know the password? At each gate the right word must be spoken, for the daemon world-ruler, the planetary spirit, is jealous of his power, and it is only the higher power of the appropriate divine name which will force him to grant passage. Let the gnostic die with the nine passwords clearly graven on his memory; and if he has lived a meditative and ascetic (or alternatively, libertine) life, the memory will not fail him at the moment of death. If he has lived otherwise he will forget and never escape from the world-onion.

But even in life the soul is a captive balloon indeed, tethered to matter—yet a captive balloon can make trial trips, and the trial trips of the soul are visions and ecstasies. These have a fixed pattern—it need not surprise us that the gnostic's trances should have resembled one another, for we dream what we have thought especially when the dream is self-induced by suggestion. The dream, then, takes the form of a rising through the spheres one after another into the height of heaven; and this is given a naive physical interpretation—the soul really makes the trip while the bodily bond is temporarily suspended. An early Christian-gnostic book describes it for us. A band of devotees was gathered, repeating to one another maxims of Higher Thought—words of faith and truth—when they heard a door being opened and the voice of the Holy Spirit. (This appears to mean, as is seen from what follows, that one of their number (Isaiah) began to speak ecstatically, and the others took this as a sign that he was getting detached from his body and a door in the sky was being opened to let his spirit through.) Then all gave glory to God who had thus vouchsafed a door in an alien world, and vouchsafed it to a man. And as Isaiah was speaking in the Holy Ghost in the hearing of all, he became silent and his mind was taken up from him and he saw not the men that stood before him, though his eyes were open, for he was seeing a vision. And the angel who was sent to make him see was not of this (lowest) firmament, nor was he of the angels of glory of this world, but he was from the Seventh Heaven. Then the circle of the prophets recognized that the holy

Isaiah had been taken up. There follows a description of his journey through the spheres to the throne of God, and of the curious things he saw, for example, the spiritual bodies of the saints still on earth, hanging on pegs in heaven awaiting the souls that should wear them. Other accounts of the heavenly journey reach poetic sublimity.

Ecstasy, then, is valued as an evidence of spiritual detachment, that the captive balloon of the soul is not too closely tied; and so is magic, as a token of the power and dominance of spirit. The Church Father Hippolytus, in his refutation of all heresies, has a very amusing section on ancient conjuring and magic. It is his view that the gnostic magicians obtained their effects by an elementary knowledge of chemistry and mechanics. The worthy man is somewhat uneasy at telling his reader so much as he does, for fear the reader, absorbing such chapters as 'How to produce the appearance of a fiery demon', might set up in the magicians' business himself. The most elementary tricks went down in that simple age: Alexander of Abunotichus ran an oracle on a stuffed snake with a speaking-tube inside it; while as for Apsethus the Lybian—I think I must tell you about him as a means to finish a paper which will otherwise never end. Apsethus the Lybian, says St Hippolytus, had an excessive desire to be reputed a god. So he collected a vast number of parrots—such birds abound in Libya and they are excellent mimics of the human voice. He kept them in an aviary and taught them to say 'Apsethus is a god'. When they had practised this for a sufficient time, he released them. They spread all over Libya proclaiming their gospel, and the Libyans, concluding Apsethus to be a god, brought him abundant offerings. Some of the birds penetrated as far as Greece spreading their teacher's fame, until a man of that country caught and collected as many of these feathered prophets as he could and, caging them, taught them to tell a different tale: 'Apsethus caged us and taught us to say Apsethus is a god.' Released in due time, they proclaimed their recantation, which the Libyans hearing came together and resolved on burning Apsethus.

CRITERIA

Infallibility and Historical Revelation

The subject I propose to discuss is a relation—the relation of ecclesiastical infallibility, however conceived, to the historical revelation. On the one side of the relation I broaden the theme; on the other side I narrow it. I broaden it on the side of infallibility, for I do not confine it to the papal office or to any organ of the Catholic Church. For the purposes of my discussion you can place infallibility where you like; anywhere, that is, in the living Ecclesia. On the other side I narrow the theme, for there are many matters which might be thought to concern or to require infallible decision; but I propose to consider no other matters beside those which constitute historical revelation. Whatever else an infallible voice may be called upon to define, the content of the revelation historically given through the saving incarnation must by all agreement find a place.

My concern is with the effective hold upon the Church of the once-for-all enacted events which are the foundation of faith. In expressing this concern, I do not wish to assert any particular doctrine of the balance between Scripture and tradition or of the balance between primitive datum and subsequent development. I mean to take common ground—ground common, anyhow, to all confessions which even claim credal orthodoxy; for I take it all agree that the Church is bound by historic title-deeds in some manner. And what I want to discuss is the part that can or should be played by infallible living authority in making the control of the Church's title-deeds upon her faith and her practice effective.

To talk of title-deeds is admittedly to talk metaphor. There are no title-deeds. If we mistake the metaphor for literal fact, we allow ourselves an all-too-tempting simplification of the issues. Title-deeds are legal instruments, and as such carry with them an implicit reference to a legal authority which will determine their interpretation and enforce their provisions. Indeed, apart from their reference to such an authority they would be of no force or validity. They ought to be so written and so phrased that their intention is unambiguous and that all sound lawyers must agree as to their practical bearing. But no document can be so drawn as to provide against every contingency, and some documents are not so well drawn as they should have been. Never mind; though the document admits of contrary interpretations the magistrate is empowered to interpret it. If the necessary law is not in the document, the magistrate makes the law required; in the last resort, the court of law is a law-factory. The decision of a first court may indeed be upset by a court of appeal, but ultimately, law is what ultimate authority determines. And there is no scandal or paradox in that; for though law has regard and should have regard to what is factually true and to what is morally just, law as such is neither ideal justice nor factual truth; it is the standing will of public power, and will is what it wills to be.

There is no need to enlarge at the present time on the harm that has been done by the abuse of juridical analogies in theology; and if I now proceed to draw out the fallacious parallel, it is not with the suggestion that any of my hearers would wish to support it. The parallel is this: the Church has her title-deeds in the New Testament, in primitive tradition, in whatever else you like to name: title-deeds drawn not by man, but by the Spirit of the Living God. Shall we then accuse Almighty Wisdom of folly—of instituting statutes without reference to a visible authority whose decision will make them effectively binding? Heaven forbid! Did not Christ in fact confer upon the apostolic college, under the headship of Peter, the power to bind and to loose?

I said that the legal parallel was fallacious; and so it is, but not wholly so. Christ's language about binding and loosing was drawn from the vocabulary of what we may not too misleadingly call the canon law of the Jews, and his use of such language implies that law and legal decision would have a part in the new Ecclesia. In the sphere of legal discipline it was indeed necessary that there should be an effective authority; and, with the divine assistance, Peter and his colleagues were to make law on earth which would have the sanction of heaven. For their law would be the will of the body through which Christ worked here below; and it would be heaven's will it should be obeyed. Here we have, if you like, a divinely authenticated law-factory; and the claim, if astounding, is still acceptable.

It is when we turn from binding laws to saving facts that the legal comparison becomes so very questionable. A law-factory may be all very well; but a fact-factory is another thing entirely. And the core of dogmatic faith is concerned with facts, with what God did in human flesh almost two millennia ago. Now it is the nature of facts to show themselves to a candid, patient, and relevant investigation. Facts are not determined by authority. Authority can make law to be law; authority cannot make facts to be facts. Facts show themselves by evidence, they are not established by authority.

Note that it is when we begin to talk about authoritative pronouncements upon matters of dogmatic fact that the notion of infallibility really comes in. If Peter and his colleagues make law, in applying the Lord's precepts, or in spiritualizing Moses, their law is the law of Christ's Church, the best (if you will) that God's Spirit can make with human instruments there and then, and, as such, to be obeyed as the will of God himself. But to call Peter *infallible* in this connection is to misplace an epithet. Infallibility is a habit in inerrancy, a conformity to some objective standard. If Peter makes good law, it is good, not inerrant, not correct. To make it seem so you would need to import the notion of a perfect conformity of Peter's decision with a foreordaining will of God, conceived as a creative blueprint, or Platonic idea, which Peter faithfully copies. But you will observe that this is precisely the reverse of what Christ promises to Peter. He does not promise him infallible correctness in reproducing on earth the eternal decrees of heaven. He promises him that the decisions he makes below will be sanctioned from above. Doubtless the divine will always anticipates us, just as the divine grace always prevents us; but there is no occasion here to think of any other precedent will than the will of God for what he will do in Peter, Peter being such as he is. If Peter makes as good law as he can make there and then he is doing the will of God.

But whereas there is no need to think of legal decisions as faithfully representing paragraphs in a pre-existent *codex juris divini* laid up in heaven, there is every need to think of pronouncements upon gospel verities as representing (or should I say, expressing) histories pre-enacted upon earth. In this province, there is no good definition which is not correct, nor any perfect definition which is not absolutely so. It is no use having good ideas about Mary's conception or about her assumption if she was not in fact thus conceived nor thus taken up. Peter can loose the rule of circumcision and bind the rule of kosher-butchery upon the faithful without being either correct or incorrect; it is enough he should be wise. But wisdom will not suffice for Peter's umpteenth successor to be justified in dogmatizing the immaculate conception; it is necessary that Mary should have been conceived immaculate. And if any living authority is to be infallible in deciding that she was, that authority will need a *charisma* of a very particular kind: either a *charisma* for perfectly appreciating historical evidences, or a *charisma* for miraculously knowing historical fact over the heads of the evidences, or, indeed, in default of any.

Of the alternative views of the *charisma* I have just suggested, we shall in fact be bound to vote for the second or more extreme; the former and more modest simply will not do the job. A perfect wisdom or enlightenment in judging evidence will merely enable one to judge on the evidence then available and according to the techniques and topics then in force for the interpretation of that evidence. If the evidence changes and the modes of interpretation change, we may hold that a decision which was perfectly correct within scholastic terms of reference is, to the best of our present belief, factually false. For example, it was fair enough to argue that *Ave plena gratia* was a divine assertion that Mary had the plenitude of grace; and you could then go on to work out what that amounted to, with an infallible propriety of judgement. But the angel did not (we now remark) speak in Latin, nor even in Greek. What he is probably meant by St Luke to have said is '*Shalom bath-shalom*,' 'Peace, daughter of peace,' i.e. 'Blessing on you who are blessed indeed'; which, since the Greeks said in greeting '*Chaire*,' 'rejoice', not 'Peace' (on you), presented St Luke with a translator's problem, very neatly solved by the pun χαῖρε κεχαριτωμένη as we might say with a similar assonance but a different sense, 'Hail, thou that art hallowed.' If St Jerome had seen his way into St Luke's Semitic background, and wished to preserve the word-play, he might very well have written '*Salve, quam salvam vult deus,*' but he chose to write '*Ave plena gratia*'. Now suppose that an interpreter of infallible wisdom was drawing dogmatic conclusions from that text in an age when it was taken for granted that authorized translations were inspired comments on the sense of the original. It would then be wise, or subjectively justified on his part to draw conclusions about Mary's plenitude of grace. But if in so doing he was to be not only subjectively justified, but objectively correct, in drawing these conclusions he would need to be guided by an inspiration which by-passes the evidence and guarantees by miracle the conformity of his judgement with objective fact about Mary's state in grace. And so no *charisma* of infallibility will serve but one which has this purely miraculous character. The infallible interpreter does not perform a supernaturalized human act, where Grace elevates the working of wisdom. He is enlightened with regard to a fact for which he has no justifying evidence by a direct fulguration of deity.

But I am digressing. Returning into the main stream of my argument I may sum up what I principally wish to say at this point. It is that infallibility looks like being a hybrid notion, arising out of a confusion between the two functions of making law and of interpreting evidence for fact. A true law-maker is neither fallible nor infallible, but simply sovereign. An interpreter of fact is neither sovereign nor infallible, but (at the best) illuminating. On the side of law, statutes or title-deeds are made effective by a sovereign authority applying them; on the side of fact, historical reality achieves its impact upon us by a complete openness, or exposure of our minds to all the evidences, and a complete integrity in the weighing of them. Well, if that is my case, may not I just as well close it at this point? Have not I said my say? Ah, but whatever you may have been thinking of me, I do really know that the matter is not as simple as that. Allowing that infallibility is a hybrid notion, the confusion would never have arisen if the lines were as hard and clear as I have drawn them. I have talked as though the divine events of the saving incarnation were just like any common or garden historical events; and as though their binding control over our present belief were of the same nature as the binding control of any other secular histories on our opinion of them. And that is, of course, simply absurd.

So now let me start making the subject if not as difficult as it is, at any rate far more difficult than I have yet allowed it to be.

How do the saving facts of the incarnation differ from common facts of history? First, no doubt, by having as it were one foot in time and one foot in eternity, so that the saving acts of Christ are present with us now in a way in which the virtuous acts of Aristides are not. Nevertheless, our redemption has a place in past history and is historically known; we are not free to rewrite the Gospels from the impressions we form of Christ's bearing upon us today. It is what we are constantly tempted to do, but in so far as we yield to the temptation, we escape from the control of history and cease to be subject to an historical revelation. And it is precisely this historical control that I am concerned to discuss.

Second, the saving events are seen as such only if they are accepted as the acts of God, and the acts of God are not appreciated as such by a mere flat historical judgement, as are the acts of Caesar or Napoleon. They are spiritually discerned. The point is sometimes put in the form that saving history consists of facts plus faith; but that way of talking is most dangerously misleading and I would almost say downright apostatical. Saving history consists of fact and fact alone, for God fully and really entered the created sphere and acted under the conditions of created existence; and so his acts, however purely divine, were historically factual. It is not the facts but our apprehension of them that bifurcates; the human in Christ is historically known, the divine is spiritually discerned. The discernment is not something subsequent to the facts, for Christ saw the supernatural character and efficacy of his own action, and indeed acted out of that discernment; the discernment and the action were together from the start. Christ knew what he did humanly and meant what he did divinely; both the knowledge of the action and the discernment of the intention passed into the Apostolic Church. The saving facts were proclaimed as a gospel, that is, not as a mere narrative of human facts but as a declaration of God's redeeming acts; and in so far as they were thus proclaimed, they challenged the hearers to undergo an awakening in themselves of the same discernment as that which informed the proclamation.

Now it is obvious from painful facts of history that the discernment of the divine action in the redeeming facts is not a matter of a simple sensitivity for spiritual things, like the fineness of ear which enables those who have it to hear the cry of bats. We do not either simply appreciate the divine in the facts or else simply fail to appreciate it: we interpret it, and we may do so inadequately or erroneously; and no mere historical expertise or scholarly soundness in settling the human facts will assure a correct reading of the divine meaning. It is had by faith, and faith is the possession of the Church. Jesus Christ was the supreme interpreter of himself; his apostles continued the interpretative work, determining truth of doctrine for their contemporaries with an authority not to be gainsaid; and since Christ by his own promise is with and indeed in the apostolic ministry, must not the Church always possess an infallible organ of interpretation—infallible not, of course, with regard to every trifle, but in determining the limits of tolerable doctrine, and in dogmatizing those things necessary to salvation?

Can we not, then, divide the field amicably between the fallible historian and the infallible dogmatist? The historian establishes his facts; the dogmatic authority regulates the interpretation, and why not infallibly? What rival authority is to challenge him? Very pretty: but it will not do. For to begin with, there is the absurdity here so often complained of in Aristotle's conception of science. Science is a rigorous deduction from premises; but the premises of the Aristotelian physics are established by the merest guess-work; they are said to be evident, but they are not; so that we have rigorous reasoning from speculative grounds; and however rigorous the reasoning, the conclusions it produces can be no more solid or certain than the grounds from which it proceeds. And so it must also be, if we have an infallible dogmatizing of the interpretation to be placed on the facts established by a fallible history. One who with infallible correctness establishes the theological sense of human facts only probably inferred, cannot give us an infallible guidance concerning the saving acts of God. But this is not the whole of the trouble; there is worse to follow. We were working with a simple division of the field between the historian and the dogmatic authority; the historian was not to concern himself with theological interpretation, nor the dogmatic authority with history. So far we have shown that the dogmatic authority must concern itself with history; for it must build on an historical foundation. We will now proceed to show the reverse—that the historian must concern himself with theological interpretation. This is so because the dogmatic authority is bound not only to interpret historically accredited facts; it is bound also to interpret in some sort of continuity with the interpretation made by Christ and his apostles, the interpretation which formed the faith of the primitive Church. There is no need for me to go into the difficult question as to what constitutes an acceptable continuity of dogma, or when doctrinal developments can be considered legitimate. Whatever views we take on those agonizingly difficult issues, it remains that the dogmatic authority must claim to be in genuine line with the apostles' theology; and such a claim involves a judgement as to what the apostles' theology was. And here once more historical scholarship butts in; for it is an historical question, not merely what humanly happened in Christ, but what the apostles understood to have happened divinely in him. The question, what theological interpretation of events the apostles held, is an historical question, a matter of reading evidence, of interpreting the literal sense of texts. We cannot accept the bare allegation of the living Church that what it propounds was implicitly or seminally contained in the faith of apostolic times; we have got to see whether it appears on historical grounds to have been so contained or not; and historical judgements are fallible.

It is my special concern, as a reformed Christian, to emphasize the necessity of a constant overhaul of dogmatic development by the standard of Christian origins; and 'Christian origins' can only mean in practice the *evidences we have* for Christian origins; and they come down pretty nearly to the New Testament writings, and the primitive sacramental usages. It is clear enough that the contemporary Catholic Church in communion with the Pope is most eager to embrace whatever is sound in the reformation principle; to prune the somewhat luxuriant growth of Catholic practice and opinion with the pruning-hooks of primitivity. What I have to point out is that to admit primitivity as a judge or as a control is to submit to scholarship or historianship; and the scholar or historian is fallible; his work is endlessly corrigible, or subject to revision. Now a fallible historian and an infallible dogmatist make strange bedfellows, anyhow in the case where the infallible dogmatist accepts from the fallible historian data upon which he infallibly dogmatizes.

I realize, of course, that my main contention in this whole argument wears superficially the face of paradox. For what am I saying? That Christian developments must be anchored to Christian origins, and that the anchor-chains will only be strong if the links composing them are weak—the links of infallible authority would be less effective in binding us to our origins than would the most fallible procedures of historical science. But if there is a paradox here, it is a paradox which the modern world is happy to swallow every day for breakfast, lunch, and dinner. Until some time in the early eighteenth century it was commonly supposed that the truth of nature could not be effectively binding on our minds unless it informed us through infallible reasonings derived from incontestable axioms. We have now most thoroughly repented of any such belief. By admitting the purely provisional and wholly corrigible character of our physical investigations we have learnt how to expose ourselves to the truth. It is a matter of choosing between appropriate procedures admitted fallible and pretended infallible procedures proved inappropriate. It does not help for an instrument to be infallible if it is the wrong instrument for the job. A foot-rule is, within certain terms of reference, a virtually infallible instrument; but that does not make it any more useful for the purpose of measuring intellectual capacity.

Now it must seem to the rest of us that the papal communion is today engaged in making a somewhat delayed catch-up and is moving out of an Aristotelian into—what shall we say—an Einsteinian world. Indeed, the Italians have a word for it. At the same time the strongly traditionalist stance of the Church prevents her from ever unambiguously burying her dead; and so, instead of putting a tombstone over infallibility we are to rally round and give its moribund image a shot in the arm, and a suit of new clothes; so that, like Ahab smitten to death at the battle of Ramoth-Gilead, it may be stayed up in its chariot until the going down of the sun, lest the troops of God's Israel should scatter on the mountains as sheep having no shepherd. Whether I should describe the predicament as comic or tragic, I am at a loss to decide; but anyhow it is a predicament that must awaken our liveliest sympathy, or concern. We must see that the Latin theologian is simply not in a position to write infallibility off; he is obliged to save the name even if he virtually drops the thing; he must go through the motions of what used to be called *coloratio*, or 'putting a complexion upon', the inconvenient item—as it might be upon some unwelcome sentence of a formidable authority. In the thirteenth century *coloratio* belonged to science; now it has changed its sphere and found a place in politics; and perhaps the Church may still be called infallible, as the Crown is still called sovereign in England, or as dictatorship is called democracy in East Germany. And perhaps if we are to put ecumenism first, then instead of carping at infallibility we ought to join in the game of giving it a false beard and whiskers, while merely making sure that it hasn't got any teeth.

But that is not the note on which I wish to conclude. For while 'infallibility' appears to me a misnomer, the last thing I want to do is to depreciate the Church's authority or to underestimate the gravity of her obligation to give dogmatic guidance. And one of the most manifest advantages to us of a reassembly of our confessions under the papal aegis would be the strengthening of such guidance so far as it affects ourselves. So now I want to make some sort of amends for my polemics and to correct the onesidedness of my previous remarks.

One of the great pleasures for me of the present occasion is to find myself in the same room with Fr Wamsley, after so many years—I do not like to think how many. If he recalls—but why should he?—the subject of a discussion we had together on one of the last occasions when we had much leisure to talk, he might, with his characteristic gentleness, interrupt me here. 'Surely', he could say, 'you have radically changed your mind. Now the scientific historian is your blue-eyed boy; you are prepared to make him an independent authority upon whose decisions the voice of the Church's faith must humbly wait. Not so when you and I talked together in the garden at Cuddesdon. I had propounded to you a problem about the virginal conception of our Saviour. I asked whether we are bound in reason and in honesty to settle the physiological fact on purely secular grounds of historical testimony and biological analogy, before admitting any supernatural considerations to our counsels. Are we to lay down the precept, "First judge the evidence or your facts, then see whether they have any religious bearing?" Or should we take account of the (presumed or possible) religious bearings of the facts, in estimating the value of the evidence for them?' Such was the problem; and the decision of our joint wisdom was for the second alternative. It would be absurd to judge the claim that

Jesus was virginally conceived as though it were a newspaper report about a physical abnormality occuring to a woman otherwise unknown. The claim about the virginal conception was brought forward only when Jesus had risen from the dead and was acknowledged Son of God. No one was asked to believe the claim except on that background of faith and no one is expected to believe it on any other background today. The question, how does any common man come into the world? is a question presenting no special problem; the question, how did the Son of God come into the world? is a question presenting a problem, to which the virginal conception has seemed the divinely appropriate answer. Historically speaking, the evidence, though not cogent, is possible. If Jesus was virginally conceived, it is very reasonable to suppose that the story should be kept within the family until the firm establishment of the Church's faith; and there is no difficulty in conjecturing how the secret might have passed into the knowledge of our first and third evangelists. The evangelists have set it before us with a great deal of typological adornment, but it seems plain that they meant to affirm the fact; and they were not contradicted by an indignant Church—quite the reverse. We concluded in our Cuddesdon garden that an orthodox Christian ought in reason to believe the virginal conception, while an unbeliever ought in reason to disbelieve it. But that was not all. It did not appear to us a black-and-white affair, 'Chrétiens ont droit, Payens ont tort.' Besides considering orthodox Christians and flat Pagans, we considered the heterodox positions of certain neo-Protestant theologians; and we saw that, though Christians of a sort, they were inevitably going to disbelieve the virginal conception in view of their total expectations about the way that God would act in the drama of our redemption. And so—I imagine Father Wamsley as saying—'You did not then think that history dictated to faith; you thought that faith dictated to history. Nor would any faith do; faith had to be a right faith. If, then, mercy has given us a sure guide in the voice of the Church to establish a right faith, the historian gets his orders from dogmatic authority—and not vice versa. Have you now changed your mind? And if so, why?'

I will now stop playing Fr Wamsley's hand out of dummy and will play my own. No, I will answer, I have not changed my mind, unless it is a change to become firmly settled in a position once held tentatively. The intervening years have served only to disgust me with the inconclusiveness and the irresponsibility of supposedly scientific New Testament scholarship or supposedly neutral historical investigation of Christian origins. Great systems of organized and co-operative folly take the field and establish themselves as the academic orthodoxy of the day. To the detached observer, the theological or philosophical bias animating much of this work is obvious; sometimes the *parti pris* is unconscious, sometimes it is openly professed. There is no such thing as a neutral or purely scientific study of Christian origins, whether we are concerned to establish the history of events or to interpret the primitive theology of them. If I am to see myself as taking a hand in historical scholarship, I should hope to approach the evidence in the faith of the Church, and by the beaten path of Catholic conviction. But the Catholic historian, however Catholic, is as much an historian as any other. He has Catholic expectations, he cannot force facts. Nor can he neglect to use any of the instruments, techniques, or logical models which the art of history or of hermeneutic has developed in his day. My *a priori* expectations may be as Catholic as you like, but they will not allow me to make such deductions from *Ave plena gratia* as a scholastic theologian might make; not will they allow me to postulate a continuous invisible tradition of Mary's assumption running through the primitive Church like water through a lead pipe and leaving no trace on the visible history. A Catholic historian will be as obedient to facts as any historian—indeed, in so far as he is the ideal historian he will be ideally obedient. It still follows, therefore, that Catholic dogmatic thought about the saving facts is corrigible, not incorrigible; for history, including Catholic history, is corrigible; and what is corrigible cannot be called infallible, or only by emptying out the sense of infallible to an absolute vacuity.

I have been discussing the relation of the infallibility idea to the control of the Saving History upon the Church's faith; that is all. It has been no part of my endeavour to do justice to what is most vital in the infallibility idea. But with whatever irrelevance, I should like to say something about it, in a sort of footnote, before I conclude. Infallibility is an expression of the faith that God will effectively guide his Church in the way of truth and of salvation. For how can he be said to do so, unless there is in the

Church an ultimate and substantial *charisma* of truth? Through toil and tribulation, and tumult of her war—through an unending tension and debate between schools of thought within the Church—between the Church and her critics, between theological faculties and pastoral authority—it must be our faith that God guides the Church into truth, that the Catholic mind settles ever more and more firmly on essentials; and it is the function of supreme ecclesiastical authority to express the Catholic mind as faithfully as possible from time to time as circumstances may demand or topics become urgent. Where, then, does infallibility reside? I reply, nowhere. Infallibility has the status of what Emmanuel Kant called a regulative, but non-constitutive idea. I apologize for the jargon. He meant an ideally perfect model to inspire our study of an elusive subject matter. For example, we may usefully approach the investigation of physical nature as being the creature of a wise artificer. It will lead us never to despair of finding in nature more and more of the rational order we look for. It will not justify us in spotting the particular intentions of God, nor in forcing the facts to any preconceived pattern of what a God would do with them. So, then, with infallibility. God, we are to say, is an infallible guide and the guidance takes effect in the history of the Church, through God knows what confusions and backslidings and refusals of co-operation. By holding such a faith we are led to look for God's guidance with all seriousness, to respect the decisions of the Church, and to do our own dogmatic thinking in the humble but serious belief that it is an item in the great divine process. But infallibility is not to be spotted, pinned down, identified with an ecclesiastical organ, or demanded on a given occasion. Infallibility is not an oracle you can consult.

When I talk to enlightened Latin theologians I form the impression that their working belief is what I have just attempted to sketch. It is an article of faith that the Church must be ultimately infallible and that God will at need move her to defend essential truth. But they are almost morbidly shy of tying infallibility down. The Pope is the mouthpiece of infallibility but it is terribly unwise to specify either the occasions on which he has infallibly spoken or the degree of precision that is to be given to the verbal form of his utterances *qua* infallible. An unsympathetic empiricist would say that such theologians want both to have their cake and eat it—they want the consoling assurance of infallible guidance and they want their freedom from all concretely incorrigible dogmatizations. I prefer to put it differently, and more sympathetically, since I hope I share the faith which I suppose the idea *de facto* to express. So I prefer to call infallibility a regulative idea, in the Kantian sense. Only, since most of us are not Kantians, I prefer still more to call infallibility by another name, which enables us to bring it right down to earth. Our faith is that God is infallible, the Church is not; she is *indefectible*.

And that, I suppose, is my *irenicon*. I will have infallibility, if it is indefectibility cast into the guise of a Kantian idea. But I shall need to be assured that the utterances which dogmatized the immaculate conception and the corporeal assumption need not be held incorrigible. It is this sort of thing that frightens me so much; in those two decrees we have the alarming appearance of an infallible fact-factory going full blast.

Can Myth be Fact?

The word myth is used in several senses, and varies with one's anthropological theory. I ask no more than that my use of the word may be allowed to pass. A myth is a traditional tale which purports to describe real happenings; for example, that the Olympian Gods came down *incognito* and paid surprise calls on the householders of Lycia to see what entertainment they would get, and were driven from the door by all except Baucis and Philemon, whose unfeigned kindness they rewarded with material blessings, while overwhelming their inhospitable neighbours in a general inundation. But such a story does not commonly impress us by any very firm grip on historical reality; no one, probably, is prepared to date it, it floats uncertainly in the great ocean of previous time. Its interest lies not in its claim to historical truth, but in its expression of some universal idea, in this case the idea that the Gods preside over the rights of strangers, in serving whom we serve the heavenly powers; that care for the stranger pays in the end, for heaven will bless the hospitable man and blast the churl. The reason why myths become current and maintain their hold is the expressiveness of their symbolism and the importance of what they symbolize. They seem to obey in their style and formation certain profound laws of the human imagination, and to handle in their subject matter certain central concerns of the human heart, especially its social and religious concerns. For this reason they tend to conform to certain types and even to reappear in different cultures with an identical content. For example, we read in Genesis how the Lord God also came down to earth, mysteriously manifest in a group of three travellers, how Abraham and Sarah showed a hospitality equal to that of Baucis and Philemon and were rewarded by a miracle of fertility, the birth of Isaac: whereas the wicked men of Sodom, attempting outrage against their heavenly guests, were overthrown with fire and brimstone. The story is here pinned on to the bituminous desert around the Dead Sea, as in its other form it was pinned to the Pisidian swamps.

Myths were presumably taken for historical fact by simple-minded antiquity. Men were not content with general principles—for instance, of hospitable duty and divine reward. They wanted to feel the conviction that these principles were the actual working forces of the universe; and they found the evidence for this in the record that at some time the powers in control of nature had expressed these principles in one perfectly clear, typical and significant event. The myth was a guarantee that man's beliefs were not mere ideals or aspirations but the very laws of being. It was the same with ritual myths. The man of primitive culture has been taught that to perform a certain ceremony will bring him rain; he does his ceremony to the accompaniment of a recitation: such and such an old hero of his tribe had been taught the ceremony in the direst extremity of drought by a kindly god, had performed it, and been rewarded with abundance of water in that very day.

As civilization and sophistication proceed, men let go the historical belief in their myths. The first expression of this is a Euripidean indignation against the ancient imposture, but second thoughts bring a more mature attitude. Men become tired of kicking the fallen idols, when no one any longer worships them; it is better to pick them up while they have still some noses and ears among them and place them in museums of history and art. And so the myths, robbed of the substance of historical fact, are rescued by the pedagogue and the philosopher; they will serve as Sunday school lessons in piety or morals, and as allegorical pegs for preaching Stoics to hang their sermons on. It now becomes the business of the philosophers to unearth from the mythic form the profound but implicit wisdom of antiquity, and to state it explicitly as universal truth. The mythic story no longer guarantees the general truths, as it did to the simpler age; on the contrary, the general truths must now be proved in their own right, and the validity of the myth depends on them.

Things had reached this pass when civilized ears first heard of Christianity. The Christian story of redemption looked outwardly like a myth; it was born in the very age which was dissolving myths in allegory, yet it resisted such treatment and claimed for itself to be the only myth that is hard historical fact.

That Christians defend the factual character of the story of redemption is obvious; it is not so obvious that they admit its mythical character too, and indeed the *word* 'mythical' would commonly be rejected by them, for 'mythical' suggests false, imaginary. We are using 'mythical' in a somewhat special sense, we must confess; but in this sense of ours, Christian orthodoxy not only *admits* that the story of redemption is mythical; it *claims* that it is, and makes a special point of the claim. Take as your evidence that most orthodox theologian, St Thomas Aquinas; no one suspects him of putting up useless novelties, of defending boyish paradoxes. And this is what he says (he is explaining the unique character of the biblical record). In the pages of the Bible, he tells us, we have, as in any other book, words which express historical facts, and by means of the words we get hold of the facts. This is the first layer of meaning, but there is another. For just as the words were used by the evangelists to signify the facts, so the facts themselves had already been used by God to signify further facts, i.e. divine or supernatural facts; and as we use the evangelists' words to get hold of the historical facts, so we are to use these historical facts in order to get hold of the supernatural or divine facts which God has expressed through them. How is it possible, St Thomas asks, that the facts of the Gospel history can be a language through which a further layer of facts is expressed? It follows, he replies, from the omnipotence of God's creative power. He controls facts no less completely, far more completely, indeed, than I control words. And so, as I shape my words to express my meaning, with what seems to me perfect freedom, in like manner God has what really is absolute freedom to shape historical events into an expression of his divine meaning. The conclusion from this is plain. Men may construct a myth expressive of divine truths as they conceive them, and the stuff of the myth will be words. God has constructed a myth expressive of the divine truths he intends to convey, and the stuff of the myth is facts. And this can very well be, because God's control of facts is infinitely more complete than our control of words: as it was in the beginning, he said the *word*, 'Let there be light', and there was light. In this text of Genesis there is already human imperfection. We do not really mean that God first uttered a word, a noise in the air, or even the voiceless image of such a noise within his mind, and that then a second event, the light, obediently jumped into existence as your dog may jump into the room when you have whistled for him. There were not two events, first the speaking, then the shining. The shining of the light was itself the speech, the utterance of God; facts do not *obey* God's words, they *are* his words.

This sounds all very fine, and people can accept it in a certain sense without meaning in the least what St Thomas and Christendom as a whole are trying to assert. People may say: When I say 'God', I mean 'Nature'. Now it is obviously all right to say that all facts are Nature's words, through which she expresses to us her universal truths, which we call her laws. If my kettle boils at 100 degrees centigrade we have a fact which I cannot make, but Nature makes, and I can, in a poetical mood, describe this fact as a word through which Nature shouts into my ears:

All water boils at a fixed heat:
This is the rule, so do not hope to cheat.
Fall into line, or eat your cabbage raw:
May Heaven incline your heart to keep this law.

As there are physical laws of Nature, so there may be moral and spiritual laws; as physical facts are the words through which physical truths are dictated to us, so human facts are the words through which moral or even spiritual truths are dictated to us; the misery and self-frustration of bad men, and the serene happiness of saints, are all positive or negative evidence for the inexorable laws of our spiritual nature.

Quite so, and who denies it? But it is evidently not this that Christians mean when they describe the story of Christ as a factual myth. The difference is not difficult to grasp. Consider two sentences in both of which the verb to express is used: (*a*) Every commonplace event *expresses* the truth of universal laws; and (*b*) Such and such a poem *expresses* the feeling of springtime or first love. Now ask yourselves whether the word 'expresses' in the two sentences means the same thing. Plainly it does not. A commonplace event expresses universal laws simply by conforming to them, but the poem expresses its subject by creating a uniquely appropriate symbol of it. Now when St Thomas says that God, through his creative control over facts, has caused the Gospel events to signify to us realities beyond themselves, he means this second thing: he means that God has bent and shaped these particular facts into a perfectly expressive symbol of a unique truth he wished to convey to us. Guide-books sometimes describe a cathedral or a palace as a 'poem in stone', and in somewhat the same sense we call Christ's birth, life, and death and resurrection a myth not in words, but in the flesh and blood of human history.

So far we have been doing little more than to define. This, we say, is what Christians mean: God is the only myth-maker who can make his myths out of hard fact; the story of our redemption is such a myth. Christians do believe this. But we are not supposed to be asking, Do Christians believe that myth and fact can coincide? That's too easy. We are supposed to be asking, Can it really happen? And we have got nowhere towards the answering of that question so far, except by reminding ourselves that God is almighty. This is scarcely even the beginning of an answer, being far too general. We may know that God is almighty and therefore might do anything, but we are concerned not with what he might do but with what he does. In fact, almighty power is seen to be exercised in sustaining the operations of Nature according to Nature's laws, and if we are asked to believe that God has worked in quite a different and special way, shaping the half-chaos of historical fact into the perfect expressiveness of a poem, turning the undramatic stuff of life into something more significant than Shakespeare's masterpieces; if we are asked to believe this, we are inclined to say: Show how it fits in with the rest of the world we know.

This is a reasonable challenge; we will try to take it up. The most satisfactory way to do so seems to be the historical way. It is alleged that a mythic pattern got a grip on actual fact in Jesus Christ's existence. Well, can we see this happening? Can we see where the mythic pattern came from, and how it was built into the facts? If we can watch the alleged process, we may be able to satisfy ourselves that it either is, or is not, the sort of thing that could take place.

If we look for *the* mythic pattern fulfilled in the gospel, we may well be baffled by the multitude of claimants; one of the astonishing things about this story is that it seems to fulfil, and more than fulfil, all the figures of myth conceived by all the prophets. We must confine ourselves to one. Let us take the Son of Man, since if there is one thing clearer than another, it is that Jesus applied this title to himself and along with the title the myth for which it stood.

The myth of the Son of Man is no other, of course, than the story of Adam. Son of Man is a Hebrew expression which just means Man, with a special added emphasis on his human character by which he differs from beasts below or angels above; as we might say 'a human being' to get the same emphasis. The Hebrew for the Son of Man is Ben-*Adam*. Adam, in the story, just because he is all mankind, is compared, not with other men, but with beasts over whom he was set to rule, and the God in whose royal likeness he was created.

Now the myth of Adam is, to start with, a far more serious affair than the myth of Philemon and Baucis. Philemon and Baucis simply illustrate a general principle of hospitable duty and divine rewards. The myth no doubt added solidity to people's belief in the principle, as we supposed, but (clearly) they could have got on without the myth, the principle could have stood up by itself. The myth of Adam is a very different matter. It does not illustrate a principle, it expresses the whole fact of man's existence, created and fallen. It attempts to describe in its own mythic way a fact inescapably real. We cannot escape from the facts that man occupies a certain place in the order of being; and that he is acutely aware of failure to fill that place, of guilt, moral frustration, and of an inability to reconcile himself to the prospect of physical death. This is an actual situation which really has come about, and the myth of Adam endeavours to describe it. You may quarrel with the description or the explanation it seems to give, but you cannot deny that the facts are facts, for those facts are you. There is (by contrast) only one indubitable historical fact that *Philemon and Baucis* deals with, and that is the existence of some particularly dismal swamps in Pisidia with a small and fertile island in the middle; and that is not what the myth is really about.

What is more, this is a myth which cannot be allegorized or evaporated into general statements without losing its force. Something happened (so the myth is telling us) in the relations between man and his creator. Well, the intelligent modern Christian is inclined to say: Quite so. Men, evolved from the ape or however else called by Providence into their rational and

CAN MYTH BE FACT?

godlike state, gradually and piecemeal misused their newly born faculties and so lost their innocence before civilization began. So our culture has sprung from a race, not of barbarians simply, but of crooked barbarians. Such a statement as this sounds very reasonable and harmless, far better than the tale about the apple. It is indeed a safe sort of statement, but like most safe statements it is an almost completely meaningless one. Whatever really happened between primitive man, his conscience, and his God, it certainly was nothing like a text-book generalization, it was the individual drama of someone's existence. Even supposing that it happened piecemeal all over the world and in different men, if there were indeed many thousand Adams, every one of them was the Adam of his own soul, to each of them it was personal reality, none of them saw himself as the instance of a statistical generalization. So, if you want to have any idea about the reality of the dawn of human reason and the fall of man, you have got to see it in a living instance, and if you won't have the myth of Adam you have got to make up a novel for yourself to replace it. Try, by all means, but I wonder if you are likely to do better.

The myth of Adam is, of course, no mere novellistic attempt to describe what the experiences of the primitive man may have seemed like to him. It is an attempt to express the drama of his existence with a clarity of which he himself would have been incapable, to bring out better than he knew it its significance in the destinies of heaven and earth. And for this purpose it brings to bear every central and elementary symbol which human life affords. It handles the contrasting natures of man and beast, of man and God; the fountain and the desert; the charm of forbidden fruit and the slippery hostility of the serpent; the pain of childbirth and the toilsome quest for bread; the shame of nakedness and the intricacies of sexual function; the image of God to which we are born and the dust into which we resolve. How can all this various stuff of human existence be woven into a single symbol, expressed in words that fill three of four pages? Well it just is so: the inspired human imagination is capable of this. It was not accomplished in a day; it was the work of ages, written and rewritten, the gross purged, the inessential dropped, new insights embodied.

On the fifth day of creation, this story tells, God had called up the monsters out of the sea, to dominate for their little hour, but on the sixth day he made man in his own image, and set him over all his works. This was the last creation, and man's the final dominion: he had no successor, for on the seventh day God rested from his works for ever, and through that eternal Sabbath the empire of man should endure. Such was the creator's purpose; but then came the fall, when Adam, the viceregent of God, had put himself under the serpent. And indeed the men of later days looking about them saw that while Adam still in a manner reigned on earth, it was the image of the beast, not the image of God, that reigned in the heart of man, and especially in the throne of princes. When would the purpose of God be fulfilled? When would he put down the beast and enthrone the Son of Man, the Man in the image of God?

Such thoughts possessed the mind of the writer of Daniel. It is, says he, as though the stages of creation are being repeated in the stages of history; as though we have reached the fifth day, or age, the age of the monsters from the deep; for what more bestial, more monstrous, than the soulless idolatrous empires which one after another rise to crush the people of God? When shall we reach the sixth 'day' of the world, when God will reveal the Son of Man and put the monsters down? And so, in his vision he sees it. It is the fifth day; the four winds of heaven, the fourfold breath of God, break loose on the great sea, and up come the monsters, which are the heathen predatory empires, to work their wicked will. But the sixth day is to come. 'I beheld till thrones were set, and one that was Ancient of Days did sit, his raiment white as snow, and the hairs of his head like pure wool: his throne was fiery flames, and the wheels thereof burning fire. And as for the beasts, their dominion was taken away, yet their lives were prolonged for a season and a time. I saw in the night visions, and behold there came with the clouds of heaven one like unto a Son of Man, and he came even to the Ancient of Days and they brought him near before him. And there was given him dominion, and glory, and a kingdom, that all the peoples, nations and languages should serve him; his dominion is an everlasting dominion that shall not be taken away, and his kingdom that shall not be destroyed (Dan. 7.9, 12-14).'

So far we have seen the myth of the Son of Man, a myth, and nothing but that; a myth first used to decipher the past and then thrown forward on to a shadowy screen in prophecy of the future;

it has not yet grasped present fact nor translated itself out of words into flesh and blood. Now we reach the crucial point, the point on which our present inquiry turns. Jesus, standing in the High Priest's court, accused of many things, is silent to most, but himself chooses the issue upon which he wills to die. Am I the Christ? 'I am,' he says, and adds from himself, not in answer to any charge: 'And ye shall see the Son of Man sitting on the right hand of Almighty Power and coming with the clouds of heaven (Mark 14.62).' He takes to himself the part of the promised Adam. He takes it; but how does he perform it? How do we see him *being* the myth?

The prophet who saw the vision of Daniel 7 applied one part of the Adam story alone. God has decreed that the divine image in mankind must have the dominion: in other words, the Son of Man must reign. And this Jesus also says; he said it to the High Priest. But there is another part to the Adam story. Adam is not now on the throne, nor is he in Paradise: he is naked, ashamed in the wilderness of his self-chosen misery, ploughing among thistles, and destined to die. The new Adam must take up his destiny where it is and work his way through it and out on to the further side: otherwise put, the Son of Man must suffer. And this also Jesus says in so many words. He does not simply say it. No sooner has the voice of the baptism, 'Thou art my beloved Son', ceased ringing in his ears than the spirit of his destiny carries him into Adam's wilderness to be with the beasts, as Adam was, and to be tempted by Adam's old enemy, and succoured, as Adam was believed to have been, by the angels of God's grace. Where Adam fell, he stood. Do this and that, the serpent had said to Adam, and make yourself your own God. If thou art the Son of God, says the tempter to Christ, do this and that: show your divinity and claim it by self-chosen arbitrary acts of power; subject yourself to me and possess yourself of the universal dominion promised to the Son of Man. No. Adam grabbed, but Christ renounced. The birds have nests and the foxes holes: the Son of Man hath not where to lay his head. Yet in that very state of renunciation he raised the standard of his kingdom, and God's. He solemnly founded a new mankind in a group of twelve apostles; in the name of the Son of Man, that is, the eternal judge, he forgave sins on earth. In the name of the Son of Man, whose dominion is to last through the Sabbath of eternity, he claimed jurisdiction over the token-Sabbath kept by Israel on the seventh day; the Son of Man is lord of the Sabbath also; the man created on the sixth day rules the seventh and subjects it to the laws of divine compassion. His royalty and his renunciation exist together absolutely, each heightening the other; the Son of Man hath dominion on earth, he says, and, presently, 'the Son of Man came not to be ministered unto, but to minister, and to give his life a ransom for many (Mark 10.45).' Because he is the fulfilment of Adam, he goes back behind Moses to the perfection of the Creator's first intention. For the hardness of your hearts, he says, Moses gave you such a commandment, but in the beginning it was not so: for it is written, Male and female created he them: therefore shall a man leave father and mother and cleave to his wife, and the two shall be one flesh: what God hath joined, let no man put asunder.

On Adam's day, Friday, the sixth day of the week, his humiliation was fulfilled. 'Art thou the King of the Jews?' said Pilate, and in that title he died, having first been mocked with purple and crowned with thorns. He died and he reigned, as he had foreseen, through the fabled instrument of Adam's death: the tree of wood. On the seventh day, the sabbath, his body rested from all its works, as God did from his, and on the first day of the new week, in rhythm with the beginning of God's creation, with the *fiat lux* which called light out of darkness, something happened to the women carrying perfumes, to Peter and the Twelve, which they did not doubt to call a new creation. For 'that which is born of the flesh is flesh, and that which is born of the spirit is spirit: marvel not that I say unto thee, ye must be born anew.'

Can myth be fact? The only answer we hoped to find to this question lay in another. Since it is the Christians who say that myth was and is fact, we ask, how do they say it came about? And what we have seen is the slow formation of the perfect, the typical myth of Adam: its taking up and projection into the future by such prophets as him we call Daniel; its acceptance by Jesus as the meaning of his destiny, so that he sets out to *be* the new Adam, the Son of Man. Now in so far as he lives this poem, it may seem as though all we have is a private obsession with an idea. That Jesus does not talk or behave like the obsessed is a point that has often been made, but let it pass. But when we come to the climax of his action, the myth gets out of hand: he, as a helpless human victim, cannot make it any longer. Did then that Creator-God, of whom St Thomas Aquinas spoke, take up and finish the work, making the tormentors of Jesus and his fugitive disciples unknowing instruments of it; did he bend and shape historical fact by that control which is his alone into the expressive completion of the redeeming mystery? Did he (above all) actually raise up Jesus from the dead, and enthrone the Son of Man at the right hand of Almighty Power, so that the divine image might reign in a kingdom both of Man and God, through the union of redeemed men with the enthroned Christ?

These last questions are not answered except by faith, faith in almighty power and in the testimony of Christ's apostles, and so 'Can myth be fact?' brings us back to omnipotence after all. But we began by assuming God's almightiness. What we set out to show was that, in the alleged instance, his almighty act was somehow one piece with the rest of his action in nature and in man; and this we have attempted to do. The revelation of the myth which is fact did not begin suddenly in the first century; it began when men, first reflecting on the paradoxes of their destiny, were inspired to start the weaving of the myth of Adam.

The Theology of Morals

No so-called branch of theology is a separate science sufficient to itself, and moral theology perhaps least of all. We understand by it the systematic description of human duty, as human duty is interpreted in the context of Christian faith. Even this is too wide a description; for the duties of prayer and spiritual self-discipline in their more intimate detail are certainly duties, yet they belong to mystical and ascetical theology; while sociology is also reckoned a distinct science, yet it deals with a tissue of human duties. Whatever lies between these two extremes is the subject matter of moral theology. It has been found convenient to group certain questions under the one heading, and the convenience still exists.

Moralism, no doubt, is a serious danger, particularly to moral theologians: if we begin to think that Christianity is a system of duties, we have relapsed into Pharisaism. But for Christians as for everyone else there exists the problem, 'What should I do?' And unless we can resolve our perplexities, we are hindered from drawing on the sources of grace, for who will be a martyr in a cause concerning which he stands in doubt? And what martyr would be justified in bleeding for an unexamined idea? Now it is to the 'martyr' conception of obedience that the gospel summons us. Are there duties which I owe to God because he is God and I am a man? Let me know what these are, and I will faithfully implore his aid to enable me to fulfil them.

The realities in which moral truth is founded were marked out by our Lord in his answer to the divorce question. The relation of the sexes, said he, was established by the Creator through the fashion in which men were made. Israel through unspirituality (hardness of heart) had fallen to a lower custom, which Moses had regularized. He himself proclaims a return to perfection—to the full intention of God. This is the doctrine of St Paul also. Put off, he enjoins, the old man corrupt through sinful lusts, and put on the new, who is being restored to knowledge, renewed after the pattern of his Creator. Christ recovers to man his true nature, and the recovery of that nature is the recovery of knowledge—knowledge of God and knowledge of ourselves. If the likeness of God is straightened out in us again, it shows us both what God is, and what he intends us to do in imitation of him, within the assigned limits of our being.

Moral theology, then, reposes on what human nature is, and on what, being such, it owes to God. And this stands, even though we do not place a literal interpretation on the Genesis story. Our Lord says, 'In the beginning. . .', but the principle of his argument will hold good so long as the production of the human race is allowed to have behind it a unitary divine intention, an intention which man could have known to some extent by sincerely reflecting upon his own existence, which he failed to recognize through 'hardness of heart,' and which is recovered in the restoration of humanity in Christ. But while this doctrine is independent of a superstitious view of Genesis, it is vain to pretend that it is independent of the whole account which as intelligent men we give ourselves of the universe, and of man's place in it. There is a popular perversion of evolutionism which supposes that it is no longer respectable to think of man as a definite species. Species continually change, and 'man' is the name for a certain series, or direction, of changes. Civilization develops through endless phases, and man is always the man of the moment.

Were this true, no code of morals could be put forward for man in general. Monogamy might be proper for Palestinians of the first century, and a temperate promiscuity for us; and so with other precepts. But it is not true. Biological evolution tends to the production of types which have a relative stability. If our biological type shifts, it will surely not be along the line of an artificial civilization, but by the abandonment of a worked-out course of development, and a jump into some growth upon which our elaborated culture could not be grafted. If that ever happened, there might be a new creature. We have nothing to do with him. He might or might not be capable of a revelation; if he were, he would need one other than ours. There is nothing to be said for regarding human history as the development of new species. It is always variations on the theme—what, in the world in which we are placed, are we to make of the species that we are? It is reasonable, then, to suppose a single divine charter for the human race, which, if not the endowment of Adam, is still the vocation of his offspring.

The theme is constant, but the variations are unending: man cannot be understood out of his historical phase. We must, then, distinguish as best we can between what belongs to manhood wherever it is not frustrated, and what to the legitimate variety of cultures. It was the duty of St Paul's women to veil their heads, it may not be the duty of ours. But it is another matter when people begin to suggest that (say) the Christian family does not fit into the present structure of society. So much the worse for the family? No, so much the worse for the society—a society which has economic discouragements for marriage at a reasonable age, which denies to many the privacy or accommodation of a home, which acclimatizes its members to mass-pleasures, mass-labour, mass-emotions—the subject is a well-worn one but will serve for illustration. We have to determine, first, what is the essentially human in all circumstances, and, second, what is consequentially human in these or those.

The gifts of grace recover to us the pattern of true nature and enable us to develop its capacity beyond what nature can. But where and how, in fact, are we to find the moral truth that springs from these, and realize in knowledge what we have by redemption? We have, says St Paul, the mind of Christ. But if this is a possession, how do we lay our hand on it? Some have taken their stand on the letter of Scripture, others on the inward light of the conscience. Scripture alone is no sufficient guide to the problem, 'What should I do?' here and now, while to follow conscience alone is to desert historical revelation altogether, and to be each his own Moses.

If we hold that grace restores and perfects nature, we must also hold that Christ restores and perfects natural moral 'sense' or 'reason' (call it which you will). The experience of accepting Christ is the experience of finding our moral reason rising into harmony with Christ's maxims, with the spirit of his life and the beauty of his death. If we could only hold our reason there, while it judges the questions Christ has not judged, or applies the principles that he outlined! Turning from him to ourselves we slip again; our regenerated mind is more receptive than creative; we can love the good where Christ has revealed it: we cannot design it with a firm hand elsewhere, not even when we have prayed. And this not only through imperfect spirituality, but also through lack of prudence, and misunderstanding of the issues involved in a given question.

Yet it is certain there can be no other authority than the moral reason lifted into harmony with the mind of Christ. To guide this reason the Holy Ghost is given. Yet whose reason? The task of knowing the truth is co-operative; we look for it in the Body of Christ. We have to use our reason, and yet that reason can be illuminated by the reason of others, and can be lifted to their truth as it can be lifted to the truth of Christ. And, where our own powers of observation and thought are not adequate to a question, we are bound to trust the opinion which we have cause to think most widely based, most Christian, and most wise, and to consider every opinion that has weighty backing of this kind.

The mind of the Church of Christ, more particularly in moral questions, is like a more elaborate, more unwieldy, immensely more slow, yet far more sure, copy of the individual mind. The individual mind is not made up immediately and intuitively on difficult questions; moral views and sentiments develop themselves, and only after much reflection and various experiences does one come to prevail. Meanwhile, and before a solid conviction is reached, we may be forced to act on a provisional conclusion—a procedure which by no means need prejudice the issue, but rather stimulate the internal debate. So it is with the mind of the Church, except that here the debate is not internal but external, and the several views are incarnated in several men. Christ has promised that his Church shall not fail, and that the Spirit shall lead her into the full truth. We do not find that he has guaranteed her against falling into false conclusions by the way, or promised her oracular certainty on every question as soon as it is raised. On some questions there has come to be a settled mind in the whole Catholic Church, which affords us practical certainty. And, where certainty is not forthcoming, it is often the duty of ecclesiastical authority to legislate, because interim corporate agreement is necessary for practical reasons. It is then the duty of the Christian to obey, unless he has invincible scruples of the sincerest kind. But it is not his duty to stop thinking (or writing with due discretion), since how else is approach to be made to a surer conclusion?

The duty, then, of the moral theologian may be threefold. First, as a lawyer, he can establish what moral church legislation is in force, and what it means, and how it applies to instances. His second function is like that of the so-called 'voice of conscience'—of the memory-conscience, that is, the conscience which shows a red light when we are about to go against a principle that we have already accepted and formed into an habitual belief. So the moral theologian must be the memory-conscience of the Church, and, through historical knowledge, keep to the fore conclusions formerly agreed. Yet we know that the memory-conscience has no licence to be uncritical: I have always to consider whether the former decision really covers the new instance, or whether new circumstances have not produced a new question—as is the case with the morals of war. There was, perhaps, in the later medieval period, an agreed mind on this subject. War was an evil, but justifiable as means to the avoidance of a greater evil. It is now fairly asked whether war has not so changed its character as to make this doctrine inapplicable. No one could justify *a given war* as a means to immediate good. We think of war as a threat, a sanction, which produces good rather in so far as it is not applied (for it stabilizes legitimate sovereignties); but which must, alas, be applied if challenged by aggression, though its application is an almost unmixed evil in itself and in its consequences, as with deterrent punishment of criminals, which does harm in the main to its victims, and good only to those that are deterred, and fails the more of its purpose the more it is used. Can war be justified in this sense? This may appear to be quite a new question, and not soluble by appeal to the past.

This brings us to the third function of the moralist—to act as a part of the reasoning function of the Church's mind, through which new issues are determined. Here he does not speak with authority, or only with the so-called authority of the expert; and experts disagree. He is not so much an authority as a disputant worth hearing. There cannot, indeed, be experts in morals as there are experts in physics. The moralist can (in this function) supply data only to the saint, who, when he has fully understood, is the better judge.

As soon as moral theology becomes a science, the faculty is sure to be staffed in the main with men who have more learning than wisdom and less spirituality than either. And so the danger arises that the scribes will copy one another down, and the traditions of lawyers be set up as the mind of Christ; that there will be no discrimination made between the by-laws of former authority and the agreed conscience of the Church; that the opinions of the half-Christian majority that has thronged her doors since Constantine will be codified alongside the doctrine of the saints, if only they have managed here and there to influence the ecclesiastical statute book. Against this evil stands the Protestant denunciation of a secularized Church. Everything must be referred back to the original criterion, and judged by the gospel, as the Lord used the law of love to judge the case-law of the rabbis; it must be proved—tested, that is, not demonstrated—by Scripture. This vital requirement in no way sets aside the need of learning; it only demands that the learned should be Christians, in mind as well as in heart. Nor does it provide any simple panacea, any formulated remedy. Faithfulness to the mind of Christ is not to be secured by a fetishistic attachment to the text of the New Testament, read with or without Calvin's commentaries.

The contents of moral theology allow of a simple division—on the one hand rules and precepts, on the other the principles for their application. It is one thing to have a law, it is another thing to know, as the Scripture says, how to use it lawfully; and it is here that the principal difference between Christianity and Pharisaism arises. The error of the Pharisees did not lie in the effort to think their morals out and discover the bearing of general precepts on particular instances. Such an effort is absolutely necessary, and how far it is to be carried is simply a practical question. At what point does detailed systematization begin to defeat its own uses? To make moral pedants of us, and to obscure the real situation which confronts us instead of illuminating it? The point is hard to fix, but wherever it lies, it is the point at which we ought to stop. The Pharisees did pass that point; but our Lord blames them not so much for this as for their principles of application—for setting aside the law of God in order to hold fast a man-made tradition, for wrongly estimating the weight of several precepts where precepts seemed to conflict.

Readers of the Bishop of Oxford's moral works are likely to infer from his lucid discussions that it is in principles of application that moral theology is now strong, while it is comparatively weak in positive law. In the first centuries of Christianity it was otherwise: the Church was clear in her moral requirements but clumsy in dealing with consciences. She knew what Christ demanded, in times and circumstances not so far removed from the apostolic. But she had not mastered the philosophic and psychological subtleties of the structure and working of the human conscience. Yet with patience and good will these were bound to emerge, and once known are known for ever, being in scope timeless and universal, and valid so long as man is man. It is far otherwise with positive precepts. Some of these, indeed, belong also to man as man, but it is not about them that there is sharp perplexity in Christian minds. It is about those that define the duties of the human creature in relation to a changing environment. Whether the case of contraception is altered by cultural changes, since St Thomas pronounced against *venena sterilitatis*; whether we have to say 'So much the worse for his maxim' or 'So much the worse for our culture'; how (if we accept the latter alternative) individual Christians are to behave themselves in this culture, until it can be amended. When is capitalism not the sin of usury? What is a reasonable standard of life, and where does criminal luxury begin?

About these burning questions, is there a Christian law worthy of respect? And until there is, will Christianity itself be respected? One has only to think of these problems to see how utterly barren and lacking even in superficial plausibility is the solution: 'Every Christian must think them out for himself in view of his own circumstances.' No doubt, until we have better guidance, we cannot do otherwise; but most of us will certainly arrive at false conclusions. The appeal to 'a man's own circumstances' is simply evasive, for these are not questions on which Christians can afford to disagree, nor do they turn on what is peculiar to this man's circumstances or that man's. Everyone knows the strength lent to Roman Catholicism by a hard-and-fast rule, anyhow on some questions. It may be that Rome, confronted with the dilemma between clear definition and avoidance of error, is sometimes inclined to prefer the more practical alternative, and in this is not to be imitated. But that is no excuse for our abandonment of the effort to surmount the dilemma and reach definition; and the pity of the present state of affairs is that there is among us so little moral theology at all which is both learned in the past and concerned with the present.

For whom is moral theology? First (if what we have just said be true) for moral theologians; it cannot be well taught while it needs to be rethought. Second, for confessors; and if all parish priests have to exercise this office as a court of first instance, then there ought to be men in every diocese who specialize, to whom confessors can refer and penitents be referred. But third, for the whole Christian people; for they need to be helped in the formation of a sound judgement and saved from the unwitting commission of harmful acts, and parochial preaching ought to be of such a kind as to serve this end, so far as definitions are available, and to stimulate thought within the limits of moral probability where they are not. For where we cannot define, we ought at least to be able to find the limits between which the truth must lie, to be able to say that this at least, and that, are wrong—as, for example, in the case of usury or capitalism. We can agree, perhaps, that men are not irresponsible for the uses to which they voluntarily lend their money; that they have not a 'right' to raise whatever dividends they can, without respect to the good either of employees or consumers; that it is criminal to spend beyond a certain proportion of a high income for one's own pleasure—and so on. If these are truths they are worth preaching, even though a wide area still remains for doubt—such as the whole justification of the economic and class system in which we live.

And as it is with this question, so it is with others. If we are allowed to suppose for a moment that contraception is not simply to be forbidden, can the field of tolerable disagreement about it be defined, so that some uses could be ruled out by consent? Can we say that it is simply immoral for healthy persons to marry with the intention of having no children or less than some desirable number? Can we define within any limits (or wholly prohibit) the beginning of marriage with a period of voluntary sterility for the sake of pleasure and convenience? Can we define the legitimate weight of the economic factor? What standard of life is it right (if ever right) to preserve at the cost of family limitation below a certain number? When is a danger to health really a danger? Are wives with professions in a peculiar position? And so on.

Over these burning questions we are inclined to behave as puritan opinion does over proposals to tax or regularize betting. To do so, they say, would be to approve what you leave unrepressed and to legitimate that from which you profit. And therefore, since you cannot in fact dissuade people from this diversion, the best thing you can do is to put your head in the sand and refuse to recognize what exists. So with capitalism, or contraception, or anything else that is felt to be a trifle shady. And so we leave the public with the idea that we have a personal distaste for the *bête noire*, but are not seriously prepared to press this. No effect is produced: how could it be? If the consciences of other men are less beautifully adjusted than ours, we can but appeal to the moral reason they have, to recognize manifest abuses; and it is difficult to see how else one is to begin their further education, or set them on the road which may lead them to appreciate at last the damnable impiety of wagering a sixpence—if that is the noble pitch to which we hope to raise them.

The alternative policy would be to lay down clear rulings of wide generality and apparent severity, and then grant dispensations according to a certain list of exemptions. There seems little to be said for this. If we have not got consent of the Church that this or that is wrong in principle, we cannot make the definition. If we have, the exemptions must be exceptional and few, or the rule is overthrown. And such a plan presupposes a different relation between clergy and people than in fact exists for the most part among us. We are committed, for good or ill, to proceed more by education of the conscience of the congregation than by the exercise of authoritative direction privately and in detail.

But in spite of this, our moral theologian has no need to give up in despair on every question to which he cannot answer 'Yes' or 'No' in the form in which it is asked. He can aim at definition within limits. And we have no need to give the impression that what we cannot yet define with common consent of the Church is actually a matter of indifference. Nor shall we give that impression, if we constantly set moral rule in the context where it belongs—the context of whole-hearted service of God. There is no state of mind more deplorable than that of the man who scrupulously observes rule and religiously avails himself of dispensation, and thinks of his duty in terms of how much indulgence is permitted, not how God may best be served and his neighbour's good promoted. But this attitude needs only to be described to be abhorred by any healthy mind. Moral rule must be taught as a definition of the bounds within which man's one great purpose can be achieved—the glory of God. Which is merely to universalize the maxim—the Sabbath was made for man: man was not made for the Sabbath.

This brings us back to the point from which we started—the wholeness of theology. Moral rulings are not offered to men who disbelieve the substance of the creed: they are presented to faith, not to fear. It is often true that, as the old Protestants liked to say, you must awe men with the law before you can gladden them with the gospel; the first appeal of religion is the conscience. Nevertheless this is a transitory phase. It is only in those that walk 'not according to the flesh, but the spirit' that 'the ordinance of the law is fulfilled'.

Free Will in Theology

'FREE WILL' is to be defined in general as intentional action uninhibited, or alternatively as the power so to act. The idea of will adds nothing to the idea of action, so long as action is taken in its full and personal sense; for personal action is such in so far as it is voluntary. To call it voluntary, or the expression of will, is to negate a negation about it—to exclude the suggestion that it is something less than a piece of genuine personal doing. It is a further point of refinement, to take up will—the voluntariness of voluntary action—and to distinguish an exercise of it which is free from one which is not: a man may act with conscious intention to do what he does, and yet not seem to merit the description of being a free agent. The assertion of free will has no significance except in relation to some constraint it is intended to exclude. The force of the term has varied, and still does vary, with predominant interest in various types of constraint; and it is this variation of topic which makes the history of the notion.

The notion of freedom as such plainly derives from the distinction between the freeman and the slave. So long as freedom of will is simply equated with freedom of status, no point of philosophical interest arises; freemen are men who do what they like, slaves are men who do what they are told. But reflection will suggest that in many things slaves do what they choose, and in some things freemen are liable to constraint, being subject (for example) to kings. Nor can kings themselves do whatever they wish; they must obey the gods, or suffer the consequences. The development of legal practice leads to systematic thought on the topic. A man is not to be held accountable for actions which were not his own. The slave's action under orders is his master's. But equally on occasion a freeman might be coerced to act against his will; whose, then, is the action, and whose the responsibility?

Written shortly before his death in the Autumn of 1968 for the *Dictionary of the History of Ideas* (New York, Charles Scribner's Sons, 1973).

Sophistic Doctrine An early Greek philosophical position regarding freedom was the simple denial of all intrinsic limitations upon the pursuit of voluntary aims. Moral convention and social structure are mere conveniences of life, and can be made the instruments of masterminds who know how to get outside them and to manipulate them. Such was, or was said to be (e.g., by Plato, *Republic* 336b ff) the doctrine of certain fifth-century Greek Sophists who claimed to teach well-placed young men the art of success in public life. In opposition to this doctrine, Socrates and Plato shifted attention from external to internal constraint—from the rub between one's own will and one's neighbour's to the rub between one's reason and one's passion or appetite. A man's true self was his Reason; to be free was to rule one's passions; it was no true freedom to make one's fellow men the instruments of mindless appetite or of exorbitant ambition.

Plato and Aristotle In the *Republic* Plato boldly inverted the historical order. The philosophical notion of inward sovereignty does not arise through the interiorization of political relations; it is the other way about: men acknowledge political sovereignty through first recognizing the intrinsic right of Reason to rule their souls, and then accepting sovereignty in the State—'the individual writ large'—as the outward embodiment of the same Reason (*Republic* 534d). Political sovereignty is to be valued as supporting Reason in the individual, and keeping it on its throne. We are not enslaved by a genuine exterior sovereignty; we are liberated by it. Here is the beginning of that famous philosophical paradox, that a right choice of service is the only freedom.

The model or parable exploited by Plato is hierarchical. Suppose a household presided over by a master capable of finding the path of right reason for himself and the other members of it, while they have no such capacity. If he lets himself be run by his inferiors, he will be enslaved and they (through the resulting chaos) will be unhappy. If he maintains control, he will be free, and they will be both outwardly well-circumstanced and inwardly content, for they can feel the intrinsic rightness of rational direction, even though they cannot find it for themselves. Such is the position of the rational self in relation to the passions or appetites. Reason persuades passion; passion merely overbears reason (*Republic* 548b, 554b–d).

Plato, and after him Aristotle, introduced several refinements into the doctrine in their progressive realization of the necessity for reason to train the passions themselves, and to take them into partnership as fellow-initiators of right intentions. It remained that essential freedom was the freedom of thoughtfulness to find the right path; particular and practical choice was to be seen as general reason finding expression under given circumstances. A man had no freedom to invent principles of good life, for they were laid down in the nature of things. Free thought would lead to agreement about the Good, as it would lead to agreement in mathematics (Aristotle, *Nicomachean Ethics* 1106b).

To be rational, then, is to be free. But does it lie within a man's power to be rational? Does effort of will suffice to bring the passions into line? Plato and Aristotle make no such unequivocal claim. They discuss the psychology of struggles for self-mastery (Plato, *Republic* 439e ff, *Phaedrus* 246ff; Aristotle, *Nicom. Ethics* 1145-7); they show how ruinously our very judgement of what is good can be perverted by an ill-formed character (*Nicom. Ethics* 1113a). They feel no concern to inquire whether or not every soul that is capable of hearing the philosophical gospel is capable also of winning her interior battle and finding felicity. Their concern is rather to vindicate the free power of Reason as such to perform its function of moralizing human existence. It is a hopeful enterprise, even if hope lies rather in conditioning the next generation than in self-culture. Such an attitude was natural, considering that the whole discussion arose out of a critique of city-state life. Reason was to prevail by being socially projected, and embodied in institutions, above all in schools.

Aristotle lived to see the collapse of city-state autonomy; but the cultural mission of his pupil, the all-conquering Alexander, was still conceived as the planting of Greek self-governing cities the world over, to drill men into rational freedom. Plato made some concession to the individual's aspiration after the freedom to save his soul, by the myth of transmigration. One's effort in this life might not take one far; but it might suffice to enable one to make the choice of such an embodiment or destiny in one's next life, as to allow of one's going further (*Republic* 617e).

Later Greek Philosophers. The progressive overshadowing of city autonomy by monarchical empire after Alexander provided a soil for Stoicism, a philosophy which both made the individual the captain of his soul, and at the same time related his strenuous self-government to the governing mind of the Universe. It was still the ideal to let Reason rule; but Reason was now seen as embodied in the Universal Order, the recurrent cycle of world-process. Since the cycle must fulfil its pattern, and universal Reason (of which the individual's reason is but a function) must prevail, the new problem is theoretically posed of the relation between the individual's exercise of freedom and the operation of a universal, rational necessity. The official solution lay in the doctrine of Relaxation—though it is the Universal Reason which functions as our rational mind, it relaxes its operation in us to what is (initially) the mere rudiment of actual rationality; and from that starting-point finds its level in us by and as our personal or free endeavour. So far from feeling himself oppressed by the World-Reason, the Stoic embraced it *con amore* and, by willing in the line of Cosmic Will, enjoyed that freedom which is escape from all frustration. (For the spirit of this ethos, see Marcus Aurelius, *passim.*) If one asked whether the sinner or fool could *resist* Cosmic Destiny, one was put off with such sayings as that God leads good will by the hand and drags recalcitrance by the hair. In practice a man was offered the choice of being the victim of fate or the partner of providence; how men could have such a choice was, no doubt, theoretically insoluble and must always be so in a strictly pantheist system.

The contemporary rival to Stoicism, the School of Epicurus, taught an out-and-out libertarian individualism (Diogenes Laërtius,x.133-4). The philosopher shook from his shoulders both the burden of politics and the burden of cosmic destiny, and pursued an amiable, cultured life at his own sweet will, under the leadership of the laudable and tranquil emotions. It must surprise the modern reader to observe that Epicurus supported his doctrine of freedom by a strict atomic materialism. Everything, including the human soul, is a chance constellation of atoms. But he does not conclude: 'So we do what the atoms make us do'. He insists: 'Our choices are ours to make'. The explanation of the paradox is that the ancients were not obliged to view the movements of matter as the realm of inflexible regularity. Reason it was that imposed order; be rid of Cosmic Reason, leave matter to itself, and there might be scope for the self-determination of a soul which atoms had transiently blown together.

Epicureanism proved to be a deviation which was not followed up. The settlement of world-empire in the seemingly everlasting Roman dominion and the infiltration of oriental attitudes towards divine monarchy favoured a philosophical development building on Stoic foundations, but tending towards an elevation of the Supreme Principle into an absolute transcendence over the world. Neo-Platonism, as this development is called, reached maturity in the third century A.D. In so far as the system viewed the human soul as an emanation from the universal being rather than as a part or function of it, it allowed a more intelligible basis for the substantial distinctness of the human agent and so for his freedom to determine his own relation to the Divine. Emanation proceeded in a cascade of descending steps, and man embraced within his being an epitome of nature's sinking scale, from spirit above to mere matter below. He had in his faculty of desire a corresponding scale of 'loves', each with affinity for its own objects. His freedom of choice essentially lay in the power to identify himself with one love or another, and supremely with love for the Supreme.

Christendom It was as a doctrine of free will that Neo-Platonism was embraced by St Augustine at the turn of the fourth to the fifth century. It afforded him deliverance from the crude heresy of Christian Manichaeism. In common with other forms of Gnosticism this sect attributed the genesis of mankind to a cosmic defeat by which elements of 'light' were captured and enmeshed in 'darkness'. The Neo-Platonic psychology gave arms to Augustine in which to appear as the champion of God's good creation. By a shift in the level of his love, man, created in the divine image, had become the author of his own degradation. Being free, he had misused the power of choice (*Confessions*, vii. 3-21).

So far, Augustine was all for free will. He was soon to face in another direction. There was nothing arbitrary or accidental in his change of front. There were special emphases in biblical and Christian theism which tipped the balance of the Neo-Platonic system. Neo-Platonic deity is not seen as the Judge of men's souls, fixing their eternal destiny according to their merit; and so there is no urgency in the inquiry about the degree of a man's personal responsibility for his character or attitudes. If men are wise and holy, they are wise and holy; they can be influenced towards such a desirable state, and their own choices or resolves will help. The absolute question, how much could have been expected of any one soul, has no practical importance. It is another thing for the Christian who sees himself placed before the bar of the Eternal Judge.

But while on the one side Biblical Theism sharpened the sense of a free choice of will determining one's salvation or perdition, on another side it called it in question. The God of the Bible is conceived as sovereign will, the creator of all things by fiat, and the saviour of men by interposition. How then can the creature's will be anything but the instrument of the Creator's, and how can the salvation of the elect be the work of any but God? Neo-Platonism conceived of God not as sovereign will, but as supreme perfection; less perfect beings were the outfall and overspill of his being, not the creatures of his will. He was their saviour only in the sense that he was their true God, and that without the pull of his attraction no one would aspire after him. But equally if one did not aspire, the attraction would have no effect. On these terms it was scarcely meaningful to ask whether the turning of a soul to God was its work or his.

Augustine felt able to save man's free will on the side of the Creatorship of God. The Creator had *chosen* to confer on his human creature much such a free will as Neo-Platonism taught, for had not he created man in his own image? But on the side of Redemption no such concession could be made. Redemption was a rescue of the perishing, a sheer seizure of minds incapable of loving God through their own act or choice. Though created free to love God, man had lost that freedom by his disobedience or irreligion. Mankind, apart from the grace of salvation, was sick or corrupt; it needed to be restored or healed by God before it regained freedom to love God. Fallen man might indeed exercise free choice in the pursuit of such objectives as he was capable of loving; he could not give himself the higher love. Restored by grace, he would choose freely on all levels, except in so far as his unredeemed condition still hung about him (*De Spiritu et Litera, De Natura et Gratia*).

Augustine's teaching provoked vigorous reactions from Christians who feared it would enervate spiritual effort. It would be wiser, said Pelagius and Julian, to see in salvation God's provision of indispensable means, means which it lay in the free choice of man to employ or to neglect. Augustine rejected that doctrine as inadequate to the Christian facts and as conducive to spiritual pride. We do not reach out our hands and take salvation; salvation takes us. The controversy drove him into extremes. God had eternally predestined whom he would elect to salvation and his saving will was irresistible. None who truly aspired to salvation, indeed, were denied it; but their aspiring was by God's predestination and grace.

Augustine carried the day against Pelagianism, but the sharp paradox of human responsibility and divine predestination was found difficult to live with and was soon qualified by the Church. The Scholastics of the High Middle Ages elaborated a subtle account of the co-operation of free will with Grace (e.g., Aquinas, *Summa Theologiae*, prima secundae quaest. cix-cxiv). But the balance of interest for them was somewhat shifted by their adoption of a Neo-Aristotelianism drawn from Mohammedan sources. The system derived from Islam an overwhelming concern with the absolute sovereignty of the Creator's will over all created things and events. The human agent, like every other creature, was a secondary cause instrumental to the sole primary cause, God. The Christian philosophers laboured to find a place for free will under the all-determining and all-foreseeing mind of God (ibid., pars prima, qu. xiv art. 13; qu. xxii art. 4). Within the created system, says Thomas Aquinas, there are chances genuinely open to the choice exercised by human free will; human decision is as real a cause as any other finite cause. But that does not stand in the way of our acknowledging the whole system, including the human volitions it contains, as the effect of divine ordination. It is a superstition to suppose that a divinely ordained effect must operate by a process of mechanical determination rather than by one of free choice. It would be misleading, then, to say that I was *bound* to do what I freely decided, since there is no binding in the case. It remains that I was *going* to do what I did. It must surely be objected that if this is a harmless tautology, it does not give reality to God's prior causality; while if it is so understood as to do this, it reduces free choice to a subjective illusion. Freely as we may act, we shall be toeing a predetermined line.

The Protestant Reformation rejected the subtleties of Scholastic Aristotelianism together with its metaphysical preoccupations. The interest of Luther and Calvin reverted to Augustine's position on salvation, which they reasserted in all its uncompromisingness. Indeed, the paradox is sharpened, in so far as Augustine is now seen as a commentator on St Paul simply, and his Neo-Platonic overtones are lost. The sovereignty of the divine will is conceived as decisive power rather than as self-fulfilling Good and the collision of omnipotent Grace with creaturely free will is uncushioned. Salvation is an unmerited gift towards which the fallen will can do nothing. Luther wrote a treatise *Of the Will Enslaved (De servo arbitrio*, 1525), Calvin carried the speculation of Predestination to unexampled extremes (*Institutes*, iii, 21-3; definitive edn, 1559). Reaction was not slow to follow; on the part of the Catholic Church it was immediate (Council of Trent, 1545-63). Within the Calvinist confession Arminius led the revolt. Strict Calvinism has since been reasserted by one reform after another, but on balance has lost ground.

Modern Physicalism Meanwhile a totally different issue has come to the fore and defined the free will question as it is now commonly understood. This is the issue raised by the development of scientific materialism. If the activity of the human person is geared to the movements of a physical body, and if that body is a system operating by rules of perfect and as it were mechanical uniformity, how can the apparent freedom of choice be real? Atomistic materialism had been a school of Greek speculation but, as we have seen in the case of Epicurus, carried no necessarily deterministic implications. The parentage of scientific determinism is rather to be found in astronomical studies. It was an ancient and a medieval commonplace that the movements of the heavenly bodies were mathematically exact and ideally predictable. Supposing the 'influences' of the stars upon the causality of earthly events to be determinative, human actions will be subject to fate. It was easy to refute the argument by pointing out that the effect of astral influence was highly general; different earthly agents reacted to it variously, and men as they might choose (Aquinas, *Summa Theologiae* prima, qu. cxv). But then the hypothesis of the mathematical physicists was that earthly bodies were composed of constellated atoms of corpuscula, of which the motions and mutual influences were as mathematically exact and as predictable as those of the stars. Physical fate seemed to have descended from the skies, and so closed in upon us as to leave no escape.

No conclusion could have been more unwelcome or more out of tune with the times. The new science was the expression of humanist self-assertion, of the resolve of strong minds to make all events, however unpromising, subject to human calculation or control. The method of physical inquiry was the voluntary invention of experimental tests and the forcing of them upon Nature; besides, as Descartes pointed out in his *Meditations* (i, iv, vi), it was only by a constant act of will that one could hold the mathematico-physical hypothesis itself in face of the contrary suasions of one's five senses. What could be more preposterous, therefore, than to make the will to intellectual world-conquest the prisoner or even the creature of the mechanism it postulated? Descartes deserves the highest credit for the firmness with which he held to both sides of the duality of free mind or will and of determinate matter; and for the honesty with which he admitted his inability to construe the operative unity of the mind–body person. There were thinkers who took the desperate course of denying free will, for example, Hobbes or Spinoza; they were violently disliked by their contemporaries.

The Cartesian position treated thought as the activity of a spiritual subject and found the immediate effect of will in the formation of mental decisions. How the clockwork body came to register or execute such decisions was beyond comprehension; all one could study on that side was the mechanism through which it did so. For practical purposes such a division of the ground was not inconvenient, and people could laugh at the rage for consistency which led George Berkeley to rid himself of dualism by reducing material objects to 'ideas', thus making will or spirit the sole substance, agent, or cause, subject only to the higher will of God.

It was a more serious matter when the proved fruitfulness of experimental physics began to suggest that its methods and basic conceptions were the models for all factual science, including psychology. It was then not merely a matter of squaring a freely-choosing mind with its mechanistically-conceived embodiment; it was a matter of squaring an experienced exercise of freedom in the mind with a causal explanation of mental experience in terms of invariant regularities. It was David Hume who first rubbed the sore of this problem in his *Treatise of Human Nature* (1739). His subtle thought continues to exercise its spell on English-speaking philosophers, and it is still widely held in academic circles that an empiricist logic distilled from the study of physical phenomena is binding upon all thought about matters of fact; and that its applicability to thinking and to behaviour makes determinism in some sense inescapable.

Solutions were bound to be attempted. Immanuel Kant, in his two first *Critiques*, conceded to Newton and to Hume that we are forced to think deterministically about both physical and mental processes, when making them an object of study; but Kant also maintained that our need so to think is an inescapable limitation of the human mind. Reality is not such, as is shown by the fact that we know ourselves called to exercise free and responsible choices in favour of the moral law. How our power so to do fits in with the actual order of nature lies (Kant thought) beyond our comprehension; what we can understand is that the very form of our cognitive processes prevents their attaining the knowledge of things as they are in themselves. Kant's solution is a rational and systematic agnosticism. His German successors attempted more positive answers by advancing bold metaphysical speculations concerning the subjective and the objective poles of existence (Fichte, Schelling, Hegel, Schopenhauer).

Modern defenders of free will insist on the abstract or diagrammatic character of our scientific knowledge but do not need to go all the way with Kant's scientific agnosticism. For the progress of the natural sciences themselves has eased their task. The scientist's model of physical reality is no longer the simple man-made machine. Nature is seen as a complex of forces, which by knotting themselves in combinations of increasing elaborateness develop astonishing new properties of joint action; and so a physical basis for free consciousness becomes less starkly inconceivable.

The Human Sciences The decreased urgency of the problem on the physical side in the present century has been balanced by increased pressure from historical, social, and psychological science. However little capable these sciences may be of attaining the mathematical rigour pursued in physical inquiry, they disclose a deep and complex conditioning of the individual by background, environment, and subconscious make-up, such as threatens to reduce the exercise of genuine choice to trivial proportions. Several thinkers have been impressed by the predominant effect of one factor or another: Marx by the pressure of economic needs and of the current system for coping with them; Freud by the twists of emotional attitude formed in us during one helpless immaturity; Jung by the individual's inheritance of ancestral archetypes of personal relation or function.

Self-creation In the face of such considerations men have looked in opposite directions for a vindication of significant free decision. A new and historicized version of the Stoic creed calls on us to identify ourselves with the march of historical process from which we should vainly hope to cut ourselves off; so let us lead it on. Such, broadly, was the attitude of Hegel; such is the attitude of Marxists today, and, in effect, of those Western optimists who are content to back the momentum of scientific and technological advance. By contrast, several schools of existentialism have put forward a parody of Augustinianism—our acknowledged conditionedness by factors of all kinds is a state of subhumanity from which we must be raised into authentic existence by deciding for ourselves what we will be and do. Kierkegaard and the religious existentialists see the challenge to self-creation as the challenge to determine your existence in the face of God; Sartre and the atheists see it as the challenge to be God to yourself—there being no other God for you.

The call to embrace historical destiny and the call to exercise self-creation, however seemingly opposed, equally exemplify a distinctively modern belief in the openness of the future. The ancients saw free will as freedom to fulfil the determinate requirements of human nature, human nature being a fixed quantity. In so far as thought later turned in a theistic direction, human nature became a God-given form, articulated in divine commands, and oriented towards God, the immutable living perfection. Even Kant, with his passion for moral autonomy, was still viewing free will as power to impose upon one's conduct a law written into the very structure of one's mind. The two succeeding centuries have dissolved the fixity of the human aim. Romanticism popularized the conception of the artist as a creator of the unique and allowed the individual life or even the common life of an epoch to be seen as a unique invention. Historicism showed the degree to which what passed for human nature had been a cultural product changing with the times. Evolutionism suggested the mutability in principle of the human species, and technology has seemed to put into our hands the means of transforming our existence beyond recognition. In consequence, freedom of will is seen as no longer limited in scope to the fulfilment of human nature, but as the power and the responsibility, whether corporate or individual, to determine in some measure the very nature we are to express.

Linguistic Philosophy The linguisticism now predominant in American and British academic philosophy offers no contribution, perhaps, to the development of the freewill idea; but it offers a fresh approach to the freewill determinism issue, seeing it as a question of adjusting to one another two modes of speech, through a careful study of the natural uses proper to each. We use the language of sheer personal action—with or without implications of alternative choice—and we use the language of event, process, etc. Actions we talk of as what we simply or freely do; events we talk of as happening. To actions we assign intentions, to events we assign causes. Of an event we ask, 'What led to it?' Of a man's action, 'What is he up to?' The problem of free will (excluding its theological aspects) will be the problem of relating these two ranges of speech to one another.

One point must first be made clear. Language which describes or mentions choiceful action is secondary to language in which we do our choiceful thinking or make our choice itself, as when you say to someone placing alternatives before you 'I opt for' A or B (J.L. Austin, *How to Do Things with Words*, Oxford 1962). Having made this point, we may proceed to show that the correlation of event-style and personal action-style speech, so far from being an oddity, is common form. In the case of your talking choice, or spoken option, you choose in view of an opinion of facts or events, which, if you do not explicitly state it, you still take for granted. Indeed, your making of your choice is a virtual affirmation of the facts in view of which you make it. Voluntary decision to act upon (supposed) facts will often be taken as a more serious assertion of those facts than a direct statement of them. If you did make the mere statement, it would be in event-style form.

Or take the case in which you are simply describing events or their interrelations. It remains true that you do the describing, and you go about it as you choose, talking backwards, forwards, or across the event-process you decribe, picking one word and rejecting another. And if I wish to understand your speech, I do not look for the causes of the vocal inflections, I look to your expressive intention. Whereas, to understand what you are talking about, I attend to the causal sequences you are describing. In fact, I am bound to do both. To understand you as speaking I must understand the facts you state and to understand the facts you state I must understand you as speaking; so inseparably are the two modes or logics connected.

But if the matter is as straightforward as this, how can we ever come to think of denying either mode of speech its rights? Why should anyone dream of reducing voluntary-action statements to the happening-by-cause category? The answer is this. So long as we are talking our way into or through choiceful acts we can use no category but the category proper to such talk—I cannot talk to myself the choice I am making, as being an event which occurs. But often we speak of choiceful actions from outside, as having been done or as likely to be done, and then it is possible for us to switch categories, and to talk of them as events—or, more accurately put, to talk, instead, about the events in which they take effect. And events as such are subject, we assume, to the category of causality—to exposition in terms of uniform sequence—and are in principle predictable from a knowledge of their antecedents. If, then, the event in which a choiceful act takes form is predictable, and causally determinate, how can that act itself be free? Such appears to be the puzzle.

The determinist case is that the causal regularity of choice-produced events should be accepted. There are two stories—one descriptive from 'within' of the way in which the choice is made, another descriptive from 'outside' of the event's position in the event-sequence. Each story is veridical in its own sphere, and there is no difficulty in letting them run parallel.

The freewill rejoinder is that a solution in that sense rests on a falsification. Two stories covering the same ground and expressed in different logical idioms may rightly be tolerated when they are both objectively descriptive stories. I may tell a story of past voluntary activity in cold detachment, and feel no great mental discomfort in doubling it with a causal account of the same behaviour. But that is because in imagination I degrade a personal story to the level of a story about a process which unrolled as it did unroll. And that is to depersonalize the story. It is only personal in so far as I identify myself in some measure with the characters or agents in it and express them as personally active from 'within'. And then the acquiescence in a parallel cause-and-effect story becomes impossible.

All the rejoinder achieves is to set aside the determinist's soothing compromise. Three possible positions remain. We may say: (1) So much the worse for the ultimate validity of the free-action language—a determinist conclusion; (2) So much the worse for that of the caused-event language—a libertarian conclusion; (3) So much the worse for both, our language in either case having a purely pragmatic value, in serving our purposes—an agnostic conclusion.

The determinist will speak slightingly of the 'subjective character' of personal experience and its expressions, the libertarian of the 'abstract and diagrammatic character' of causality-constructions, while the agnostic will cite the agelong inconclusiveness of the debate between the two other parties, and the inadequacy of language as such to the nature of things.

The defender of free will ruins his case if he overplays his hand. He must not deny the validity of causal-regularity interpretations so far as they go; but he will maintain that we have no reason to suppose, and much reason to disbelieve, that the grid of natural uniformity fits so tightly upon living processes as to deny scope to free personal action. On the other side of his case, he must avoid exaggerating human liberty. The individual is constantly subject to pressures, visible and invisible, which he often has no motive and sometimes no ability to resist; and the free options he does exercise are mostly within a range of choice narrowly circumscribed by conditions outside his control. So human conduct may often be broadly predictable. On the other hand, the libertarian is not going to admit that all the predictability in a man's conduct is dependent upon the operation of determining causes which restrict his freedom of choice. For in taking a decision, a man will follow his usual policy in such matters unless he now sees reason to revise it. If we, his friends, have formulated his policy to ourselves, we may think of the policy-rule, taken in conjunction with the circumstances invoking its application, as *causing* his action. But voluntary consistency is not subjection to any determining causality. His policy only guides the man because he goes on choosing to maintain it. It is a hard case, if voluntary freedom is only to be evinced by wild and continuous caprice.

Most difficult of solution along linguistic lines is the theological problem of free will in face of a sovereign divine will, in so far as religious conviction puts forward statements about divine initiative in the origination of human free acts which are in formal conflict with statements about the human agent's own initiative. Appeal may be made to the believer's practical understanding of what it is to exercise his will in prolongation (as it were) of God's. But no formal solution can be attempted without a prior examination of the special sense and status of statements about the Divine Subject (traditionally known as the topic of Analogy).

BIBLIOGRAPHY

As will have been seen from the body of the article, the history of the freewill idea is the history of philosophy from a certain angle, and correspondingly difficult to supply with a limited bibliography. Harold Ofstad, *An Inquiry into the Freedom of the Will* (London 1961) contains a very full bibliography as well as a thorough discussion of the subject from a semi-determinist standpoint. An out-and-out libertarian is Corliss Lamont, *Freedom of Choice Affirmed* (New York 1967). He offers a good historical survey. Austin Farrer's *Freedom of the Will* (London 1960;2e.—New York 1960: London 1963—includes a 'Summary of the Argument', pp.316-20) works largely from linguistic ground. To turn to historical positions, in addition to references in the article we may cite the following. For a classic defence of the Calvinist position: Jonathan Edwards, *Careful and Strict Enquiry* . . . (1754). For German Idealism, Arthur Schopenhauer, *The World as Will and Idea (Die Welt als Wille und Vorstellung)*, tr. R.B. Haldane and J. Kemp, 3 vols. (London 1883). For American Pragmatism, William James, 'The Dilemma of Determinism' (1884), in *The Will to Believe* . . . (New York 1897). For Vitalistic Philosophy, Henri Bergson, *Essai sur les Données Immédiates de la Conscience* (Paris 1889). For Existentialism, J-P. Sartre, L'Etre et le Néant (Paris 1943), tr. H. Barnes as *Being and Nothingness* (London 1956).

Analogy in Common Talk

I am supposed to say something about analogy in ordinary talk as opposed to analogy in metaphysics. As will perhaps become clear as I proceed, I find the division between the two areas a division very difficult to maintain. If one is to confine one's attention to explicitly analogical statements in common, non-technical use, one will find little to remark that is of much philosophical interest: whereas if one is to elucidate the element of concealed analogy in statements having no explicitly analogical form, one will find oneself to be engaged in the only sort of metaphysical inquiry which I, for my part, would wish to attempt anyhow. So I apologize in advance for my trespassing on the metaphysician's territory.

And now to my business. I do not wish (nor will you wish me, if you value your happiness) to be comprehensive. I want to get down to what is most interesting and to concentrate on that. And in furtherance of this aim I will make a rough division of the ground, for the purpose of excluding what I propose to neglect. So for the purposes of this rough and ready preliminary division, I ask, 'In what forms analogy may be said to manifest itself in current, non-technical speech?' I propose a threefold division. First, there is conscious and open metaphor, simile, or witty comparison. Second, there is washed-out and virtually dead metaphor. Third, there is stretched meaning. It is the last of these which alone appears to me to be of much interest.

Look, first, at conscious metaphor. Where metaphor is fresh and fully alive, as it is under the pen of a true poet, it suggests itself whole and entire to the mind that conceives it, as a felt analogy between two concrete things. His love is like a red, red rose: that's what strikes him. Leave it at that, and the phenomenon is of no great philosophical interest. For we know that unless our reactions generalized their stimuli, they would be useless to us: they would throw no bridges for us from one of our

---

A paper read to a graduate class on 'Analogy', Michaelmas 1968.

experiences to another. Things are felt to be alike, then, before we have sorted out the ways in which they are alike. The poet's remark might mean no more than that the opening rosebud and the young girl awaked similar emotions of pleasure, admiration, etc. But it is very likely that he is suggesting something more objective—that the girl's animal form is as perfect in its kind as the rose's vegetable form; that she is at a corresponding phase of development to that of the newly opened bud; that her personal or mental unfolding is at the same interesting stage as her physical. And as for the emphatic 'red, red', perhaps that refers to the colour of unexpressed sexuality in her; or hits him with the sort of violence which that colour does to our eyes.

To pull a metaphor like this to pieces is rather like pulling the rosebud to pieces: the charm of either is in its entirety. But as botanizing requires the one desecration, so philosophizing does the other. And when we have finished our piecemeal analysis, what have we got?—Abstractly stated formal identities between the two subjects of comparison, carefully distinguished from the irrelevant accompaniments in which they are concretely embedded. But that is banality itself. For the recognition and isolation of formal identities in objects otherwise dissimilar is the common form of all our experience—a platitude about which Immanuel Kant and others have strung together a very unnecessary number of ugly words.

Ah, but (you may protest) these formal identities between the red, red rosebud and the nubile girl—are they *all that* formal? The rose and the girl are both delightful—but is the delight awakened by the one and the other really the same thing? Both are on the threshold of maturity, but has maturity the same meaning in the two cases?—and so on with the other alleged identities.

Very well: I give you your objection. Suppose that the alleged formal identities are held together by the stretching of the common term applied to both—delightful, newly mature, or whatever. One word is used, but it hasn't a full identity of sense in the two cases. Let it be so. Is it not then incumbent on us as philosophers to try again, and see if we can't get rid of the stretchedness of the stretched term by a finer distinction? If there is a spectrum in the qualities of delight, let us exhibit it, and show how delight in the rose and delight in the girl each has its place in the scale. And so with the other stretched identities. Once again, either we can do the job to our satisfaction or we cannot. If we get rid of the stretching, nothing of philosophical interest remains in our hands; for we presumably knew before we started that common speech makes a lazy or provisional use of stretched terms which it is the business of exact thought to get rid of. But suppose, on the contrary, that we can't get rid of the stretching i.e., there is no way of saying what the metaphor says which does not employ a stretched term or terms. Then that, surely, *is* of philosophical interest—namely, that we can't do justice to our experience without employing stretched terms. Only the fact of interest is, just, the ultimacy of stretched terms—not that such terms happen to lie at the bottom of the meaning carried by a conscious and high-flown metaphor. After all, we may be able to get along pretty well without seeing girls as quasi-*rosaceae*. The interesting question is, how wide, and how important, is the currency of irresolvably stretched terms in our speech or our thought?

It is to this point that I mean to return, but first I will make a dismissive remark about my second head of classification, dead or unconscious metaphor. Romantically disposed philosophers—with whom I must reckon my own ill-judging youth—have tried to make capital out of the fact that we appear to be unable to find proper words for anything more out of the way than common physical experience and its objects; everything else is talked about by us in borrowed terms. The fact (I would now wish to say) has its interest; but that interest is historical. No doubt our first human words denoted physical objects, events, or actions; and as we extended our mental view to other realms, we made do with our existing vocabulary through metaphysical extension of our terms. But what concerns the philosophical analyst of our present experience is the intention with which terms are now used. 'To apprehend' meant originally 'to seize'. Now it means also 'to become understanding of' and 'to anticipate with displeasure'. My grandfather, bedridden and blind, appeared discomposed. What's the matter? asked my father. 'I apprehend a perspiration' the old one replied. 'I detest a perspiration. I seem to remember reading that the celebrated German philosopher, Immanuel Kant, had a rooted dislike to a perspiration.' My grandfather 'apprehended' the oncoming of a perspiration. The Bow Street runners 'apprehended' a highwayman. I once thought I 'apprehended' what that lamented metaphysician, A.N. Whitehead, meant by the blessed word *prehension*. And none of these three uses of the word 'apprehend' has any live connection with any of the others. Each simply refers to the type of action or experience, mental or physical, which it denotes.

In fact, a case like this is a typical case of the equivocal use of a term in several applications, as the scholastics understood 'equivocal'. I notice that a modern text book takes for a paradigm of equivocation 'mug, a drinking-vessel; mug, the victim of a fraud'. But this scarcely illustrates the equivocal use of a term, because it is not clear to us that we are using one and the same word in the two cases. You might as well say that *père*, a French father, and pear, a pot-bellied fruit, exhibit equivocation. For all I know 'Mug' the victim of a fraud, does not derive from mug a drinking-vessel at all, but (let us say) by shortening from Muggletonian, in allusion to the guileless innocence of simple sectarians. It is only when we are aware of a faded derivation joining two uses of a word that we take the word to be the same term at all. And such, in fact, was Aquinas's standing instance. Everyone knew that the Dog in the sky (the star Sirius) derived its name from the dog at one's gate, but since in using the word of Sirius one forgot the myth and ignored the derivation, and referred to a certain star, that was pure equivocation on that term 'dog'. We may agree with St Thomas; faded metaphor is mere equivocation and mere equivocation is just what isn't analogy.

I said I wasn't going to take any interest in faded metaphor, but I seem to be getting interested in it, and I shall take one more step. Suppose someone protests that we are treating the matter too cavalierly. Isn't it a systematic, or structural fact about our experience that we can't help expressing non-physical facts or notions in body-derived terms? Well, suppose it is. But may not it be parallel to an even more universally systematic or structural fact—that we express everything by vocal noises managed through motions of the throat and mouth? The voice is an amazingly flexible and immediately obedient instrument for the giving of signals and so we use it to express everything. But that is no reason for asserting a special analogy between vocal experience and whatever other experience the voice is used to express. There is analogy at certain points, where we have what is called onomatopoeia; but onomatopoeia is not a generally characteristic feature of language nor is it an important one. What is important is to recognize that verbal noise-signs can be purely conventional. And now to develop the parallel that concerns us. The voice, we said, is a beautifully flexible and obedient expressive instrument. So also is physical gesture, physical manipulation of all kinds; and so the shadow-form of physical gesture or manipulation, the physical imagination. As I can use my hands, so I can imagine the use of them. Here, then, is a readily available and easily manageable physical and imaginative sign language, simply crying out for symbolical employment. And it can be used, like vocal language, in a purely conventional way. Allow, if you like, that when my grandfather *apprehended* a perspiration, the word carried with it some shadow of getting one's hands on to something in the dark. That will not make the use of the term *analogical*, if the shadowy grasping of a shape of things unseen has become the mere denotative symbol for the anticipation of events to come. The characteristic of conventionalized signs is that the mind passes clear through them without attending to them: their meaning is found in their present use or application.

It is certainly a fascinating topic of psychology, or of mental philosophy, to explore the subtle relation between vocal language and this sort of undertow of bodily imagination which over so wide a field accompanies it; but it does not seem to belong to our present concern and I must let it alone. The gist of the matter is simply this: in so far as bodily metaphor becomes dead metaphor, it becomes sign-language; and a linguistic sign is not as such analogical to what it is made the sign of.

And now I have got dead metaphor off my hands, I turn to what I said I really wanted to talk about: stretched uses of terms; and more in particular, stretched uses that are indispensable, such as cannot be analysed away into exact formal identities on the one side, and distinguishing differences on the other. Of such uses I shall make two classes only. First, we are obliged to stretch a term when the reality to which the term refers is self-stretching. Second, we may be obliged to stretch a term when we are using the knowable as a clue to what is not knowable in the same sense of 'knowable'.

To take these two classes in order. Self-stretching realities are found in personal experience. You will of course understand that the stretch I refer to is a stretch in nature, or quality. The Proteus of mythology was a self-stretching entity because he could manifest the action of fish and lion, fire and water, and still be the Old Man of the Sea. This is, no doubt, a prejudicial because a really nonsensical example. No reality, however protean, is as protean as Proteus. To turn to real examples: take the scale of felt-warmth. Warmth as felt is not like heat as measured by a thermometer. It is a scale of different feeling-qualities which pass into one another as we go up or down the scale. A considerable warmth is not simply a greater intensity of the same quality as a slight warmth: it is a different quality; and yet the two are in continuous scale with one another. But neither can one abstract what is common to the two and set it apart from the distinguishing differences of the several examples. Warmth is a self-stretching, or sliding, quality, which changes its nature as it changes its altitude; and so the term which refers to it has a stretched or sliding sense, use, or application.

Pleasure or delight is another and, of course, much more important example. How simple it would be for the proponents of the hedonistic calculus if pleasure were a simple quality merely differing in degree of intensity and length of duration. But how far that is from being the case! There is a continuity in the scale of pleasures for, after all, they do come into practical comparison with one another. And yet how various are the pleasantnesses of various delights, and how various the delightings we take in them! That which constitutes my pleasure is a sliding point, and, to believe the ancient moralists, the sort of man I morally am is largely shown by where it slides to, that is to say, which form among its possible protean varieties it dominantly and characteristically assumes.

But most important of all are scales of mental action. Merely being awake and aware of one's environment becomes a different activity as it passes from bare attentions to alert observation and yet there is entire continuity between the two phases. What I do in passing from one to the other is to raise myself in the scale, the scale of attention. And so with the exercise of voluntary choice. What infinite varieties there are in the exercise of volition, between the mere maintenance of a standing policy of conduct, to the making of a mint-new decision in an unprecedented situation or at the cross roads of one's life! But I cannot forgo the use of a stretching-term; for my life, in so far as it is personal and mine, is the exercise of choice or volition, and I can no more forgo the use of the sliding, stretching-term throughout than I can forgo the use of the pronoun 'I' as common subject to all my experiences and acts.

If I have failed to give a properly philosophical account of the self-stretching realities which call for the use of stretching-terms, that may not matter just now, since there is nothing more interesting or more important for us to pull to pieces in discussion than this. So I will hasten to complete my performance by taking my second class of stretched terms—those we stretch in using the known as a clue to the unknown. The unknown I am talking about here is not, of course, that which gives no evidences of itself to us or does not confront us in any way. I am talking about what is metaphorically called the inside to the outside with which we interact. I can wrestle with a man; I might wrestle (hopefully) with a chimpanzee and (most unhopefully) with a gorilla. I know what it is like for me to wrestle with the ape and for me to be wrestled with by the ape; I do not know what it is like for the ape to be wrestling with me, or to be wrestled with by me. And yet my mind is not and cannot be a blank on the subject. I have no power to think of the ape as a mere mass of disagreeable phenomena; I cannot but suppose him to be the quasi-personal subject of the active verb 'to wrestle', and of the passive experience of 'being wrestled with'. In doing so, I am using my own voluntary physical action, my own intelligent response to challenge and pressure, as my clue to his. In this way I stretch my terms and I do not know how much they ought to be stretched. At this point the stretchiness of terms in my descriptions to myself of my own experience comes into play. My own behaviour, my own awareness, can sink to levels of the more instinctive, the less thoughtful, the more purely sensuous; and I immediately and without effort suppose the beast's action and response to be somewhat like that, only more so. I make (without any reflection) a rough and ready fit between a simplified version of human action at its least human and the phenomena of the beast's behaviour.

In the study of beasts I can, of course, be scientific if I like, and then I can get rid of stretched terms. I can disattend from, or profess agnosticism about, what it is for the beast to be a beast, and to act beastly. I can confine myself to verifiable diagrams of his recurrent behaviour-phenomena. But that is science, and I have precisely undertaken to talk about analogy not in science, but in commonsense or ordinary talking and thinking. And once we get down off our scientific high-horse, we discard such austerity and think of our fellow-creature—the ape, the dog, or the horse—not as a pattern of phenomenal disturbance in the field of our existence, but as a going concern on his own account, exercising his own being as the centre of his own environmental field.

And so, indeed, common sense, that true metaphysician, thinks of all realities whatsoever. They are revealed to us, if you like, by the disturbances they make in our field of action or of sentience; but we take them actually to be things, processes, or whatever, doing business out there in space under their own names, as it were. We take processes actually to proceed, and things to endure, and activities to be active of and in themselves; and in so speaking and thinking of them, we are using desperately stretched terms, terms stretching into the unknown or the inconceivable—for what does it mean for anything which cannot be conceived in personal terms to be itself and to act? At the outer end of the stretch, such terms are stretched indefinitely; at the inner end, they are anchored to our own existence.

It will now have become clear what I meant by saying that it is difficult to talk about philosophically significant analogy in common speech without going over the border into metaphysics. I suppose I should, in conclusion, come back to the blessed word *analogy*. To say that we use stretched terms is to say that we assert an analogy, not an identity, between their several applications. When the several applications are all equally objects of our experience, the analogy acts as a bridge. When one of the applications is not within our experience as the other is, the analogy acts as a clue.

Whether we consciously reason from analogy in each case is of minor importance. We most usually do not; we simply attribute consciousness to the frog and think we know what we mean by consciousness. But then that's just like theology, is it not? We confidently, and without any logical fuss, are accustomed to assert the life of God.

www.ingramcontent.com/pod-product-compliance
Lightning Source LLC
Chambersburg PA
CBHW070315230426
43663CB00011B/2140